DEVELOPING A SPORT PSYCHOLOGY CONSULTANCY PRACTICE

Sport and exercise psychology as a profession is becoming increasingly popular, with a growth in the number of students applying for and studying Undergraduate and Postgraduate degrees in sport and exercise psychology in recent years within the UK and International Higher Education landscape. *Developing a Sport Psychology Consultancy Practice: A Toolkit for Students and Trainees* provides logistical and practical information about becoming and working as an applied sport psychology practitioner and the critical processes involved in setting up a consultancy practice. The book focuses on three broad areas:

- Pathways into Applied Sport Psychology Practice
- Setting up a Sport Consultancy Practice
- Personal and Professional Development

Within these areas, the chapters provide coverage on topics related to UK and International training and qualification routes, setting up, operating and marketing successful consultancy practices, engaging in administrative and quality assurance processes and optimising technology for effective practice. The chapters further focus on the practitioner's journey of personal and professional development, including the importance of maintaining a healthy work–life balance for mental health, integrating self-care strategies into daily lives, developing cultural competence and engaging in lifelong learning.

This book is a valuable resource for students who are considering training as an applied practitioner, including students enrolled on undergraduate and postgraduate Sport and Exercise Psychology, Sport and Exercise Science and Psychology programmes. It is also a vital aid for current trainees and recently qualified Sport and Exercise Psychologists.

Vaithehy Shanmuganathan-Felton, PhD, is the Head of Education and Student Engagement in the School of Psychology at the University of Roehampton, UK.

Stephen Smith is a Health and Care Professionals Council (HCPC) registered Occupational Psychologist and Sport and Exercise Psychologist working in private practice and is a Partner with this regulator in assessing postgraduate courses at UK Institutions. He was one of the four original founders of the BPS Division of Sport & Exercise Psychology and has over 35 years of global delivery experience. He is a member of 'The College of Experts' – the select group of independent scientists who advise the Department of Digital, Media, Culture & Sport (DCMS) in the UK government.

DEVELOPING A SPORT PSYCHOLOGY CONSULTANCY PRACTICE

A Toolkit for Students and Trainees

Edited by Vaithehy Shanmuganathan-Felton and Stephen Smith

NEW YORK AND LONDON

Cover image: Delpixart

First published 2023
by Routledge
605 Third Avenue, New York, NY 10158

and by Routledge
4 Park Square, Milton Park, Abingdon, Oxon, OX14 4RN

Routledge is an imprint of the Taylor & Francis Group, an informa business

© 2023 selection and editorial matter, Vaithehy Shanmuganathan-Felton and Stephen Smith; individual chapters, the contributors

The right of Vaithehy Shanmuganathan-Felton and Stephen Smith to be identified as the authors of the editorial material, and of the authors for their individual chapters, has been asserted in accordance with sections 77 and 78 of the Copyright, Designs and Patents Act 1988.

All rights reserved. No part of this book may be reprinted or reproduced or utilised in any form or by any electronic, mechanical, or other means, now known or hereafter invented, including photocopying and recording, or in any information storage or retrieval system, without permission in writing from the publishers.

Trademark notice: Product or corporate names may be trademarks or registered trademarks, and are used only for identification and explanation without intent to infringe.

ISBN: 978-1-032-05149-9 (hbk)
ISBN: 978-1-032-05148-2 (pbk)
ISBN: 978-1-003-19628-0 (ebk)

DOI: 10.4324/9781003196280

Typeset in Bembo
by SPi Technologies India Pvt Ltd (Straive)

CONTENTS

List of Figures	viii
List of Tables	ix
List of Boxes	x
Preface	xi
Acknowledgments	xv
List of Contributors	xvi

PART I
Pathways into Applied Sport Psychology Practice   1
Stephen Smith

1 The British Psychological Society Qualification in Sport and Exercise Psychology (Stage 2)   5
 Martin Eubank, Moira E. Lafferty and Gavin Breslin

2 The British Association of Sport and Exercise Sciences (BASES) Sport and Exercise Psychology Accreditation Route (SEPAR)   19
 Chris Harwood, Claire J. L. Rossato, Richard Thelwell and Zoe Knowles

3 Professional Doctorates in Sport and Exercise Psychology   39
 Martin Eubank, Christopher Wagstaff and Paul McCarthy

4 International Routes to Sport and Exercise Psychology 54
   Eesha J. Shah, Nicholas de Cruz and Richard Keegan

5 The Supervisor–Trainee Relationship 70
   Stacy Winter and Tim Holder

PART II
Developing a Sport Psychology Consultancy 85
Stephen Smith

6 Setting Up and Operating a Sport and Exercise Psychology
   Consultancy Practice 89
   Hannah Stoyel and Paul McCarthy

7 Marketing the Sport and Exercise Psychology Consultancy
   Practice 102
   Paul McCarthy

8 Going Online: How to Enhance Consultancy Practice
   Using Digital Technology 113
   Stewart T. Cotterill and Olivia A. Hurley

9 Administrative and Quality Assurance Processes 126
   Andrea M. Firth and Ricardo G. Lugo

PART III
Personal and Professional Development 141
Vaithehy Shanmuganathan-Felton

10 The Mental Health of Sport Psychology Consultants 145
   *Margaret McCarthy, Tadhg E. MacIntyre, Laura McMahon
   and Hannah McCormack*

11 Practising What We Preach: Self-Care as an Avenue for
   Effective Practice 160
   Alessandro Quartiroli, Heather Hunter and Daniel R. F. Martin

12 'Doing the Work': Broaching Culture and Diversity in
   Sport, Exercise, and Performance Psychology Consultancy
   Practice – An Intersectional Consideration for Working with
   Stakeholders of Marginalised Racial and Ethnic Identities   176
   Shameema Yousuf and Rob Owens

13 Life-Long Learning: Life beyond the Training   193
   Moira E. Lafferty and David Tod

Index   *210*

FIGURES

2.1	An exemplar of feedback received during initial submission of portfolio and competency profile.	32
2.2	An exemplar from the final feedback SEPAR submission.	35
4.1	A thematic map of accreditation and the practice of sport psychology around the world.	60
4.2	A flowchart of common routes to accreditation around the world.	65
PII.1	Global Competency Model.	87
6.1	My personal timeline from undergrad graduation to moving Optimise Potential to a group consultancy.	91
6.2	Checklist for your first client.	91
6.3	Items to consider for inclusion in a client intake form.	92
6.4	Items to consider when establishing prices.	92
6.5	Aspects to consider when establishing how you will work and run your private practice.	92
6.6	Quotes from OP practitioners on why being part of a group consultancy is valuable to them.	95
9.1	Quality assurance for practitioners.	139
13.1	Relationship of CPD, CE with lifelong learning.	194

TABLES

2.1	SEPAR Knowledge-Based Competencies	22
2.2	SEPAR Skills-Based Competencies	23
2.3	SEPAR Self-Development and Management-Based Competencies	25
2.4	SEPAR Experience-Based Competencies	27
3.1	Current Enrolments and Completions in UK Professional Doctorate in Sport and Exercise Psychology Programmes	40
5.1	Supervisor Requirements for QSEP Stage 2 and SEPAR	72
11.1	McAdams' Life Story Interview Outline – Modified	166
13.1	Examples of the Differing Continuing Education Types	195

BOXES

11.1	Definition of Self-Care	167
11.2	Reflective Questions on Values	167
11.3	Reflective Questioning on Self-Care	167
11.4	Bringing It All Together – The Beginning of a Self-Care Plan	170
12.1	Essential Cultural Questions for Practitioners to Consider about Their Practice	183
13.1	The Trainee Experience	199
13.2	The Newly Qualified Consultant	200
13.3	Journey Consultant 1	201
13.4	Journey Consultant 2	202
13.5	Reflecting on Their Journey Consultant 1	203
13.6	Reflecting on Their Journey Consultant 2	203

PREFACE

Once considered a subdiscipline of sport and exercise science/kinesiology (Vealey, 2006), sport and exercise psychology has grown and evolved substantially in recent decades. Sly, Wagstaff and Mellalieu (2020) recently reflected on and summarised these developments including the impact of theoretical and practice advancements in the field, the diversification of the remit, roles and responsibilities of an applied practitioner and the shift towards working with more diverse stakeholders and performance populations. Aligned with these developments, there have been changes in the training pathways for qualification, registration and accreditation as an applied Sport and Exercise Psychologist, to ensure that those who work in the field are appropriately and suitably competent. To support and counsel applied practitioners and those wanting to practice, there are a significant number of texts and scientific literature dedicated to philosophical frameworks (e.g., Tod & Eubank, 2020), consultancy processes (e.g., Keegan, 2016) and the design, development and implementation of evidence-based psychological programmes (e.g., Maher, 2021). There has also been a growth in practitioners sharing their own reflections and case studies of working with clients.[1] However, there is little literature dedicated to the logistical and practical information about becoming an applied practitioner, the critical processes involved in setting up and operating an independent consultancy practice and the impact of working in a helping profession on the practitioner.

The Inception and Purpose of the Current Book

The impetus for this text stems from our own experience of working within sport and exercise psychology in the education sector (VSF) and private practice (SS). Having been involved in the teaching of undergraduate and postgraduate programmes in sport and exercise psychology, students have always asked me (VSF) for advice and guidance about their next steps. These relate to what training pathways they should take, how to identify and select supervisors for their training, what factors they should consider when setting up their practice, how to develop a client base, how much to charge clients, etc. These questions are not unique to the programmes or the students that I have taught, rather they are echoed by students enrolled on similar programmes across the globe. Unsurprisingly, these were also the questions we asked our tutors many, many years ago when we were completing our studies! So while the discipline is continually changing, the questions and uncertainty faced by students and trainees as they embark on their applied practice journey have remained the same. However, time to address and provide in-depth coverage of these critical topics within the curriculum of undergraduate and postgraduate programmes and courses is a recognised constraint. Accordingly, the current text has been created to enrich students and trainees with contemporary and practical information to aid them make informed decisions about their career in applied practice and equip professionals, including trainees and practitioners, with the logistical knowledge, practical understanding and entrepreneurship skills required for setting up and operating an effective consultancy practice.

The Organisation of the Current Book

The current book is divided into three broad sections, with chapters authored by academics, scholars and practitioners, many of whom are at the forefront of the discipline. Most of the chapters are also supplemented with reflections from current trainees and practitioners working in the discipline. This was important to us, as we wanted to represent the varied experiences of members in our profession and provide a range of learning moments for our readers.

Pathways into Applied Sport Psychology Practice

As a result of the legal protection of the title 'Sport and Exercise Psychologist' and regulation by the Health and Care Professions Council (HCPC), there have been several changes to the professional training routes in the UK. This section (Section I) contains dedicated chapters outlining the professional training routes to becoming a Sport and Exercise Psychologist in the UK and internationally. This includes the British Psychological Society Qualification in Sport and Exercise Psychology (Stage 2), the British Association of Sport and Exercise Sciences (BASES) Sport and Exercise Psychology Accreditation Route (SEPAR) and Professional Doctorates in Sport and Exercise Psychology. There is also a discussion of the different pathways to becoming a Sport and Exercise Psychologist in countries with and without formal accreditation frameworks in Chapter 4. This section is completed by Chapter 5 which focuses on the supervisor–trainee relationships which lie at the heart of the professional training routes and for personal and professional growth as a practitioner. To further aid understanding, these chapters are accompanied with reflections from trainees, supervisors and assessors as relevant. We believe that this is an integral part of these chapters, as they provide guidance, advice and tips to shape your decision-making and personal and professional development.

Developing a Sport Psychology Consultancy

Section II of this text is centred on developing and operating a sport psychology consultancy practice. This includes unique and frank reflections on setting up, operating and marketing a sport and exercise psychology practice as a business in the UK. Chapter 6 provides an insight into the different ways a consultancy practice can operate (e.g., Group V individual), shares advice on how to secure clients and factors to consider when setting fees for clients. While applied sport and exercise psychology is a helping profession, there is the inevitable need for practitioners to market their services to ensure financial security and sustainability. The strategies used by practitioners to market their services are discussed in Chapter 7. Digital technology is increasingly becoming part of the consultancy practice, whether it is used as part of the marketing strategy to enhance online presence or as a mode of service delivery. This became more apparent as the profession responded and adapted to the COVID-19 pandemic in 2020. Chapter 8 explores the use of digital technology to further develop the consultancy brand, engaging with social media platforms to create professional online presence and networks, and the benefits and pitfalls of using online platforms to conduct consultancy with clients. This chapter also considers the ethical challenges associated with employing online and digital spaces supported with guidance on how to navigate these challenges in a safe manner. Finally, this section finishes with a focus on administrative and quality assurance processes that underpin sport and exercise psychology consultancy. This chapter discusses the Standards of Proficiency for Sports and Exercise Psychologists and outlines the processes involved in setting up a service agreement with clients, keeping client records and engaging in reflection and supervision to enhance best practice.

Personal and Professional Development

The final section (Section III) of the text concerns the practitioner's personal and professional development. Applied practitioners are dedicated to facilitating their clients to thrive and flourish (Poczwardowski, 2019). However, very little attention has been paid to the impact that working within a helping profession has on practitioners. Chapter 10 addresses this gap by focusing on the mental health of sport psychology consultants. This line of thought is further built upon in Chapter 11, which discusses the importance of developing and integrating self-care practices to minimise the challenges of working in the profession. In 2020 the world witnessed the unlawful murder of George Floyd by a law enforcement officer in the USA.[2] A consequent positive implication, and perhaps even a legacy of his murder, appears to be that our discipline is now explicitly having the 'difficult' or 'uncomfortable' conversations about racial inequity, social injustice and inclusive practice.

Chapter 12 provides guidance on how to broach such conversations with cultural humility and offers practical advice on how to promote diversity and inclusion in your practice in a meaningful and authentic manner. This section concludes with the focus on engagement in continued professional development and lifelong learning for development as a practitioner. This is supported by practical guidelines to help you plan and steer your journey as an applied practitioner.

Over to You…

This book has been designed to allow you to read the chapters as standalone chapters, coming back to them as and when you need to. We encourage you to learn from the reflections, guidance and good practice shared by our experienced authors. Throughout the book, there are numerous reflective points and questions for your consideration. We hope that these act as aids for deliberation on the chapter but also facilitate your development and growth as a practitioner. We wish you all the best and hope that our book acts as a helpful resource as you navigate your personal and professional journey as future Sport and Exercise Psychologists.

Notes

1 Readers are also referred to *Casestudies in Sport and Exercise Psychology* journal.
2 https://www.bbc.co.uk/news/world-us-canada-57618356

References

Keegan, R. (2016). *Being a Sport Psychologist*. London: Palgrave Macmillan.
Maher, C. A. (2021). *Developing and sustaining sport psychology programs: A resource guide for practitioners*. New York: Routledge.
Poczwardowski, A. (2019). Deconstructing sport and performance psychology consultant: Expert, person, performer, and self-regulator. *International Journal of Sport and Exercise Psychology*, 17(5), 427–444. https://doi.org/dzgk.
Sly, D., Wagstaff, C. R. D., & Mellalieu, S. D. (2020). "It's psychology Jim, but not as we know it!": The changing face of applied sport psychology. *Sport, Exercise, and Performance Psychology*, 9(1), 87–101. https://doi.org/10.1037/spy0000163.
Tod, D., & Eubank, M. (2020). *Applied Sport, Exercise and Performance Psychology: Current Approaches to Helping Clients*. London: Routledge.
Vealey, R. S. (2006). Smocks and jocks outside the box: The paradigmatic evolution of sport and exercise psychology. *Quest*, (58), 128–159. https://doi.org/10.1080/00336297.2006.10491876.

ACKNOWLEDGMENTS

We would like to thank our contributing authors for bringing our vision, ideas and initial concepts for the book to life. The knowledge, expertise and experience you have shared in these chapters will no doubt be invaluable for our future generation of Sport and Exercise Psychologists. We are also grateful to the team from Routledge for their continual support and guidance from the inception to the delivery of this text.

CONTRIBUTORS

Gavin Breslin, PhD
Ulster University, UK

Stewart T. Cotterill, PhD
AECC University College, UK

Nicholas de Cruz, PhD
University of Surrey, UK

Martin Eubank, PhD
Liverpool John Moores University, UK

Andrea M. Firth, PhD
University College Football Business, UK

Chris Harwood, PhD
Loughborough University, UK

Tim Holder, PhD
University of Winchester, UK

Heather Hunter, MSc
University of Portsmouth, UK

Olivia A. Hurley, PhD
Institute of Art, Design + Technology, Dún Laoghaire, Dublin, Ireland

Richard Keegan, PhD
University of Canberra, Australia

Zoe Knowles, PhD
Liverpool John Moores University, UK

Moira E. Lafferty, PhD
University of Chester, UK

Ricardo G. Lugo, PhD
Østfold University College, Norway

Tadhg E. MacIntyre, PhD
Maynooth University, Ireland

Daniel R. F. Martin, MSc
University of Portsmouth, UK

Margaret McCarthy, MSc
Loft Performance, Kilkenny, Ireland

Paul McCarthy, PhD
Glasgow Caledonian University, UK

Hannah McCormack, PhD
Rugby Players Ireland, Ireland

Laura McMahon, MSc
The Saileach, Ireland

Rob Owens, EdD
Resolute Performance, PLLC, USA

Alessandro Quartiroli, PhD
University of Wisconsin, La Crosse, USA
University of Portsmouth, UK

Claire J. L. Rossato, PhD
University of Greenwich, UK

Eesha J. Shah, MSc
University of Bath, UK

Hannah Stoyel, PhD
Optimise Performance, UK

Richard Thelwell, PhD
University of Portsmouth, UK

David Tod, PhD
Liverpool John Moores University, UK

Christopher Wagstaff, PhD
University of Portsmouth, UK

Stacy Winter, DProf
St Mary's University, UK

Shameema Yousuf, MSc, MEd, M BACP
Empower2Perform, UK

PART I
Pathways into Applied Sport Psychology Practice

Stephen Smith

In the congested streets near Liverpool Street Train Station in old London town there are myriad hostelries and drinking dens. It was in the smoke-filled cellar bar of 'Dirty Dicks' pub in one of these streets that four shadowy figures met in the last knockings of 1989. I was one of those four psychologists gathered around the table that day and I remember the conversation well. As our heads dipped towards each other and our voices lowered conspiratorially, we all agreed that something had to be done and that we would be the people to do it – sport and exercise psychology in the UK would never be the same again.

The gang of four that day were Dr. Barry Cripps, Prof. Hannah Steinberg (sadly deceased), Dr. George Sik and my good self. We all hailed from different aspects of the psychology profession as it existed at that time – I, for example, was working towards Chartership with the British Psychological Society (BPS) for a leading occupational psychology consultancy. That organisation made millions of pounds selling consultancy and psychometric products to organisations in the UK and the world, eventually becoming the only psychology-based organisation to float on a major stock market (London 1997); my passion, however, was to build a personality questionnaire for sport rather than pander to the needs of London bankers (that may or may not be rhyming slang).

All four people gathered around that table were involved in sport and exercise psychology in one form or another but were frustrated that the governing body (the BPS) did not seem to recognise the growing importance of this field. In fact, there were a number of academic snobs who looked down their noses at it seeing it as 'Vulgar'. This included some of the leaders of the occupational psychology firm I worked for who did not have the foresight to invest in sport psychology or understand how big the market would become. However, we were not deterred and managed to persuade enough of our colleagues to formally sign and petition

DOI: 10.4324/9781003196280-1

the BPS to have a referendum on the creation of a Sport and Exercise Psychology Section. The referendum was a great success, and the Section was formally constituted in December 1992 at the inaugural symposium of the section in London. I was delighted to present a paper on the validation of a personality questionnaire for elite professional footballers. The symposium ran for two days and we had many great speakers including the famous Professor Hans Eysenck. Finally, the profession was on its way in the UK.

Looking back 30 years later, the world of sport and exercise psychology is a very different place in the UK. At that time, there were no dedicated postgraduate programmes and no professional route for individuals to follow. Even if these programmes had existed, the world of sport was not really ready. Only one top-flight football team used a Psychologist, but he was sworn to secrecy and had to call himself a Player Development Officer and never reveal his real profession. The Manager/Coach of one of the UK's home nations football teams (England, Scotland, Wales and Northern Ireland) wanted to bring me in but was clearly told by the managers of the clubs that his players came from that, if he did so, these players would be withdrawn and made unavailable for selection. The FA turned down the opportunity to have Psychologists supporting referees and the editor of one of the world's leading golf magazines had lunch with me expressing his view that 'He could never see a time when his readers would be at all interested in such things'. In the world of sport, many, genuinely, could not tell the difference between a Psychologist and a spiritualist who promised to connect you with your dead ancestors.

When organisations did utilise Psychologists, the situation was not helped by the fact that no agreed professional register existed. This enabled charlatans to get in such as the Belgian Psychologist whose previous profession had been as a drummer in a rock band and the leading 'Psychologist' who offered to cure an elite athlete's child of autism with a 20-minute counselling session. As outrageous as these folks may have been, they were, it has to be admitted, excellent marketeers which is an area dealt with in Section II of this book.

Today, in the UK, sport and exercise psychology is mainstream and core within the curriculum. It is covered in the Psychology courses that are assessed for entry into University as well as in the curriculum of a wide number of undergraduate courses. There are now (at least at the latest count) over 25 universities in the UK offering dedicated postgraduate programmes with more coming online as these words are written.

Mainstream sport itself is awash with psychological support. Almost every leading football team has a Psychologist/psychological support team embedded in their academies and now supporting the first teams as well. In times past, this might have been the odd individual working part-time but now there are whole in-house units with full-time psychologists as well as room for trainees. The days when managers and coaches did not want Psychologists involved because they confused the profession with voodoo are long gone. This has enabled the national teams to start looking at their use of psychological support. There is a whole team embedded at the

FA National Centre of Excellence to support the England National teams. Once the England team were famously useless at penalty shoot-outs and the old coaches never practised them as they thought it was 'Just luck'. Thirty years after I first presented a paper stating that personality questionnaires could be used to help select those chosen to take the spot kicks, England adopted this approach. Subsequently, they won their first penalty shoot-out in over 20 years (please note as a Scot and a fully paid-up member of the Tartan Army, I preferred it when they lost).

Almost all the Olympic Teams that the UK send have Psychologists to support the teams and individuals. Referees have dedicated psychological support and every sports magazine has a section on the mental aspects of performance. Organisations are looking at sport and exercise psychology as they recognise the importance of exercise in resilience and performance. The world is a very different place from that in 1990.

From a regulatory standpoint, there are now clear routes in the UK to being formally registered as a Sport and Exercise Psychologist. Currently, there are still a few loopholes that unregistered individuals have exploited to deliver in this area. This makes genuine trainee Psychologists question the relevance and importance of following arduous professional pathways to their conclusion. Just as I have seen massive changes in the last 30 years, I expect to see massive changes in the regulation of the profession in the next 30 – and sooner. The Professional Body and the regulator in the UK are working more closely than they ever have, tightening up regulations and loopholes making it harder for unregistered individuals to continue. This is raising awareness amongst employers of the need to only use fully qualified and registered Psychologists. I strongly advise all of you to ensure you are completely aware of the professional pathways highlighted in Section I and in your own part of the world. Sport psychology is on an inexorable path to complete professionalisation, and you do not want to be left behind.

1

THE BRITISH PSYCHOLOGICAL SOCIETY QUALIFICATION IN SPORT AND EXERCISE PSYCHOLOGY (STAGE 2)

Martin Eubank, Moira E. Lafferty, and Gavin Breslin

Qualification in Sport and Exercise Psychology

The Qualification in Sport and Exercise Psychology (QSEP) is the British Psychological Society's (BPS) independent route to Health and Care Professions Council (HCPC) Practitioner Psychologist registration and Chartered Psychologist status. QSEP was launched in 2009, and, in 2019, celebrated its 10 years of providing 'gold standard' professional training to aspiring Sport and Exercise Psychologists. At the time of writing, QSEP has contributed circa 120 Sport and Exercise Psychologists to the HCPC register and has in excess of 100 trainees enrolled (being HCPC-approved for up to 125 candidate enrolments at any one time), 60 supervisors, and 20 assessors. QSEP continues to grow in ensuring a vibrant community of support and practice.

In this chapter, we aim to provide the reader with an informative compendium of key information about this important professional qualification. Initially, the chapter discusses the purpose, aims, and requirements of QSEP training and provides a summary of the four key competencies trainees must develop as part of the qualification. The chapter then moves on to discuss the enrolment process and the role and nature of effective supervision that supports trainee practitioner development. Finally, the chapter discusses the assessment process and the methods of assessment used to evaluate trainee practitioner competence. Throughout the chapter, reflections of QSEP trainees, supervisors, and assessors provide first-hand accounts of the qualification. Reflections include how the qualification develops effective practitioners to become employable Sport and Exercise Psychologists, the nature of effective supervision, top tips for getting the most out of the supervised practice experience, and top tips for successfully navigating assessment.

At this point in the chapter, it is important to note that while the content that follows provides the reader with key information about QSEP in the context of the 'Pathways into Applied Sport Psychology Practice' section of this book, there are a number of other outputs devoted to the qualification that the reader will also find useful. Firstly, Eubank and Tod (2018) published a textbook titled *How to Become a Sport and Exercise Psychologist*, which includes details of the Stage 2 QSEP and Professional Doctorate training routes that are also the focus of Chapters 1 and 3 in Section I. The book provides detailed information on the sport and exercise psychology profession and its training requirements, and guidance on starting out and career possibilities. Secondly, the *Sport and Exercise Psychology Review* (SEPR) journal of the BPS Division of Sport and Exercise Psychology (DSEP) has three special issues devoted to QSEP (Vol. 9 No. 1, February 2013; Vol. 12 No. 2, September 2016; Vol. 15 No. 2, September 2019). These include articles discussing the qualification process, examples of trainee case studies, and insightful reflections from some of the trainees, supervisors, assessors, and key stakeholders (e.g., employers of Sport and Exercise Psychologists) within the QSEP community about their experiences of the qualification, and its contribution to enhancing professional training.

QSEP Training

The QSEP aims to provide professional training that enables the competencies required to perform the role of a Sport and Exercise Psychologist to be developed. It builds on the Stage 1 Sport and Exercise Psychology BPS-accredited training undertaken at Masters (MSc.) level, and through a process of supervised practice, aims to enable trainees to 'apply knowledge to do practice.' The QSEP is a doctoral level 8 qualification, which requires the level of work produced in written and oral assessment (viva) to evidence originality, significance, impact and rigour. QSEP consists of four key role competencies, best described as (1) professional standards and ethical practice; (2) consultancy; (3) research; and (4) communication and dissemination. These key roles fulfil the expectations of what a Sport and Exercise Psychologist should be competent to do on qualification. More details outlining the different key roles, what they entail, and the requirements for them are available in the QSEP candidate handbook.[1]

1. *Competence in being able to develop, implement and maintain personal and professional standards and ethical practice*: This competence involves compliance with the standards of conduct, performance and ethics that should govern our work. This includes (i) desire to develop and enhance ourselves as professional applied psychologists and incorporate best practice into what we do; (ii) assure the integrity of ourselves and our discipline and be cognizant of the privileges and responsibilities of the profession; (iii) ensure the dignity, welfare, rights and privacy of our service users by operating within our professional boundaries; (iv) work effectively with other related professionals and adapt our practice to different organizational contexts of service delivery.

2. *Competence in being able to apply sport and exercise psychology methods, concepts, models, theories and knowledge in consultancy*: This competence involves (i) identifying service user's needs and assessing the feasibility of consultancy; (ii) determining the aims of consultancy and planning the objectives of interventions; (iii) establishing, developing and maintaining working relationships with service users; (iv) conducting consultancy by implementing planned interventions; (v) monitoring and reviewing the implementation of consultancy; and (vi) implementing and assessing evaluation of the impact of consultancy.
3. *Competence in being able to conduct research that develops new sport and exercise psychology methods, concepts, models, theories and instruments, and translate this and existing innovations to inform practice*: This competence involves developing, designing, conducting, analysing and evaluating original sport and exercise psychology research to inform our applied practice, or to use research to solve a real-world problem that has been encountered.
4. *Competence in being able to communicate and disseminate Sport and Exercise Psychology knowledge, principles, methods to educate service users*: This competence involves (i) promoting sport and exercise psychology services and benefits to service users; (ii) feeding back information and providing advice and guidance to meet individual client's needs; (iii) preparing and presenting information to individuals, groups and organizations on the processes and outcomes of psychological interventions.

(Adapted from Eubank & Tod, 2018; pp. 18–19)

While the required competencies are standard requirements, QSEP accommodates the capacity for these to be evidenced in different ways, enabling trainees to tailor their 'on the job training' around their specific interests. On programme entry, QSEP trainees should ideally be in a role or a position to establish a portfolio of work-based opportunities relevant to the qualification to enable the competencies within the four key roles to be acquired across the supervised practice period, which can flexibly be 2, 3, or 4 years in duration. Work can be undertaken across a range of sport and/or exercise settings with different and diverse population groups (e.g., able-bodied and disability athletes, exercisers, coaches, officials, sport governing bodies, health promoters, and parents), at different levels (e.g., professional and amateur, competitive and leisurely participation), and across the age spectrum (e.g., youth athletes, adults and elderly physical activity participants).

QSEP is for those who have Graduate Basis for Chartered Membership of the BPS from an undergraduate psychology degree or conversion course, and a Society-accredited MSc. in Sport or Sport and Exercise Psychology. While QSEP is an independent training route, giving flexibility over the training plan, this does not mean that trainees are on their own. All trainees have a coordinating supervisor who acts as a mentor and support provider over the course of the qualification. Trainees may also have a key role supervisor who provides them with more specialist mentorship, for example, with the research component of the qualification. The BPS has a Qualifications Team that provides administrative support. QSEP has a designated Qualifications Officer to field questions or queries about the qualification, or to get information from a QSEP board official on a trainee's behalf. There are also electronic resources on the qualification website that provide helpful information. The qualification operates within a Virtual Learning Environment (VLE), including for assessment submission and feedback, providing an easy-to-navigate 'one-stop shop' for all QSEP-related matters. Once QSEP is complete, graduates are eligible to apply to register with HCPC as a Sport and Exercise Psychologist and practice independently under this legally protected title. They will also be eligible for Chartered Membership of the BPS (C. Psychol.) and full membership of the DSEP, the benefits of which include reduced fees for conference attendance, access to the Applied Hubs, DSEP Division days, access to the E-Newsletter, opportunity to join Research Working Groups, contribution to and receipt of the SEPR, and full access to the BPS Website and Workshops.

Trainee Reflections

Trainees are the heartbeat of the qualification and the future ambassadors for the Sport and Exercise Psychology profession. The feedback and opinion of the trainee community regarding the value of the qualification in shaping their practitioner development, and how it has helped them to become an effective and employable Sport and Exercise Psychologist is critical to the quality monitoring, assurance and enhancement of QSEP as a worthwhile and meaningful training route. As one trainee explains, the status of QSEP is important.

> For me QSEP was the best route for growing into a professional Sport & Exercise Psychologist. As part of the British Psychological Society, I felt it had an extra level of prestige and rigour that would set me up well for the opportunities I want to pursue. I was drawn to the flexibility and being able to undertake the qualification whilst working full-time alongside developing my own portfolio of work as a Trainee Sport & Exercise Psychologist.

Trainees also reflect positively on the ability of QSEP to engender the 'know', 'know-how', 'show-how' and 'do' (Miller, 1990) of some of the important common and specific active ingredients of applied practice service provision (Tod et al., 2019), and the importance of practice philosophy (Poczwardowski et al., 2004) and reflection (Wadsworth et al., 2021).

> Studying Sport Psychology at University gives you a great insight into the 'what' a Sport Psychologist does, but it is Stage 2 QSEP that really develops your practice by focusing on the 'how' and 'why'. I learned that a professional philosophy is living and breathing; guiding everything that I do but equally being shaped by my experiences. I also came to understand how reflecting is a skill in itself, and probably the most important skill a sport psychologist has at their disposal. The overall QSEP pathway brings these, and several other,

important elements together. It is one thing reading textbooks, but QSEP really embraces the idea of learning-by-doing.

In addition to QSEP's prestige and rigour and its capacity to develop competence, trainees also value its capacity to support their professional development (Tod et al., 2017; Wadsworth et al., 2020), growth (Tod et al., 2020), and individuation (McEwan et al., 2019).

> QSEP can be a demanding, stimulating and insightful experience. In approaching my final submission, I've come to look back and almost be surprised by my own progression.

QSEP Enrolment and Supervision
Enrolling on the Qualification

A trainee can enrol in one of two ways on the qualification. The first is termed 'full enrolment' and is suitable for those trainees who have already identified and secured placements and are able to complete the initial Plan of Training. The Plan of Training is a document that shows how a trainee plans to spend their time accruing the required minimum threshold hours/days for each key role and competency. The second route, 'provisional enrolment', can be used by those trainees who have yet to secure placement opportunities and are not able to complete the plan of training. The provisional enrolment route allows trainees to start the training clock and gives them time to finalise, in supervision, their plan of training. Whilst many supervisors will supervise trainees across all key roles, there may be instances where a key role supervisor will be appointed. Some examples of where this can happen include appointing a key role supervisor for the research element or engaging in an exercise/health placement where the key role supervisor for the duration of placement could be an exercise specialist. It is important to remember that the qualification is both a flexible and independent learning route, in that trainees have up to 4 years to complete the qualification and can orientate practice experiences to their own interests. As one trainee explains:

> The Qualification journey is set up to reflect the work you want to do, the experiences you wish to focus on and the commitment you can make. Whilst the learning is very much self-directed, there is a strong community out there who have either been there or are doing that alongside you.

It is perhaps this degree of flexibility that allows a trainee to shape their own journey. As one of our supervisors acknowledges:

> QSEP provides a diverse breadth of practitioner experiences that facilitate a development and refinement in one's philosophical underpinnings. It is a journey therefore of discovery and challenge, personally and professionally.

Supervision on the Qualification

Supervision is a critical aspect of trainee development and we have previously discussed in detail some of the issues surrounding the supervision of practice (cf. Lafferty et al., 2019). In this section, we briefly describe how supervision fits into the QSEP training model and through the voices of both trainees and supervisors discuss some of the key aspects of supervision as it relates to the qualification. Including how to gain the most from supervision and how supervision has shaped the trainee journey.

Although described as an independent training route, the journey from enrolment through to successful completion is scaffolded and supported through supervision, with minimum criteria and expectations specified in both the Trainee and Supervisor Handbooks. The BPS Register of Applied Psychology Practice Supervisors (RAPPS) lists those approved to supervise QSEP trainees.[2] Each HCPC-registered Sport and Exercise Psychologist on this list has approval to supervise from the Society and its Sport and Exercise Psychology Qualification Board. They will have undertaken both initial training and a commitment to attend regular update training so they are fully aware of any changes within the qualification and to engage in discussion about good supervision practice.

Finding the right supervisor is critical for each trainee. As Cropley and Neil (2014) suggest, the development and nurturing of the supervisory relationship is the capstone to grow both as a person and a practitioner. Therefore, when thinking about who to approach as a supervisor develop a list of questions, it may seem daunting to approach individuals whose papers you have read, or who you may hold in high esteem. That said, the supervisor is providing you with an important service and there is likely to be a financial cost associated with supervision. In reality, when selecting a supervisor you are the client, much in the same way as when an athlete contracts you for your psychological services. Finding a supervisor who is right for you is dependent on fit and whether a working alliance can be formed. Some important key questions that you might ask a potential supervisor include: What is their model of supervision and how do they supervise? What is their practice philosophy? How do they support candidates and what are the experiences on offer? What is the cost of their supervision?

Maximising the benefits of supervision requires work and an understanding that the supervisory relationship changes as you move through the stages of the qualification. As one trainee explained:

> Supervision is a two-way street; the more you put in the more you will receive in return. For me, I quickly discovered that I needed to embrace my own vulnerability. Supervisory meetings are not about a brave face and good impressions, but actually about exploring doubts, decisions and disagreements in a safe environment. In a similar way, this is why choosing the right supervisor is so important. Look to understand their philosophy, approach and style before settling on your choice.

We also see through this how positive supervision should provide a safe space that allows for the sharing of vulnerabilities. Development through supervision does not occur if the focus is on only reviewing the positive aspects of practice. Instead, as one of our supervisors suggests:

> My experience of supervising has evidenced the discomfort and anxiety of moving one's identity into a 'trainee' and the freedom, responsibility and accountability in self presenting/representation to potential individual clients / NGBs / Teams / Clubs etc. that accompanies this transition. The reality of training is this is an important competency to navigate early on (within the psychological safety net of supervision). I also believe a key development milestone of stage two is navigating the 'grey' ethical area of the ethical parameters of 'trainee' competence when it comes to 'real world' practice. In other words how does a 'trainee' decide, work through and know they are competent to start to engage with 'real' clients. Stage 2 plays an important role in shifting trainee practice expectations, supporting trainees as they typically move through a phase of 'imposter' syndrome and into an awareness that stage 2 is about 'firsts' and that this is necessary and normal but doesn't mean you are not 'competent' it is just a different level/expectation of competence (relevant to the trainees specific life context and history).

In essence, supervision should provide a safe space with 'active engagement and connection between supervisor and trainee' where you can share fears and concerns, and the vulnerabilities that come with the journey from trainee to practitioner. Supervisors may often share experiences and engage in what one supervisor describes as 'check and challenge discussions.' From these quotes, we can see that both trainee and supervisor see supervision as an active and dynamic process, a place of psychological safety where you gain support but are constantly evolving as a practitioner.

Critically however, it is important to remember that support during the QSEP journey might not come just from supervisors but also from peer support networks. For some, peer support networks arise from formal supervision in that some supervisors engage in group supervision. In these situations, the supervisory experience is a mix of group and individual sessions. For other trainees their supervisory experience is a more solo venture, this is why it is important to reach out to other trainees and join up with the Applied Hubs and networks, both through the BPS and DSEP and informally. Having a range of differing support networks increases the safety net around you, and peer learning can be a critical aspect of development. As one trainee explained:

> Equally, a great deal of supervised practice comes from peers. Look to build a network of others on the same journey so you can share and compare experiences. Having both formal and peer supervision presents more opportunities to explore your experiences.

QSEP Assessment

The assessment of the QSEP includes a written competency and progress portfolio that is submitted for assessor feedback on three occasions, and via an end-of-qualification oral viva examination. The first and second competency submission is assessed by two independent QSEP-trained assessors and consists of a reflective diary; a practice log; two case studies; an evaluation of Professional Competence; and a research project overview with associated ethical application or approval. For the final competency submission, trainees produce a reflective diary; a practice log; third and fourth case studies, an evaluation of Professional Competence; and a research report with ethical approval evidence. The final portfolio of competence should demonstrate how the required competencies have been developed in accordance with a Plan of Training. The final portfolio comprises evidence for Key Roles – (1) Ethical Competence, (2) Consultancy Competence, and (4) Communication Competence. A research project or systematic review can be submitted in fulfilment of Key Role 3 – Research Competence. Due to the progressive formative assessment and feedback nature of the qualification, the gaining of competence is cumulative. Trainees are required to have demonstrated the full range of competencies by the end of their supervised practice by their two allocated assessors to be able to proceed to viva, which is conducted by the same two assessors. The viva examination enables the assessors to discuss the work within the portfolio with the trainee and to confirm that competence demonstrated in each of the four key roles has been achieved. The Chief Assessor moderates all assessment reports, and on qualification completion, the QSEP board chair ratifies the outcome.

Trainee and Assessor Reflections

> I quickly found I needed to recalibrate my approach from that of doing a University degree. I eventually acknowledged that QSEP was really about empowering me, not directing me what to do. Every opportunity to submit and receive feedback is for you to interpret and learn from. It really is a process, and so it is good to appreciate that along the way. In more practical terms, I tried to make sure I was recording and writing as I went. Structuring your day or week with set time for writing reflections, reading or curating your content is very helpful too! I remember feeling a bit surprised – even embarrassed – when I revisited my first submission, but this feeling is probably the best proof of progress you'll get!

This trainee's reflection captures the ethos of the assessment feedback provided on the QSEP. In essence, good feedback, received and used in the right manner, is a great opportunity to learn and grow. At a more practical level, in compiling the portfolio of evidence there are likely to be many areas of diverse work-related experiences that can elicit the required consultancy, research and reflective products. This requires the trainee and supervisor to make decisions about what to include to best navigate the assessments. Trainees who have been able to do this successfully are able to enlighten neophyte trainees with useful top tips for completing QSEP. These include:

i. 'Don't leave your reflections to the last minute. Keep writing them as you go along on the qualification – they should inform and demonstrate your development, not be an after-thought.'
ii. 'Be regular with your writing-up. It needs to be a habit. If left for too long, it becomes much more difficult to get into the flow.'
iii. 'Keep in touch with your supervisor and have a plan. With everything I've done so far on this qualification I've made a mind map. My advice would be to map things out in a way that works for you. Be thorough and utilise the candidate handbook for precision.'
iv. 'Apply strong self-discipline to your work, work-life balance and self-care.'
v. 'If you struggle with either your writing or time management, get help from your supervisor and peers. Don't be afraid to ask or bury your head in the sand.'

Assessor Reflections

To gain a richer and helpful insight into QSEP assessment, understanding the assessment process from the perspective of the assessors is a valuable source of information and influence (see Eubank et al. 2019). To represent the assessor's voice and generate some equally useful top tips for completing QSEP, three experienced assessors were asked the following questions – (1) How long have you been an assessor and what motivates you to be an assessor on QSEP? (2) What are your top tips for trainees to get the most out of supervised practice on the qualification? (3) What are your top tips for successfully navigating the writing-up and assessment process on the qualification?

Assessor 1

Motivation to Be a QSEP Assessor

I have been an assessor since 2014. I have two main motivations for assessing. First, to try to provide a supportive development process for trainees to facilitate their progression to registered practitioners and instil a mindset of ongoing development. Second (and linked to the first), trainees have so many really innovative approaches to their work, and learning how they are developing enables ongoing learning for myself. There have been so many excellent examples of how trainee reflections/accounts have provided an alternative view of my work.

Top Tips for Getting the Most Out of Supervised Practice

i. Whilst you may not know at the outset, invest time in reviewing core values and beliefs and how they affect your practice philosophy, and subsequent frameworks and approaches to your work – this will give greater confidence when faced with situations that are potentially incongruent with your own position.

ii. Keep in touch with the literature...and I say this in a guarded manner in that no research/case study, etc., will 100% replicate your situation/scenario. However, the work can give you a stronger evidence base on which to make your professional decision. Most of us have key papers/chapters that we go back to...but also be prepared to check whether they also bias us as they are often materials that we refer to before we embark on our training journey.

iii. Don't expect your supervisor to give you all of the answers – be prepared to reflect and use them as a sounding board. You don't always have to agree and as such become a protégé – but do be clear about the rationale that underpins your points. It is ok not to know and seek time to explore, read, reflect, delve deep, and refine.

iv. Seek clarity as to what you are trying to achieve as a practitioner – what is your end goal and how might you evaluate your effectiveness?

Top Tips for Successfully Navigating the Writing-Up and Assessment Process

i. When providing reflections, try to ensure that you do so with ongoing development in mind. Try to avoid just saying, 'this is what I did and this is what happened' – what was the real learning and development that took place and how has it affected your development and ongoing work? There may be some reflections from previous submissions that are useful to refer to so that you can show the ongoing development – having a long-running development theme can be a real strength. The same can be said for CPD – what was the learning that took place? Try to refrain from just stating what the CPD was and what was covered – how has it impacted you?

ii. On writing the KR3 component, perhaps also consider a supporting document/section of the research to detail how it has/may affect your practice. Given that the work is expected to be at doctoral level 8, have a target journal in mind – there is no reason why you should not be considering some form of output from it – the same can be said for the case studies (especially those in the final submission) given the journal outlets that are now available.

iii. It is always interesting to learn how trainees approach new work opportunities – how do they engage with stakeholders/key influencers/the budget holders – how will you present yourself and what would your pitch be? This will also be influenced by the aims you have as a practitioner. However, remember that it is an interaction and that they may not meet your values...the client (whoever that is?!) is not the only one saying yes/no.

Assessor 2

Motivation to Be a QSEP Assessor

I have been assessing the qualification for a number of years. Initially, when I was first asked to become an assessor, I said yes because it was clear that there were too few assessors for the qualification, I saw it as a professional obligation to the BPS. Now being an assessor on QSEP allows me the opportunity to see how the profession is evolving. I think the difficulties of delivery during the Coronavirus pandemic have been particularly interesting. I see just how well and well placed our QSEP trainees have been to move their work remotely to maintain social distancing but also how they have adapted their work to meet the particular needs of clients during this time. By assessing portfolios of work, I am able to stay informed on professional practice literature but also see the kinds of issues that trainees are facing. Assessing work then informs my Stage 1 teaching as well as the career mentorship work I undertake with students approaching graduation or graduates after they have left the university I work at. The crossover of responsibilities to my own institution and to the professional body is extremely valuable as I can be reassured that the changes I advocate are informed by current information from people entering the profession.

Top Tips for Getting the Most Out of Supervised Practice

i. See the qualification as an opportunity to explore and try new things; the training pathway is there to act as a scaffold to allow you the chance to try new methods, read widely, and have conversations with new people.
ii. See it as that opportunity to immerse yourself in a new area, be curious and inquisitive and don't be afraid to experiment. Don't be afraid to reach out to others in the profession to observe or shadow them in practice but to also gain their insight into the profession. By surrounding yourself with others in the professional community, you will feel less isolated and hopefully more informed and confident in your decision-making.
iii. Try to gain a wide range of experiences across your time on QSEP; it can be tempting to stick with what you know or a position that is offered, but ensure that you are working across sports, at different levels, with different ages, genders, etc.
iv. Also consider gaining experience outside of competitive sport. Exercise Psychology and physical activity are forming part of the country's COVID-19 recovery plan for the improvement of health and wellbeing. There may be opportunities to provide and disseminate evaluation evidence in relation to local and national initiatives that can be used to demonstrate Key Role 4 competencies.

Top Tips for Successfully Navigating the Writing-Up and Assessment Process

i. One of the consistent issues that assessors see and comment on is the lack of literature used within reflections. Trainees need to demonstrate that their work is at the level of the qualification and therefore the reflections need to move beyond a description of the event, actions, feelings, thoughts, and plans.

Consider reading about the experience and incorporating the views from the literature on the issue. Are your own thoughts and feelings compatible with the published literature? Can your future actions be informed by literature?

ii. Read widely; some trainees tend to limit themselves to the applied practice literature from within the profession and therefore miss the opportunity to explore the wider literature for insights. If you are working on systemic issues, what can be learnt from occupational psychology? If you are working with young athletes and their families, what can be learnt from the developmental and counselling literature?

iii. Try to demonstrate progression; you can refer back to earlier reflections/case studies to demonstrate how your actions or thinking has evolved and why.

iv. Finally, consider trying different practice reflective frameworks across the qualification and discuss this in terms of your professional philosophy, therapeutic modality, etc. There are a number of reflective practice frameworks to choose from.

Assessor 3

Motivation to Be a QSEP Assessor

I've been assessing for 3 years. Having completed Stage 2 myself, I can relate to and understand trainees' experiences on the Qualification, have reasonable expectations, and offer informed feedback and advice. I appreciate supporting the development of others, by drawing upon my own learning, knowledge, and experiences.

Top Tips for Getting the Most Out of Supervised Practice

i. Read extensively. As part of my Plan of Training, I read two papers or chapters a week for all 3 years. To state a few ways that reading supported my progress, it gave me ideas for practice, helped me to navigate ethical issues, informed my philosophy of practice, supported different elements of the Case Studies (e.g., literature on needs analyses or evaluating practice), and helped me to interpret and make sense of my experiences while reflecting.

ii. Find a way of reflecting (e.g., a reflective model, use of supervision) that works for you and that helps you to achieve meaningful learning from experiences, and pursue varied learning opportunities (e.g., different sports, competitive levels, genders).

Top Tips for Successfully Navigating the Writing-Up and Assessment Process

i. Pace the workload and stay on top of the administration. Completing the practice log and reflective diary as you go is more much manageable and will support high-quality paperwork.

ii. In the Practice Log, provide brief details on the nature of the clients (e.g., sport, approx. age) and the nature of the work (e.g., 1–2 sentences on what the work involved) to support the Assessors in navigating the paperwork and in getting a feel for the work you do.
iii. In your Reflective Diary, select and share the most meaningful reflections that supported your learning and development. Demonstrate your reading through meaningful engagement with literature in your reflections.
iv. For the case studies, read some of the published examples in SEPR to have a clear understanding of what is expected. Demonstrate how the reading you are doing is informing your work.

Conclusion

Since 2019, the Stage 2 QSEP has made a significant contribution to the quality and standards of Sport and Exercise Psychology professional training in the UK. Through its content, structure, effective supervision, and assessment processes, the qualification has facilitated the training and development of a significant number of outstanding Sport and Exercise Psychologists in our field. Through the qualification's trainee, supervisor, and assessor community, we have been able to positively maintain the health and vitality of the *profession*, engender the recognised standards of professional competence and conduct to practice in our *professionals*, and support the qualification's responsibility for the development, promotion and application of psychology for the public good. On reading this chapter, it is hoped that other aspiring Sport and Exercise Psychologists will be inspired to use the Qualification to complete their own training and make their own quality contribution to Sport and Exercise Psychology service provision of the future. After reading this chapter, readers are encouraged to consider the following key questions:

- Why is the QSEP the right independent training route for me?
- What is the value of being able to produce and translate original research to develop effectiveness in my own applied practice?
- What questions do I need to ask to secure the right supervisor to best support my development needs as a trainee on the qualification?

Acknowledgements

We would like to extend our sincere thanks to the QSEP trainees, supervisors, and assessors who contributed their reflections for this chapter.

Notes

1 https://www.bps.org.uk/qualifications/sport-exercise-psychology/outline.
2 https://portal.bps.org.uk/Psychologist-search/Register-of-Applied-Psychology-Practice-Supervisors.

References

Cropley, B., & Neil, R. (2014). The neophyte supervisor: What did I get myself into? In *Becoming a Sport, Exercise, and Performance Psychology Professional* (pp. 247–255). Psychology Press.

Eubank, M., & Tod, D. (2018). *How to Become a Sport and Exercise Psychologist*. Routledge.

Eubank, M., Holder, T., Lowry, R., Manley, A., Maynard, I., McCormick, A., Smith, J., Thelwell, R., Woodman, T., & Lafferty, M. (2019). All roads lead to Rome, but Rome wasn't built in a day. Advice on QSEP navigation from the 'Roman Gods' of assessment! *Sport and Exercise Psychology Review, 15*, 21–31.

Lafferty, M., Hemmings, B., Katz, J., Cunliffe, M., & Eubank, M. (2019). Many roads can lead to Rome – Supervisors perspectives on successful supervision and its challenges. *Sport and Exercise Psychology Review, 15*, 14–20.

McEwan, H. E., Tod, D., & Eubank, M. (2019). The rocky road to individuation: Sport psychologists' perspectives on professional development. *Psychology of Sport and Exercise, 45*, Article 101542.

Miller, G. E. (1990). The assessment of clinical skills/competence/performance. *Academic medicine, 65*(9), S63–S67.

Poczwardowski, A., Sherman, C. P., & Ravizza, K. (2004). Professional philosophy in the sport psychology service delivery: Building on theory and practice. *The Sport Psychologist, 18*, 445–463.

Tod, D., Hardy, J., Lavallee, D., Eubank, M., & Ronkainen, N. (2019). Practitioners' narratives regarding active ingredients in service delivery: Collaboration-based problem solving. *Psychology of Sport and Exercise, 43*, 350–358.

Tod, D., Hutter, V., & Eubank, M. R. (2017). Professional development for sport psychology practice. *Current Opinion in Psychology, 16*, 134–137.

Tod, D., McEwan, H., Chandler, C., Eubank, M., & Lafferty, M. (2020). The gravitational pull of Identity: Professional growth in sport, exercise, and performance psychologists. *Journal of Sport Psychology in Action, 11*(4), 233–242.

Wadsworth, N., McEwan, H., Lafferty, M., Eubank, M. R., & Tod, D. (2020). Stories of critical moments contributing to the development of applied sport psychology practitioners. *The Sport Psychologist, 35*(1), 11–21.

Wadsworth, N., McEwan, H., Lafferty, M., Eubank, M. R., & Tod, D. (2021). A systematic review exploring the reflective accounts of applied sport psychology practitioners. *International Review of Sport and Exercise Psychology*. ISSN 1750-984X.

2
THE BRITISH ASSOCIATION OF SPORT AND EXERCISE SCIENCES (BASES) SPORT AND EXERCISE PSYCHOLOGY ACCREDITATION ROUTE (SEPAR)

Chris Harwood, Claire J. L. Rossato, Richard Thelwell and Zoe Knowles

The British Association of Sport and Exercise Sciences (BASES) Sport and Exercise Psychology Accreditation Route (SEPAR)

The professional development and qualification of practitioners seeking to provide psychological services in the sport industry has been, and remains, both a contentious and vital topic for discussion. This is pertinent to the ethical obligations for any practitioner to serve the well-being and care of their clients (Tod et al., 2017). This chapter will outline the purpose, aims and requirements of the British Association of Sport and Exercise Sciences (BASES) Sport and Exercise Psychology Accreditation Route (SEPAR).[1] Details of the qualifications and entry requirements for this pathway, the enrolment process, the qualification journey, a summary of the key competencies which trainees are expected to develop and assessment methods for such competencies are provided. To provide a working illustration of the scheme, reflections from a trainee who has taken this pathway and an assessor and supervisor will follow, as they share their experience of undertaking the qualification and offer tips and guidance for future trainees.

Background to BASES as an Organisation

BASES is the professional body for sport and exercise science in the UK. Originally formed in 1984, it has five Divisions that represent the breadth of sport and exercise science disciplines Biomechanics and Motor Behaviour, Physiology and Nutrition, Psychology, Physical Activity for Health, and Sport and Performance. BASES has operated a training and accreditation system for practitioners working within sport and sport science since the early 1990s. With the title 'Sport and Exercise Psychologist' legally protected by the Health Professions Order 2001 and regulated by the Health and Care Professions Council (HCPC), BASES redesigned its accreditation programme in sport and exercise psychology to meet the required HCPC regulations. In 2019, the SEPAR was launched by BASES and represents an independent training route with enrolments for 2-, 3- or 4-year duration depending on the individual circumstances of the Sport and Exercise Psychologist in Training (SEPiT) to meet the required competencies and hours of experience.

SEPAR Governance, Quality Assurance and Core Training

At the heart of the SEPAR governance and quality assurance process is the SEPAR Advisory Group (SEPAR AG) who report to the BASES Professional Standards Committee. The SEPAR AG are responsible for quality assurance (e.g., SEPAR documentation, provision of candidate feedback,), maintenance of professional ethics and standards (e.g., monitoring of equal opportunity processes, learner complaints and appeals), marketing and communications (e.g., to maintain and develop the reputation of the SEPAR and the broader role of BASES to wider society), end-user and stakeholder engagement (e.g., to determine whether the service meets members and end-user needs and expectations), assessing and alignment to the HCPC Standards of Education and Training and Standards of Proficiency (e.g., to conform with the HCPC Performance Review process). Via the SEPAR AG, the feedback from the candidate, reviewer and supervisor representatives following the first few cycles helped to facilitate the development of the core training offer to candidates: An introductory SEPAR workshop (within the first month of registration); BASES safeguarding, ethics in professional practice, reflective practice workshops; eight BASES mental health in sport and exercise [online] units (to be completed within the first 12 months of registration); and finally, SEPAR-specific case study workshops and counselling workshop (to be completed by the mid-point competence profile submission. Two further core training workshops covering 'practice philosophy' and 'equity, diversity and inclusivity in sport and exercise psychology' were introduced in Spring 2022.

SEPAR Entry Requirements and Enrolment

Following pre-application checks to confirm candidate citizenship status/residence, the SEPAR Application Process requires evidence of specific education and qualifications that candidates MUST hold at the point of entry. These are in addition to holding a minimum of Graduate membership of BASES which must be maintained throughout the SEPAR programme.

Such relevant and necessary education and qualifications include an:

i. **Evidence of underpinning psychology knowledge**. This refers to the study and assessment of individual differences, cognitive, social, biological and developmental psychology and can be achieved via one of the following:
    - a professionally accredited BSc psychology course[2];
    - a professionally accredited PGCert/conversion psychology course[3];

- the 60-credit Open University module *'Investigating Psychology'* – a course that is organised via BASES for those individuals who have not taken appropriate academic credit-bearing courses in psychology (i.e., BSc in psychology) at the undergraduate level (see information on SEPAR webpage);
- by prior recognition of underpinning psychology knowledge from a learned society/professional body (e.g., British Psychological Society in the UK and overseas equivalent)

ii. **Evidence of an MSc Sport and/or Exercise Psychology.** In addition to this undergraduate level education, a fundamental entry requirement of the SEPAR is the completion of a postgraduate/Level 7 academic programme in sport and/or exercise psychology

Alongside these educational requirements, evidence of a standard of proficiency in the English language to IELTS Grade 7 (with no less than 6.5 in any area) may be required for international applicants and confirmation from a SEPAR-accredited supervisor that they are prepared to fulfil the required supervisory role throughout the SEPAR for the applicant. Finally, the candidate will need to provide confirmation of appropriate professional indemnity cover and submit to a DBS check provided by the Government Disclosure and Barring Service.

The SEPAR requires candidates to develop standards of proficiency in sport and/or exercise psychology across four categories of competencies representing *knowledge, skills, self-development and management* and *experience*. Such competencies mirror Miller's (1990) prism of clinical competence (adapted by Mehay & Burns, 2012) in that candidates are expected to move from a position of *knowing* (where candidates know and understand the key concepts associated with sport and/or exercise psychology,) through to *doing* (where competence can be demonstrated and is integrated into practice). Throughout the SEPAR, candidates move along a 0 (no competence) to 5 (full competence) Likert scale of self-assessment whereby their evidence of growing knowledge, skills, self-development and practical experiences serve to inform the ratings (i.e., 0–5) that they propose to their assessors at initial, mid-point and end-point submissions. Details on each of these categories are presented below.

Knowledge

The thematic elements of the 'Knowledge' category that illustrate specific *knowledge-based competencies* are presented in Table 2.1 and available with further details in the SEPAR candidate handbook on the website.[4]

Candidates will enter the SEPAR with wide-ranging undergraduate educational experiences and knowledge from their courses (e.g., Sport and Exercise Science, Sport and Exercise Psychology, Psychology). Postgraduate experiences and knowledge development have a more 'standardised' approach although the structures, learning, teaching and assessment strategies, and focus of expertise within courses will often vary. As such, it cannot be assumed that the necessary 'knowledge' competence will have been achieved.

TABLE 2.1 SEPAR Knowledge-Based Competencies

1. Knowledge

Theme	Competency Number	Competency
		Candidates should know and understand the key concepts associated with the scientific knowledge base in:
Sport & Exercise Psychology		
	1.1.1	The nature of sport and exercise psychology
	1.1.2	Motivation, confidence and participation for sport, physical activity and exercise
	1.1.3	Group and team based theories
	1.1.4	Gender, diversity and cultural competence
	1.1.5	Contemporary topics in sport and exercise psychology
	1.1.6	Mental health
Sport Psychology		
	1.2.1	Performance enhancement
	1.2.2	Psychomotor learning and sport performance
	1.2.3	Understanding of special issues in sport psychology
	1.2.4	Coaching psychology
Exercise Psychology		
	1.3.1	Epidemiology of physical activity and health
	1.3.2	Physical activity promotion strategies
	1.3.3	Special populations in physical activity and exercise
Complimentary Areas to Sport & Exercise Psychology		
	1.4.1	The sport sciences and allied professions
Issues in Professional Practice		
	1.5.1	Current issues in the professional practice of sport & exercise psychology
	1.5.2	Frameworks for applied sport & exercise psychology
	1.5.3	Approaches to counselling

Given the more 'standardised' approach to the MSc level knowledge development for candidates, they will be able to claim a **baseline competence rating of 2** for the 'sport and/or exercise psychology' competencies (1.1, 1.2, 1.3 and 1.5). To meet the threshold competence levels in these areas (which is viewed as a 4), candidates will then be required to engage in ongoing personal study/development. The competencies in 1.4 (complimentary areas to sport and exercise psychology) have a different rating scale. Given that candidates will have had varied exposure to the disciplines outside of sport and exercise psychology (e.g., physiology, biomechanics, nutrition, physiotherapy/massage, performance analysis, performance lifestyle and, strength and conditioning) throughout their prior educational experiences, it is difficult to assume any consistent prior level of knowledge. Further, with candidates unlikely to work solely in isolation, it is essential for them to have, at least, a working knowledge of alternative sport and exercise science/medicine disciplines. In summary, the 'Knowledge' category is for candidates to rate their current competence regarding 'what they know' and 'how they understand key concepts'. Candidates are not required to detail how they use their knowledge in practice; this is evidenced through their skills development.

Skills

The competency themes for the 'Skills' category, as well as the specific *skills-based competencies*, are presented in Table 2.2.

TABLE 2.2 SEPAR Skills-Based Competencies

2. Skills

Theme	Competency Number	Competency
		Candidates should be able to:
Communication and Presentation Skills		
	2.1.1	Demonstrate the ability to communicate effectively using verbal and non-verbal approaches with specialist and non-specialist audiences via presentations
	2.1.2	Demonstrate the ability to communicate effectively using verbal and non-verbal approaches with specialist and non-specialist audiences via verbal reports
	2.1.3	Demonstrate the ability to communicate effectively with specialist and non-specialist audiences via written reports
	2.1.4	Demonstrate the ability to communicate effectively using verbal and non-verbal approaches with specialist and non-specialist audiences via creative/non-standard methods
Needs Analysis		
	2.2.1	Assess the performance-related demands of the particular sport or exercise context
	2.2.2	Assess organisational structure to inform evaluation
	2.2.3	Understand the requirements of team member audits/ intake interviews
	2.2.4	Identify clients' expectations, needs and requirements in order to appropriately negotiate the priorities of the client
Understanding and Use of Research		
	2.3.1	Justify decisions made for consultancy from that of a research-informed practice position through case formulation
	2.3.2	Offer a research overview to client/athlete/coach/parent in an appropriate format to justify practice
Intervention Design		
	2.4.1	Select appropriate interventions based on needs analysis outcomes or intervention

(Continued)

TABLE 2.2 (Continued)

2. Skills		
Theme	Competency Number	Competency
Consultancy Skills		
	2.5.1	Discuss and explain the rationale for, the use of sport and exercise science interventions
	2.5.2	Negotiate roles and responsibilities in relation to client and/or stakeholder needs
	2.5.3	Recognise the need to use interpersonal skills to encourage active participation of service users in consultancy sessions
	2.5.4	Apply technical frameworks in action in order to achieve agreed client outcomes
	2.5.5	Work effectively with other professionals, support staff and others (e.g., medical team) as part of a multidisciplinary team
	2.5.6	Build and sustain relationships with a range of clients and stakeholders
	2.5.7	Use counselling skills to optimise the consultancy process
	2.5.8	Demonstrate a logical and systematic approach to problem-solving
Evaluation in Professional Practice		
	2.6.1	Understand requisite elements to offer a single case design/single case study
	2.6.2	Select elements of evaluating intervention effectiveness appropriate to the agreed outcomes
	2.6.3	Select and assess elements of consultant effectiveness appropriate to the role, consultancy expectations and service deliverables
	2.6.4	Demonstrate the need for ongoing monitoring and evaluation in order to revise intervention plans where necessary

The 'Skills' category of the SEPAR focuses on the *candidate's development of critical interpersonal and technical skills that are associated with their effective delivery of services* as a sport and exercise psychologist. The engine room of being a sport and exercise psychologist is represented by the processes that the practitioner engages in practice from the 'beginnings' to the 'ends' of working with a client or organisation (see Keegan, 2016). First, candidates must demonstrate an awareness of how effective communication can be affected by culture, age, ethnicity, gender, religious beliefs, nationality, sexuality and socio-economic status. It is expected that candidates can demonstrate evidence of communicating appropriately in different formats across a range of audiences. Second, candidates must be able to illustrate competence in needs analysis and an understanding of the client's context through appropriate psychological assessment methods and information gathering. Applying their knowledge of the best available research literature in the field and synthesising the information gathered from the clients aids in the execution of accurate case formulation. This enables the candidate to develop appropriate interventions based on client needs and then to execute their intervention and support to their client through skilful consulting and the use of strategies that are evidence-based. Finally, it is important for SEPiTs to have systems of monitoring and evaluation of their applied work in place. Practitioners need to be aware of the effects of their work and to monitor changes as their work takes its course. In addition, the evaluation of work by key stakeholders (e.g., client, coach, parents/carers) is important both during and at the end of a performance phase or period of consultation.

In sum, the 'Skills' category of the SEPAR challenges the candidate to illustrate 'why' a client may need a particular type of support (i.e., appropriate evidence-based needs analysis and assessment skills), to select 'what' strategies and areas of work are most pertinent to helping the client and to showcase 'how' they go about such work in a professional and competent manner with a skilful application of relevant techniques.

Self-Development and Management

The competency themes for the *Self-Development and Management* category, as well as the specific *self-development and management-based competencies*, are outlined in Table 2.3.

TABLE 2.3 SEPAR Self-Development and Management-Based Competencies

3. Self		
Theme	Competency Number	Competency
		Candidates should be able to:
Defining a Personal Approach to Sport and Exercise Psychology activities		
	3.1.1	State and justify their own philosophical approach to practice
	3.1.2	Demonstrate an appreciation of the different contexts in which they may function (e.g. Sport vs. Exercise; Insider [National Governing Body] vs. Outsider [Private Practice])
	3.1.3	Know the limits of their own practice and when to seek advice or refer to another professional
	3.1.4	Be able to practice within the legal and ethical boundaries of their profession
Development of Own Practice		
	3.2.1	Analyse their own strengths and weaknesses and identify areas for personal development
	3.2.2	Understand the value of reflection on practice and evidence engagement in the process
	3.2.3	Demonstrate a commitment to, and engagement with, professional development through continuing advancement of own knowledge, understanding and competence

(Continued)

TABLE 2.3 (Continued)

3. Self		
Theme	Competency Number	Competency
Ensuring Professional Compliance and Duty of Care		
	3.3.1	Maintain records appropriately and in line with data protection requirements
	3.3.2	Promote and implement robust policies and protocols relating to health, wellbeing, safety and security of themselves and their clients
	3.3.3	Promote and ensure compliance with all relevant regulatory requirements and quality standards
	3.3.4	Demonstrate an understanding and compliance with relevant codes of conduct (e.g., BASES, HCPC) to ensure ethical and safeguarding principles are applied in practice
	3.3.5	Understand the principles of duty of care, professional standards, quality control and quality assurance
Management of Resources, Risks, Self and Others		
	3.4.1	Demonstrate the achievement of desired outcomes with the effective management of resources and risks
	3.4.2	Effectively manage resources and risks to ensure the wellbeing of self and others
	3.4.3	Demonstrate effective leadership through the ability to guide, influence, inspire and empathise with others

The essential focus of the 'Self-Development and Management' category is to ensure *that candidates have appropriate regulatory systems in place* – both at a personal and business level. For example, meeting safeguarding and insurance requirements for trading as a business/sole-trader, illustrating their application of ethical knowledge by making appropriate ethical decisions and pursuing ongoing professional development opportunities. This competency also challenges candidates to reflect upon and draw together their personal and professional values in helping them to discover, define and redefine their approach to practice as a sport and exercise psychologist. At all submission points of the SEPAR, we ask SEPiTs to provide a reflection piece regarding their emerging practice philosophy, how this might influence day-to-day work and how they plan to ensure congruence between their philosophy and behaviour. This approach allows candidates to demonstrate the evolution of their practice philosophy across the SEPAR period as part of their personal and professional development.

Experience

The competency themes for the *Experience* category, as well as the specific *experience competencies*, are presented in Table 2.4.

TABLE 2.4 SEPAR Experience-Based Competencies

4. Experience		
Theme	Competency Number	Competency
Sport and/or Exercise Participation		
	4.1.1	Competitive/practical experience as a sport performer and/or exercise participant/exercise contexts
	4.1.2	Experience of insights into stakeholder (e.g., parents, family members, sponsors) demands
Allied Professions		
	4.2.1	Experience of working with practitioners in the disciplines of sport science and/or allied health professions (e.g., doctors; nutritionists)
	4.2.2	Experience of working as part of a multidisciplinary team to support athletes
	4.2.3	Experience of coaching, team leader and/or management roles
The Sport and/or Exercise Psychologist		
	4.3.1	Experience of working as a practitioner with a range of sport and/or exercise types
	4.3.2	Experience of working as a practitioner with a range of populations
	4.3.3	Experience of working as a practitioner with clients on a one-to-one basis
	4.3.4	Experience of working as a practitioner with clients in group and/or team settings
	4.3.5	Integrated sport or exercise psychology support to coaches and/or exercise leaders

Throughout the SEPAR process, it is essential that the SEPiT gains 'Experience' of working with a *range of populations throughout their training experience*. Executing their developing skills in various sport or exercise contexts (e.g., active, sedentary, those with medical conditions, senior athletes, coaches, youth age groups, individual vs. team sports, etc.) means that candidates will become sport and exercise psychologists as opposed to sport-specific psychologists, or exercise psychologists with experience of only one sample population.

Competency in sport and/or exercise participation to appreciate what it is like to be an athlete/exerciser who has experienced some form of competition/programme is viewed as important. Additionally, the SEPAR expects the candidate to develop competencies in working within a sport science, sports medicine, health and clinical exercise support team. The emerging roles for a sport psychology or exercise psychology consultant not only include working *through* the coach/allied health care professional, but also *with* the coach/allied health care professional. In addition, support staff in the allied professions are not immune to needing psychological support at times and is an appropriate service for the sport and exercise psychologist to conduct. Working in an integrated fashion with other sport/exercise, science/medical personnel (e.g., fitness coach/dietician/physiotherapist) can ensure a more interdisciplinary service for the individual, particularly with respect to lifestyle management, goal setting plans and rehabilitation programmes.

In sum, this Experience category serves as an indicative map or blueprint for the range of contexts and populations in sport and exercise where candidates are asked to apply their *knowledge*, *skills* and benefits of their *self-development and management*.

Your Pathway, Your Choice

Beyond demonstrating competence across their portfolio of activity, the main challenge for SEPAR candidates is to evidence sport and/or exercise psychology-related activities to the level of **3,200 hours/400 days**. As a general rule, candidates are advised that if they are working in a part-time capacity on the SEPAR, then either a 3- or 4-year registration period would be more appropriate for them to complete the required number of hours.

To complete the SEPAR process, irrespective of the length of registration, candidates are expected to:

1. Demonstrate and evidence the minimum required level of competence across the four categories of competence;
2. Evidence engagement in minimum of 3,200 hours of activity (400 days equivalent). These are broken down into:
   a. *Application/consulting* – 2,700 hours of consulting [900 hours of direct contact, 900 hours of planning, 900 hours of reflection];
   b. *Continuing Professional Development (CPD) and supervisor-led activity* – 275 hours;
   c. *Dissemination and citizenship* – 225 hours of (e.g., teaching, research, observed practice, role play, promotion of the industry);
3. Be observed in practice (live or via video) by their supervisor for a minimum of 20 hours (with documented evidence of observations);
4. Complete an initial (3-month), mid-point and final portfolio of evidence submission. Following the mid-point review the candidate and the review team will engage in a formal interview (e-meeting) to discuss candidate progress and developmental needs;
5. Produce three case studies, one at the mid-way submission point and two at the final submission point;
6. Be able to provide three references from clients who are able to offer insight into the candidate's practice (e.g., autonomy, ethical issues, effectiveness) and their suitability as a safe, effective and independent Sport and Exercise Psychologist.

The Initial 3-Month Submission

For all candidates, there is an initial 3-month competency submission where by the candidate, supervisor and, ultimately, reviewers agree 'where the candidate is' within the first 3 months of their SEPAR journey. In this submission, the evidence-gathering process is fundamental in that the candidate is asked to provide relevant evidence against the rating they have claimed on their competency table. the SEPAR provides several templates that can be used to record evidence of relevant activities that illustrate competence. In this first submission, many of the ratings will be very low and the candidate (with the assistance of the supervisor) is asked to plan activities and set goals to move the candidate up the competency rating ladder in terms of Knowledge, Skills, Self and Experience. In this respect, the competency profile includes a current rating of competence, a target rating of competence for the mid-point review and activities/actions that are set to enable the target goal to be achieved. Once submitted, the external SEPAR reviewers attached to the candidate will appraise the competence submission and offer extensive feedback to the candidate and supervisor.

The Mid-Point Submission

At the SEPAR mid-point submission, the candidate documents all necessary evidence to support their progress made across the ratings since the initial (3-month) submission. This means re-rating themselves against each competency and then setting their new targets for the final period (i.e., second half) of the SEPAR. Candidates will outline the remaining activities for meeting these goals in readiness for their final submission. Upon receipt of the mid-point reviewer feedback, candidates will also have a mid-point review meeting to discuss the 'process-related' rather than 'knowledge-related' aspects of their development, and to allow the candidate to discuss their progress and remaining developmental needs. In this mid-term submission, the portfolio of evidence compiled by the candidate is more sizeable and several elements are required here in addition to the ongoing evidence of activity collected by the candidate across logs of practice log, CPD and supervisor-activity, dissemination and citizenship, supervisor observation and supervisor report form which provide an appraisal of the candidate's progress against the four core categories of competence since the initial submission.

The candidate is encouraged in the SEPAR to use innovative ways to introduce and highlight any key areas of progress and development over the previous term for the reviewers as part of a synopsis of their experience. In this respect, we encourage candidates to submit a 5-minute video file where they share their perspectives as well as key goals for the upcoming term. This enables the candidate to interact more personably with the reviewers and sets up the e-meeting for further discussion. Finally, candidates are required to submit one formal case study of practice up to 4,000 words following a SEPAR Case Study template and at least one formal Client Reference which allows the reviewers to critically appraise the processes and skills 'at work' undertaken by the candidate through supporting one client in depth. Such case studies are important in illustrating the know-do pathway to competence (Mehay & Burns, 2012) where candidates can demonstrate how their 'knowledge' informs their 'know-how' and their 'show-how' in terms of 'doing' effective work with a client. Reviewers will state whether candidates have/have not met the targeted competence levels at the mid-point of their SEPAR and offer detailed feedback and an agenda for the mid-term e-meeting.

The Final Submission

The final submission should document all necessary evidence to support the progress made across the ratings since the mid-point submission and outline any activities of note to be completed post-SEPAR. If the review team agrees that the minimum level of competency has been achieved across all areas, then the candidate will be deemed as SEPAR completed and eligible to apply for registration with the HCPC.

The final submission requires submission of the same logs as the initial and mid-point submissions to be uploaded into the candidate's portfolio 'portal' for review, a final video or cover summary highlighting progress and development since the mid-term review, two further formal case studies following specific SEPAR Case Study templates and at least two further formal Client References as endorsements of the candidates work. If candidates have not met the targeted competence levels at the final point of their SEPAR period, the reviewers will make recommendations for any additional work that needs to be completed. This will result in a resubmission that will be submitted after either 6 or 12 months, with the former being the preferred option.

A Practitioner's Reflection on SEPAR and Supervisor Tips

When first enrolling on the SEPAR programme, my expectations were to go through a process in which I would gain HCPC but also learn from other practitioners, and attend various workshops and CPD events along the way. To gain HCPC registration, I elected to undertake the SEPAR over a Professional Doctorate as I already held a PhD; in addition, I could use my existing BASES Accreditation (Psychological Support) to claim for some of my hours and competencies via the Accreditation of Prior Experiential Competence (APEC) route. Furthermore, within the SEPAR pathway enrolment, I was able to access a suite of workshops as part of my core training as well as having the opportunity to attend various CPD events such as division days within BASES. Therefore, I selected the SEPAR pathway over the BPS Qualification in Sport and Exercise Psychology (Stage 2). I was unsure what the experience would be like, given this was a new training pathway. I wanted to learn as much as possible from the process and hoped that it would be a helpful learning experience and a way to potentially enhance my applied practice along the way, through discussion and exploration within a peer supervision group.

My journey began in February 2020 with my expectations of the process twofold at this point – the first, gaining HCPC registration and the second, to be able to gain knowledge and experience from working with others going through the process. I also felt that it was a good opportunity to reflect upon my own practice and identify areas of potential development that I could further work on during my enrolment to enhance applied practice. Being an Accredited Sport and Exercise Scientist (Psychological Support) in conjunction with BASES, I was able to enrol on SEPAR with an accelerated route being APEC. This route is for 1 year if enrolled on a full-time pathway and takes into account previous experiences from my existing BASES accreditation (Psychological Support). I would encourage candidates to talk to at least two supervisors before making their decision (readers are referred to Chapter 5 for further guidance on the Supervisor–Supervisee relationship). Arranging initial meetings with supervisors is a good way to ask questions about their supervision style and to see if their way of supervision will be suited to your individual needs. It is important to remember that you will spend at least 2 years with your supervisor. Once the decision is made, a contract should be produced between the supervisor and the supervisee, this is where expectations can be set out and you can be clear about how much contact/feedback is offered during your time on the programme.

I felt very excited about embarking on this journey, in addition to being enrolled (finally on my path to HCPC registration), I was also welcomed into a supervision group, which consisted of practitioners from a variety of different psychology backgrounds including sport, clinical and exercise. This allowed me to learn from other practitioners and hear about their experiences working in the field. The group's experience varied from the English Institute of Sport (EIS) practitioners, Premier League, clinical psychologists and those working around mental health. Therefore, this made a great forum to share and explore different opinions and practices, and share experiences of the journey. Being part of this group complemented individual supervision, giving another space to explore different scenarios within applied practice and an opportunity to ask questions within the discussions. Having this space allowed us as a group to explore ethical issues, recent events that we could talk through with the group and broad questions that the group may have had. During my time enrolled on the SEPAR, I met with several members on an individual basis to talk over specific ways of practice within specific sports. This helped to develop my knowledge base and widen my network further. This group is still something I attend to this day to explore various topics related to applied practice.

Self-Assessment of Competencies, Planning and Feedback (from Reviewers)

The next phase of the journey was to complete my initial competency profile for submission. Approximately 1 month after my registration to the SEPAR, I attended the online SEPAR 'Introductory Workshop' for applicants. This helped to gain familiarity with the administration, process of reviewing, expectations for the qualification and clarity on how to present and complete the documentation for the initial review, with live demonstrations on how this could be completed. I saw the completion of the documentation as an opportunity to showcase activities and applied work I had previously undertaken, relating these directly to the competencies on the profile. However, there were several competencies that I had not previously considered to evidence, and the completion of the competency profile aided in identifying areas for development. Therefore, completing this process allowed me to identify clear areas that I could focus on over the next year. I submitted my initial competence profile along with my portfolio of evidence and practice, CPD and dissemination and citizenship log. I tried to make evidence mapping as clear as possible with reference to the competency and where the evidence could be located within the portfolio and practice logs.

Highlighting areas that need further evidence were easy to identify, especially after receiving feedback from the two reviewers. The feedback contained many highlighted areas to give me a clear structure regarding areas I could provide more evidence for over the next 12 months. An example of reviewer feedback can be seen in Figure 2.1.

From the feedback received I was able to devise a clear plan to demonstrate the competencies that needed further information to help complete the profile. The feedback was clear and concise, and I was able to highlight specific areas from the feedback to build developmental points to focus on over my duration on the SEPAR. For instance, this included reflections of working with clinical populations or with various charities and the further submission of case studies within the final submission in order to address the feedback provided (see Figure 2.1). During this process, my supervisor and I were able to also identify areas for specific development and, using feedback from subsequent observations, able to demonstrate competencies further. Key resources were highlighted regarding development, for example, reading other case studies within the *Case Studies in Sport and Exercise Psychology* (CSSEP) journal publication. Being part of the supervision group also allowed me to talk through various experiences such as navigating new contracts and talking through various scenarios that posed challenges to me during my time on SEPAR.

Do you, the Reviewer, agree with the levels of competence claimed in this category?
If no, which competencies require consideration (and why)?

1.3.3 - There is a lack of evidence around work with special populations that we would like to see further information on. Acknowledging the work with Boccia, it would be valuable to see some reflections around other special populations, either through self-directed learning, or reflections on work.

FIGURE 2.1 An exemplar of feedback received during initial submission of portfolio and competency profile.

Competency Development and Supervisory Support along the Journey

Having a plan in place based on the initial competency profile, I was then able to reflect on activities that were carried out over the next year helped by the new peer supervision group I was part of. This allowed discussion of various cases, ethical issues and other situations we found ourselves in during our time enrolled on the SEPAR. For example:

- An insight into the supervisee's 'practitioner' world and associated challenges
- Sharing of experiences (e.g., casework, ethical scenarios, working across client groups within an organisation, confidentiality and MDT concerns, referral processes, working within boundaries)
- The development of case studies and providing critical review/peer supervision
- Discussion of key applied-focused/contemporary literature
- Observation reflections (across all members of the supervisory group)
- Sharing insights to practice philosophies and practice frameworks.

With two practitioners within the group attending the delayed Tokyo 2020 Summer Olympic Games, this gave some interesting material to discuss in terms of preparation for the games and various disruptions due to the climate. I also sought support from members of the group in a one-to-one environment to discuss various issues. Having access to this group allowed me to complete various competencies, especially within the area of 'Self' and in particular, *ensuring professional compliance and duty of care and management of resources, risks self and others*.

During this time of the SEPAR journey, my supervisor not only attended the group meetings but was also able to offer one-to-one support with cases. My supervisor was also able to observe me during my practice, which was helpful to have a highly experienced individual give feedback to me regarding my practice and allowed further time for reflection.

Writing My Case Study and Professional Development: Reflective Account

Having completed most of the activities I had planned regarding demonstrating more evidence for several competencies and areas for improvement, I was then tasked with deciding which case study I might write up as part of my submission. I decided to pick a case study that had taken place more recently within my applied work and that demonstrated a clear process that led to specific interventions with the client. This enabled me to clearly demonstrate some of the key competencies. My supervisor suggested that all group members review a recent journal submission from CSSEP to structure the case study – the guidance for submissions to CSSEP has now been adopted as the general template for SEPAR case study submissions and include the following subheadings:

Introduction
- Consulting philosophy
- Initial assessment and case formulation (ethical considerations, initial assessment/intake, intake interview and baseline questionnaires, measures)
- Evidence-based intervention and insight to processes of work
- Monitoring and evaluation (assessment phases, post-intervention questionnaires, follow up questionnaire)
- Results
- Reflection
- Significant factors, goals and future application

I found writing the case study an enjoyable experience, reflecting on the processes that you go through as a practitioner, also allowing for further reflection. Implementing this further, I have started to utilise a similar structure to the case study to record client notes, and then have used these notes to reflect upon my ongoing work with a client. Going through this process also helps to keep clear records of the applied work being undertaken, and as a reminder of how you might organise client meetings.

Competency Profile Completion and Organising Myself

The competency profile helped with various aspects of my journey. Firstly, to showcase experiences and knowledge, but also to identify areas of development. After the initial rating of the competencies and reviewers' feedback, it was important to organise my movements and work allocation. I was also a full-time member of staff working at an academic institution during this time, and therefore organisation and time management were key to the successful completion of the process. During this time, it was important to 'block out' time for peer supervision monthly meetings and to include time within this to reflect on the experience. Keeping track of all the activities that you undertake during the journey, can sometimes take its toll along with trying to reflect on every session conducted or every discussion you might have with peers. Therefore, it was important to remind myself that this needed to be completed as evidence and could help to gain higher ratings in certain competencies. The feedback regarding the final submission (Figure 2.2) helped to signpost where I might take my experience further and gave various suggestions where I could submit some of the work, I had produced for the SEPAR qualification for publication. This was useful and demonstrated the value of the work I had undertaken as part of the SEPAR process.

Final Recommendation, Tips and Guidance

Regarding recommendations, as a practitioner completing this process, it has been a rewarding experience that has allowed me to reflect on my practice, be part of

(For End-Point Submissions Only)

Reviewer comments on the candidate's suitability to be considered as SE PAR completed (in relation to the candidate's ability, based on the reviewer perceptions of the evidence presented, to practice as a sate and autonomous applied sport and/or exercise psychologist):

Throughout this process Claire has shown an openness to challenge and has taken on board the feedback that Nichola and I have provided. This is a strong application, and we whole heartedly recommend that Claire be considered tor APEC completion.

Well done

Going forward, our recommendations for Claire would include:

- as planned for in her portfolio. it is hoped that she will look to supervise, and review, SEPAR candidates in the future.
- To continue to engage with the group-based supervision evident within the final submission portfolio, in addition to wider CPD activities.
- consider submitting work to The Sport and Exercise Scientist - https://www.bases.org.uk/spage-resources-the_sport_and_exercise_scientist.html;
- - consider submitting [anonymised] case study/ future case work for peer-review (e.g., Case Studies in Sport and Exercise Psychology) - https://journals.humankinetics.com/view/journals/cssep/cssep-overview.xml;
- - consider submitting [anonymised] reflections/philosophy development for peer-review (e.g., Journal of Sport Psychology in Action - http://www.tandfonline.com/USPA;
- - keep abreast of relevant research via the Journal of Applied Sport Psychology - https://members.bases.org.uk/spage-resource_library-journal_ of _applied_ sport _psychology __jasp __.html:

FIGURE 2.2 An exemplar from the final feedback SEPAR submission.

a wider community and allowed me to meet other colleagues and practitioners within the field. I found the peer supervision group especially rewarding, being able to share experiences of practice and listen to other trainee experiences, learning from their reflection processes and knowledge base. It is vital that you find a supervisor who will be able to support you through the process and give you the support you feel you need. You need to also be open to advice and constructive criticism. With reference to reviewer feedback, it is useful to signpost your responses and developmental activities directly to the feedback provided, this will allow the reviewer to locate this and cross reference what actions you have taken to address the feedback provided. Furthermore, it is useful to think about publishing and disseminating via a range of approaches and various aspects of the journey, whether that be in the form of reflection or a case study submission to a journal. This will help the profession further and share applied experiences with a wider audience.

The Role of the SEPAR Supervisor

Although the role of the SEPAR supervisor and associated duties are detailed within the SEPAR Supervisor Handbook, following a review of discussion with some of the registered SEPAR supervisors, the authors thought it beneficial to share some of the top tips for supervisors embarking on SEPAR supervision. Whilst the following does not represent an extensive list, the suggestions do reflect several consistent tips for consideration.

i. *Know the route.* Whilst it may seem obvious, given the increasing number of training routes that confer eligibility to the HCPC register, one of the top tips reflected the need for supervisors to 'know the route' and be familiar with the processes. Whilst there is bespoke training in place for individuals wishing to become SEPAR supervisors, many are likely to supervise across more than one route. The SEPAR has some stark contrasts to other routes in terms of, for example, the presentation of evidence, the core training, no requirement for research and the overall structure of the training route.

ii. *Agree on roles and responsibilities prior to agreeing to supervise.* Although many individuals may enter into supervisory agreements in good faith to support individuals through the process, there is a requirement to confirm roles and responsibilities and to clarify exactly what the supervisor–supervisee relationship will look like. Given that many supervisors are likely to charge for their supervision services, it is recommended that prior to any relationship commencing that there is agreement between each party to what the expectation of the other is and what process should be followed if there are any perceived shortfalls. As part of this process, it is suggested that a declaration of accountability is made known and signed up to.

iii. *Be a critical friend and provide honest appraisal.* Although supervisors will have many duties within their role, they should not lose sight of the importance of being a critical friend and providing honest appraisal. As such, being prepared to challenge and critique the candidate (albeit in a supportive manner) can be an essential component of the role and one that many candidates can really benefit from. By providing honest appraisal of candidate development and performance, the supervisor may also need to consider their own communication approaches to ensure that the feedback is provided in a manner that the candidate can reflect and synthesise prior to going again.

iv. *Support the development of documentation.* Supervisors are strongly encouraged to engage in the process of documentation development, and this is especially the case when considering the importance of mapping the evidence to the competence levels being claimed. Not only will the supervisor be required to provide supporting documents to verify the content of each submission, but they should also be aware that their name will be associated with the work that will be reviewed. As noted above, the extent to which documentation development will take place should be agreed at the very outset of the supervisor–supervisee relationship.

v. *Engage in active supervision.* As noted throughout the SEPAR documentation there is an expectation that observation takes place and this may be either live (in-person/online) or recorded, depending on the candidate and supervisor situation and/or location. Supervisors should, therefore, engage in active supervision where observation opportunities (of the candidate and supervisor) are made available. Further to this, being an active supervisor can take many forms and many may set specific role play scenarios to work through, for example, case formulations, ethical scenarios, client presentations, intake meetings and evaluation sessions.

vi. *Facilitate independence.* Although one role of the supervisor is to support the candidate to a stage where they achieve the necessary competence to be able to work autonomously, it is strongly suggested that they do so within a framework that always provides ongoing mentoring and supervision post-qualification. Whilst the relationship will inevitably develop into more of a peer relationship, an overriding view of all supervisors is that ongoing professional supervision is critical to the ongoing development of practitioners.

vii. *Acceptance of 'where the candidate is' on entry.* One of the ongoing challenges for supervisors is managing the expectations of candidates, especially when there is a desire from them to move straight into applied practice despite [many] having just completed a 'knowledge-based' MSc qualification. Again, this reaffirms the importance of managing candidate expectations at the outset of the process given the potential for candidates to be faced with a myriad of ethical and professional practice challenges; many of which would be novel and daunting to them. It is the case within the first 6–9 months of the SEPAR that candidates ease themselves into professional client work and focus on knowledge, self and skills-based competencies that build their confidence and readiness.

viii. *Engage in supervisor reflection.* Many supervisors engage in supervision for the rich ongoing development opportunities that are provided through the process. To fully embrace such opportunities, supervisors are encouraged to utilise reflective practice so that they can capture the wide array of creative approaches to practice. Not only does the reflection provide ongoing refining of the supervision role, it can also influence the supervisors applied practice. As such, whilst there are the inevitable expectations that candidates will have of their supervisors, the supervisors will invariably benefit in many ways from engaging in the process too.

Conclusion

In summary, the SEPAR provides a contemporary, inclusive and comprehensive training route option for trainees. The suite of core training workshops is a unique offering and the engagement of wide-ranging stakeholders on the SEPAR AG ensures that the programme 'keeps pace' with the sector. Following reading this chapter, readers are encouraged to consider the following key questions:

- How do the core training opportunities included with the SEPAR compare to other routes so that my ongoing trainee activities can be maximised?
- Is there clarity to what I need to do, and by when – what evidence do I need to provide?
- Am I clear on the process for finding a supervisor and ensuring that we have agreed expectations?

Notes

1 https://www.bases.org.uk/spage-professional_development-separ.html
2 In the UK, this would typically be a undergraduate degree accredited by the British Psychological Society. For an international applicant, the equivalence would need to be demonstrated.
3 In the UK, this would typically be a postgraduate course accredited by the British Psychological Society. For an international applicant, the equivalence would need to be demonstrated.
4 See pre-application information on the SEPAR webpage.

References

Keegan, R., (2016). *Being a Sport Psychologist*. London: Palgrave Macmillan Education.
Mehay, R., & Burns, R. (2012). Assessment and competence. In R. Mehay (Ed.), *The Essential Handbook for GP Training and Education* (pp. 414–426). London: Radcliffe Publishing.
Tod, D., Hutter, R. I., & Eubank, M. (2017). Professional development for sport psychology practice. *Current Opinion in Psychology, 16*, 134–137. https://doi.org/10.1016/j.copsyc.2017.05.007

3
PROFESSIONAL DOCTORATES IN SPORT AND EXERCISE PSYCHOLOGY

Martin Eubank, Christopher Wagstaff and Paul McCarthy

Professional Doctorates in Sport and Exercise Psychology

Professional Doctorates (PDs) in Sport and Exercise Psychology represent the British Psychological Society (BPS) and Health and Care Professions Council (HCPC) approved Higher Education Institution (HEI) route to Practitioner Psychologist registration and Chartered Psychologist status. There are currently three PDs in the UK, run by Glasgow Caledonian University (GCU), Liverpool John Moores University (LJMU) and the University of Portsmouth (UoP), all of which provide a professional pathway for those who wish to undertake their Sport and Exercise Psychology training within a university environment. Since their launch, the programmes have recruited well and have begun to make a meaningful contribution to the HCPC register (Table 3.1).

As co-authors of this chapter, we hold the formal role of PD programme director in our respective institutions. In writing this chapter, we felt it was important to come together to consolidate our knowledge and experiences of running PDs and provide the reader with insights about what we believe to be influential professional qualifications that have evolved the UK professional training landscape. Initially, we discuss the purpose, aims and entry requirements of PD training, including the key competencies trainees must develop as part of the qualification to meet the required standards and some of the distinguishing characteristics of university-based PD training. We then move on to discuss our perspectives as programme directors regarding the unique selling points (USPs) of a PD. This places particular emphasis on the value of taught continued professional development (CPD), formal and informal supervision to establish a community of practice, and the nature and importance of research and practice. Finally, we draw on the reflections of a cross-programme group of PD trainees to provide accounts about what attracted them to train via a PD and its key strengths as a training option, top tips for getting

DOI: 10.4324/9781003196280-4

TABLE 3.1 Current Enrolments and Completions in UK Professional Doctorate in Sport and Exercise Psychology Programmes

Institution	Enrolments	Completions
Glasgow Caledonian University	14	7
Liverpool John Moores University	24	11
University of Portsmouth	25	3

Note. Data correct as of April 2022.

the most out of supervised practice and successfully navigating the writing-up and assessment process and how the PD helped them develop into competent Sport and Exercise Psychologists. We deliberately brought together a representative cross-programme working group and tasked them to generate a joint 'community of practice' response to some key questions we posed. We hope you find their reflections illuminating and insightful, particularly if you are considering the PD as a possible route for your own training.

Professional Doctorate Training

The PD represents a qualification that, by meeting the HCPC and BPS standards, offers a route to practitioner psychologist registration via a doctorate award (Eubank & Forshaw, 2018). The development of a PD programme for Trainee Sport and Exercise Psychologists is arguably more challenging than an independent route qualification, based on the fact that there are a greater number of regulatory authorities to satisfy. PDs have existed within the Higher Education system for many years and yet the PDs we run differ from what might be labelled 'traditional PDs' in a number of ways. Traditional PDs run by universities are set up for industry professionals who identify a real-world problem, typically within their workplace, and enrol on a university PD to conduct research to get answers that can subsequently inform industry policy and practice (Eubank & Tod, 2018). While this form of 'real-world research' can occur in our PDs, trainees are not, by definition, industry professionals doing an applied research PhD; rather, they are 'qualifying psychologists in training', reflecting a profession-specific form of PD undertaken by early career practitioners for entry into an occupation (Costley & Lester, 2012). This emphasises an education and training process that develops 'service providers' and helps trainee practitioner psychologists develop the required knowledge, skills and characteristics needed to meet the needs of clients.

Within the higher education sector, scholars have identified that PDs can provide an excellent training vehicle and motivation through which to create our own industry professionals (Wellington & Sikes, 2006). In developing PDs for our sector, it was important to be mindful of what the industry requires, which is where our BPS Standards for the accreditation of doctoral programmes in sport and exercise psychology and the HCPC Standards of Proficiency and Education and Training for Practitioner Psychologists are key. To create a university-validated, professional statutory-regulatory body (PSRB) accredited and approved PD that confers a doctoral award, Chartered Psychologist status and HCPC registration, three sets of regulations need to be met. Getting this right, while challenging, yields an excellent product that is attractive to applicants who want all the above benefits and end-goals from one programme. These outcomes can be realised via the environment and support that a university infrastructure and all its resources offer, in a more timely manner than pursuing the component parts via separate programmes of work (e.g., a PhD and an independent route qualification). Getting it right means high quality

> practicum training that enables professionals to serve their clients more effectively, meet new and more complex 'real world' needs along the way and even transform the organisations and settings in which they work. While such changes are a product of good applied practice, they can be enhanced through original and high quality research that generates new knowledge about a real-world problem in the workplace or how to practice more effectively.
>
> *(Eubank & Forshaw, 2018; p. 143)*

The purpose, aims and entry requirements of PD training have similarities to the independent route qualifications outlined in Chapters 1 and 2 of this book. The importance of a supervised practice-based experience that meets the required standards of education and training and enables the standards of proficiency of an HCPC-registered Sport and Exercise Psychologist and BPS Chartered Psychologist to be demonstrated sits at the heart of the purpose of all the PDs. While the competencies may be operationalised differently across the three programmes (prospective applicants are encouraged to read the HEI course information and discuss this with the respective programme directors), the competencies are the same. The programmes are designed to enable trainees to demonstrate the required standards through the research and practice work they undertake. To demonstrate the required competencies, PD programmes provide authentic learning-oriented assessment, such as research papers, applied case studies, reflections on practice and viva voces to capture a trainee's 'on the job' training and development across the range of sport and/or exercise settings and diverse populations. Pedagogically, this form of assessment provides real, relevant and valued assessment that promotes deep learning and identity development, while also facilitating the quality, meaning and depth of feedback processes and self-evaluation of learning through reflection on research and practice (Costley & Armsby, 2007).

Compared to the other independent training routes, the research required to evidence originality, significance, impact and rigour within a university doctorate framework is heightened. While an ability to evidence the ability to *understand* and *draw on* research to inform practice is a cornerstone of all our pathways to registration, the volume of assessment devoted to *doing* research in the PD is greater. Eubank and Forshaw (2018) make the case against the flawed suggestion that doing research has no place in a qualification for practitioners, arguing that conducting research improves the practitioner psychologists' ability to understand and draw on its findings and consequentially produces a more competent practitioner (Armsby et al., 2017). PD trainees are thus encouraged to see research as an integrated component of their work and to develop work of publishable quality, both in their empirical research papers and applied case studies.

Those who have a Graduate Basis for Chartered Membership (GBC) of the BPS from an undergraduate psychology degree or conversion course and a Society-accredited MSc. in Sport Psychology, or Sport and Exercise Psychology, meet the qualification-based PD entry requirements. When applying for a PD, good personal statements and references that affirm the motivation, attributes, skills and personal qualities of the applicant are also key. In applying to the programmes, PD applicants are also required to self-source their own opportunities to undertake research and applied work. Having such opportunities secured and agreed in principle before programme commencement helps the trainee to 'hit the ground running', helping to ensure planned progress and development from the outset of training.

As with all training pathways, the availability and quality of good human and learning resource to support the trainee's development is key. On enrolment, PD trainees become part of a community of practice represented by all the trainees on the programme operating as one cohort. Through a combination of expert-led teaching and trainee-led learning both within and across cohorts, trainees are not isolated. Rather, an environment is created where they can share practice and experiences with each other and develop an effective peer learning and informal supervision network. Formal PD supervision is provided by appropriately qualified academic staff employed by the HEI offering the programme and is covered in the university tuition fee. That is, supervision does not have to be separately sought and costed by the trainee. Besides receiving sport and exercise psychology specific training and development through supervision, PD trainees can access the same central resources afforded to research PhD students. In most universities, a doctoral academy or equivalent exists to support a student's doctoral level study and enhance 'doctoral-ness'. This includes access to excellent training and development courses, such as training in specific research methods or academic writing and presenting.

In our experience, many trainees who have enjoyed studying the prerequisite degree qualifications at GCU, LJMU and UoP decide to stay and complete their PD at the same HEI. Familiarity with the HEI's location and infrastructure, the significant human and learning resource that remains wrapped around the trainee from the point of enrolment and relationships with staff that are already well-formed are key attractions for many trainees to 'stay put' and finish where they started!

The USPs of Professional Doctorate Provision: A Programme Director Perspective

While there are points of difference in the way we structure and deliver our training provision that make each PD programme distinct, they all comprise some common characteristics that enable us to 'walk in step' with each trainee from entry to graduation. We discuss some of these characteristics in this section, which are unique to a university-based doctoral training experience.

Taught Continued Professional Development Content

Being taught doctoral programmes, our PD trainees are afforded face-to-face and remote taught sessions across their enrolment period, which support their development of professional practice competence and the completion of professional practice placements/work that inform their programme assignments and portfolio of work. Essentially, this facilitates a bespoke CPD programme of activity, the content of which is owned by both the programme staff and trainees, to ensure that specific training and development needs are met. Professional development sessions are led and delivered by a combination of internal programme staff, external guest speakers and the trainees themselves, who can present examples of their work or on professional practice topics for discussion with the peer group cohort. Sessions are largely available and delivered to the whole programme cohort, which facilitates valuable cross-cohort interaction and discussion across trainees at different stages of the doctoral programme. In this form of training provision, the trainee need not be working in isolation, which is often the disadvantage reported by trainees undertaking independent training routes. In contrast, the programme cohort effect afforded in an HEI setting creates a community of practice that engenders its own self-serving peer network.

Given that our PDs are oriented towards practising as a Sport and Exercise Psychologist (as well as but not just research like in a traditional PhD), we focus more intently on applied practice in the taught elements. Typically, the themes of the taught sessions fall into strands of applied psychology that span the 'know', 'know-how', 'show-how' and 'doing' of professional practice (Miller, 1990), including approaches and interventions relevant to the sport and exercise psychology domain, research (and how it informs evidence-based practice) and the ethics and professional standards pertinent to research and practice. These strands parallel the key standards outlined by the BPS and HCPC for accredited doctoral programmes. Practising to become a Sport and Exercise Psychologist focuses on the learning and practice of key consultancy approaches, processes, interventions and skills/techniques that can then be applied in face-to-face practice placement or work settings across each year of enrolment. Throughout the programme, trainees have the opportunity to engage in professional development sessions, where through personal development, peer group and individual supervision, they discuss cases from their caseload and debate and reflect on diverse professional practice challenges, including ethical scenarios they have encountered and the ethical decision-making process and outcomes they have generated.

The formal taught element of a PD programme is a key point of difference from the other training routes detailed in Chapters 1 and 2, which are more reliant on the training provider and the sector offering CPD opportunities, some of which have an associated cost. This is not to say that PD trainees don't need to undertake CPD outside their programme, but that a significant amount of CPD is provided in-house. This also includes 'no cost' university training courses aimed at doctoral trainees (e.g., how to write for different audiences as both a practitioner and a researcher), a resource that PD trainees can access by virtue of being enrolled as a student at the university. PD trainees also benefit from being immersed within a postgraduate research and training culture that enriches personal and professional development beyond the traditionally isolated independent routes.

Supervision 'Plus'

Similarly to the other training routes, one-to-one supervision (from an HCPC-Registered Sport and Exercise Psychologist) is a fundamental component of the PD training provision. In contrast to the other training programmes that require the trainee to find one co-ordinating supervisor from an approved list or register, PDs provide a supervisor pool from within their own university staffing base. It is common for doctoral programmes in universities to require the allocation of at least a 'lead' and a 'second' supervisor to each doctoral trainee. As a consequence, PD trainees often have multiple supervisors, with the identification of the supervisory team being negotiated between the staff and trainee. Furthermore, the other Sport and Exercise Science or Psychology staff in the school/department are an accessible resource and will readily give their expertise and guidance to a trainee in an advisory capacity. Consequently, the quantity of supervisory/advisory support and guidance available to the PD trainee is substantial and the quality of supervision is controlled by a combination of having staff who are HCPC-registered Practitioner Psychologists and other non-HCPC-registered staff who can draw on their sport and exercise psychology expertise and supervisory experience in research and applied practice to make excellent second supervisors. The university will also likely have a minimum requirement and process for the trainee to arrange supervisory meetings with their team, to promote the expectation of the trainee that meetings are sufficiently regular and frequent. At the doctoral level, this is normally monitored through the creation of supervisory meeting records and the conduction of some form of annual progress review.

While the academic staff provide the formal supervision to the trainee, the creation of a peer network structure (alluded to in the 'taught CPD' commentary above) can usefully extend to support opportunities for peer supervision. In our experience, it is common for a cohort to work together for mutual benefit or through the creation of sub-groups or clusters, where self-directed learning and developmental feedback are emphasised. This form of learning and development through informal supervision provides an additional and valuable layer of useful interaction, diverse input and exposure to a bigger and broader range of knowledge, and is a feature that trainees often highlight as a distinct benefit of their PD training experience.

Research-Informed Practice and Practice-Informed Research

Our PD programmes require the trainee to conduct and produce research outputs to a significantly greater quantity that the other training routes, where one (e.g., QSEP) or no (e.g., SEPAR) research products are required. In deciding on the research plan, there is flexibility of choice to suit the trainee's interest and passion for particular research topics and processes. The research products may be conceptually linked, as they would be in a PhD, or they may reflect different conceptual interests and topics. Whichever the case, supervisors work closely with their trainees to ensure they generate research that demonstrates competence, rigour, originality and impact.

The research is expected to be at the doctoral level and therefore of publishable quality. Trainees write their research assessments as 'submission ready' documents for review and publication in peer-reviewed journals and there is already substantial evidence in our trainee population of systematic review, empirical study and case study publications. These outputs contribute to the growth and proliferation of underpinning research in applied sport and exercise psychology, expand the research output and impact of supervisors and other staff involved in the work and grow the research profile of the 'owning' school/department. They also represent significant benefits to the trainee to strengthen their professional network and reputation, curriculum vitae and employability prospects. Moreover, having aspects of their PD work published prior to the viva voce examination is helpful in explicitly evidencing to examiners that the work is at the doctoral level.

A key aim for us as Practitioner Psychologists, researchers and lecturers is to reduce the research-practice gap. This gap reflects the void between what happens in research (e.g., evidence-based practice) and the realities of everyday practice. Indeed, we can address some weaknesses of evidence-based practice with practice-based evidence. Practice-based evidence means systematically collecting client-reported data of a practice goal or outcome. Practitioner Psychologists can examine whether the evidence-based practice we choose to inform practice has a meaningful influence on the clients we serve. We can pinpoint where evidence-based practice is not working for the clients or what changes might support more favourable outcomes for them. We can share these lessons among trainees, staff, service users and carers, through conferences, books and peer-reviewed publications. We contend a PD programme that requires and produces high-quality research products is uniquely placed to enable practitioners to engage in research to answer real-world questions through practice-informed research and to translate the research finding to inform policy and practice.

From this prologue, we hope you can appreciate the orientation and direction of our learning and teaching approach to train the next generation of sport and exercise psychologists. We believe trainees learn more effectively in shared learning and teaching systems and settings, so we attempt to provide an opportunity to facilitate share learning experiences across the trainee cohort within the doctoral framework as much as possible. Trainees learn alongside other doctoral trainees' training in their discipline and from staff experienced in teaching and practising psychology. Such a learning and teaching environment can also enable cross-disciplinary fertilisation of standards of education, training and proficiency, for example, with Health or Counselling Psychology where doctorates in other domains of psychology may also be offered within an institution. As such, we feel more agile to meet the needs of service users and carers and the core elements of equity, diversity and inclusion.

The USPs of Professional Doctorate Provision: A Trainee Perspective

To provide a trainee perspective on undertaking Sport and Exercise Psychologist training via the PD route, a diverse and inclusive working group of seven trainees from across the three PD programmes was assembled. For this chapter, the group was tasked with generating a joint response to the following four questions: (1) What attracted you to train via a Professional Doctorate and what are its key strengths as a training option?; (2) What are your top tips for getting the most out of supervised practice on the Professional Doctorate?; (3) What are your top tips for successfully navigating the writing-up and assessment process on the Professional Doctorate?; (4) How has the Professional Doctorate helped you develop into a competent sport and exercise psychologist?

We empowered the PD trainees to undertake a form of analytical integration of reflections and key themes from their discussions related to our questions. Therefore, in this section of the chapter, the narrator or 'we' changes to that of our PD trainee cross-programme group in the form of a 'composite voice', which we hope maintains a personal connection to the themes.

Key Strengths of the Professional Doctorate Training Route

The themes developed from the trainee discussions in response to 'What attracted you to train via a Professional Doctorate and what are its key strengths as a training option?' were: A combination of applied and academic work; the structure and support provided; the value and quality of qualification; enhanced employability; access to university services.

1. *A combination of applied and academic work.* We, trainees, feel that the PD offered the chance to not have to choose between a solely academic (via PhD) or applied career (QSEP/SEPAR). To elaborate, without the PD, trainees who do not wish to specialise in either applied practice or academia only would be required to explore completing both the QSEP/SEPAR and a PhD as separate multi-year programmes of work, adding many years onto an already lengthy development process. By this point in their careers, we have completed a three- or four-year undergraduate degree, a majority will also obtain a Master's degree and, in some cases, also a conversion course. Through our PDs, we can

develop professionally in both academic and applied arenas simultaneously, and within one qualification and one place, which is an attractive prospect.

2. *The structure and support provided.* Within the PD, as trainees, we instigate regular (at least monthly and, in some cases, weekly) contact with our supervisors, in both one-to-one and group settings. PDs also offer the opportunity to work with multiple supervisors, other staff in the department, and to draw on human (e.g., administrators, librarians, and societies, and postgraduate research peers) and system (e.g., finance administration support for grants, professional development funds for conference attendance) resources within the university context. The extra structure (through teaching, learning and assessment) and supervision (both applied and research) in addition to the direct access to a peer group help us become better practitioners, both as trainees and by the end of our qualification. The programme helps to provide us with security during training, through assistance in finding placements, group formulation, one-to-one supervision and peer support. We feel that the foundation received during this qualification allows us to finish with more knowledge and experience within both research and applied work compared to alternative pathways, as well as more access to learning relevant skills (e.g., counselling skills). For some of us, the PD means we can continue working with supervisors and within institutions that we are already familiar with and where we have a sense of support (e.g., continuing onto the PD directly from a Master's degree) via prior working relationships with university staff.

3. *The value and quality of qualification.* A key feature of the PD that attracted us to join the programme was the doctoral recognition of the qualification beyond graduation. The nuances of qualification routes to become a Sport and Exercise Psychologist are only somewhat known within the sport and exercise science and medicine context and haven't stretched beyond that. Having a 'Dr' title opens up doors in different fields, as that is a universally recognised standard of competency and is valuable to employers. As trainees, we feel that this more than makes up for the difference in workload that must be undertaken on the PD, compared to other training pathways.

4. *Enhanced employability.* We have found employment across a range of contexts. Some of us have developed 'sole-trader' consultancy companies, some are employed in the UK's high-performance system within the world-class programmes of national governing bodies or in professional sport clubs, and others have gained academic positions and positions on journal editorial boards despite their early career status. While it might be too early to tell if we are better placed for gaining employment over independent route-qualified peers, we do feel we possess a more rounded professional preparation and readiness for a sustainable career given our more developed critical thought/research reasoning skills. Moreover, we are undeniably better placed when applying for roles in academia than our peers who complete independent routes, given a doctorate is 'essential' criterion for permanent academic roles in the area of sport and exercise psychology at UK HEIs.

5. *Access to university services.* PDs provide the opportunity to undertake training with access to all the services offered within a university environment. Academic resources such as an online library, learning and teaching facilities, statistics support, postgraduate development courses (which are not or less available while working independently via other training routes), as well as general pastoral support, and being immersed within a research culture, are a huge advantage of the PD route. Fundamentally, the assessments, such as writing academic papers, would have been much harder to achieve without access to a university library. For many of us, it is important to qualify in the most 'time and effort-efficient' manner possible, and the PD seems to be the best vehicle to facilitate that progression. We perceive it to be the most complete and supported learning experience available within our field.

Top Tips for Getting the Most Out of Supervised Practice

The themes developed from the trainee discussions in response to 'What are your top tips for getting the most out of supervised practice on the Professional Doctorate?' were: Being clear and taking an active role; trying to impress vs. vulnerability; learning from others; reducing feelings of isolation.

i. *Being clear and taking an active role.* The key to getting the most out of supervision on a PD is to know clearly what it is exactly that you want to get out of it! Being clear about what you want to achieve within a supervision session, whether it's one-on-one or within a group, helps you as the trainee to be accountable for how effective your supervision is in assisting in your practitioner development. Depending on the structure of the PD course, supervision can be some of the only dedicated face-to-face time with your own supervision team, so it's important to be collectively clear about what you want and expect from those sessions. Is it informal or boundaried by a set agenda (e.g., formulation or learning about different therapeutic approaches)? We have also found it helpful to build relationships with people outside of our immediate supervision team, such as other university staff members, joining regional networks or committees and attending networking and training events (e.g., workshops, webinars and conferences). This helped to provide us with variety within our professional development and increased the breadth and depth of our learning.

ii. *Trying to impress vs. vulnerability.* It's important to stay active in your role as the supervisee, and not just be a passenger. At the start of training, it's quite common to feel pressure to 'show off' your knowledge, skills or experiences in supervision sessions. Yet, for many of us, our most valuable supervision experiences came when we expressed our own vulnerability to others. Supervision can be a place to explore safely what we don't know, rather than feel obligated to demonstrate what we know. Trainees are ultimately in the driving seat of supervised practice; you will get out of it as much as you're prepared to put in.

It's important to remember to 'bring' issues from both the professional and the personal domain when meeting with your supervisor, because who you are as an individual, and the experiences in your own personal life, inform how you develop throughout the course. This shapes your identity and practice philosophy (Poczwardowski et al., 2004; Quartiroli et al., 2022; Tod et al., 2020; Wagstaff & Quartiroli, 2020).

iii. *Learning from others.* We feel that the ability to engage in peer supervision is very refreshing and not something always experienced by practitioners on different pathways. Being able to learn from others' experiences helps you to realise that everyone's in the same boat. For many of us, having regular peer supervision was especially helpful during COVID-19 lockdown restrictions, when feelings of isolation were enhanced.

iv. *Reducing feelings of isolation.* In general, being in a cohort of peers and regularly attending group supervision meetings and taught sessions reduces our sense of isolation, as it helped us to get to know other people in our cohort and re-introduced a more sociable element to professional development, including an easier and less daunting setting in which to do role play. We have found that playing an active role in supervision also reduces feelings of imposter syndrome and helps to clarify professional beliefs and values (cf. Hings et al., 2020). This active role also assists in greater understanding and exploration of our approach to professional practice, which is helpful in quieting self-doubt and insecurities that everyone experiences throughout their training.

Top Tips for Successfully Navigating the Writing-Up and Assessment Process

The themes developed from the trainee discussions in response to 'What are your top tips for successfully navigating the writing-up and assessment process on the Professional Doctorate?' were: Being organised, having a clear plan that meets your needs, and using the available advice.

i. *Being organised.* The key to submitting assessments for the PD is to be organised. Each course has different requirements; some have staged submissions and others are arranged so that you structure the timing of submissions yourself. Some people may find self-imposed deadlines useful in getting through the assessments in a steady and consistent manner, while others may prefer meeting deadlines organised by the programme. Although there are small nuances in the presentational requirements and assessments from programme to programme, they are very similar in terms of the effort you need to commit and the amount of work that must be produced by the end of the course. Break things down into manageable sections and be prepared to find flexibility and adaptability in how you manage your time.

ii. *Having a clear plan that meets your needs.* We feel it is important for future trainees to thoroughly explore the different PDs available and consider their assessment submission structure when choosing where to apply. Studying in a programme format that helps support your unique learning needs through having autonomy about the choice of, for example, research topics or consultancy approaches to meet the assessment criteria (as opposed to working against your own preference) will play a significant role in your ability to meet the programme's requirements. There are more submission requirements on a PD than QSEP or SEPAR, so at times it can feel like you're spinning a lot of plates. We found that this challenged us to learn to adjust, becoming more proactive and independent in our professional development and equipping us for the often sporadic and varied nature of the sport and exercise psychology field. Be open to having to change your plans; life often throws a 'spanner in the works', so taking the time to revisit and revise plans can help you stay on track and avoid feeling overwhelmed.

iii. *Using the available advice.* We found being aware and making use of the different facilities and resources available via our universities to be very helpful in assisting with academic writing and submissions. Making use of the additional support you have access to at University can ease the pressure of training a little. Through our PD enrolment, we can access university libraries and their staff, online learning modules, teaching and learning resources and have wide access to databases and journals. Many of us would have found the research components of sport and exercise psychology training significantly more challenging to complete without having these resources available to us. Your supervisors, academic tutors and peers are a vital support network, don't be afraid to ask for help! We have found that bouncing ideas off peers or seeking clarity from tutors has helped us to understand what's required from our assignments, consider different perspectives and ultimately enhanced our confidence as trainees.

Developing into a Competent Sport and Exercise Psychologist

The themes developed from the trainee discussions in response to 'How has the Professional Doctorate helped you develop into a competent Sport and Exercise Psychologist?' were: Qualification recognition, Transferrable skills, Diversity of experience and Supportive relationships.

i. *Qualification recognition.* Ultimately, as a group of trainees, we feel that a PD offered the most supervision (one-to-one and peer) and the most widely recognised 'stamp of approval' of the available training routes. A PD qualification means others in the sport and exercise fields (both applied and academic) can make certain assumptions about the professional standard of your training and qualification. It also means that potential employers can be assured that your training was both supervised throughout by a registered Practitioner Psychologist and that you have engaged in both rigorous academic research and applied work within the field. They can also be confident of the standard of the qualification, as PDs are overseen and regulated by PSRBs beyond the university institutions themselves. Holding a doctoral title and the ability to apply for HCPC registration on completion are highly valuable, not just for employers but also for trainees who want their developmental journey, proficiency, associated qualification and professional title to be professionally regulated and publicly recognised.

ii. *Transferrable skills*. An additional benefit to PDs is that the wider recognition of an academic doctorate qualification awarded by a university (as opposed to applied qualifications such as QSEP or SEPAR) means that they may be more transferable to employment opportunities beyond sport and exercise. This transferability allows us to transition into alternative roles more easily than trainees on other pathways. The employment field is also changing in a way that reflects the value of the PD pathway. University lecturing posts typically now seek applications from individuals with both academic and applied expertise, so that future trainees on their programmes can learn from those who draw on application experiences in the classroom and contribute to quality assurance requirements for accreditation from PSRBs. The duality of our qualifications is more valuable than ever and, hopefully, our employment prospects will continue to grow.

iii. *Diversity of experience*. For many of us, the diversity on offer within the relationships (supervisor, staff, peer group and more) we have made through studying in our PDs has been most impactful to our development. Discussing philosophy, ethics and applied work with trusted others is a real benefit. Trainees arrive to PD programmes from different routes and with a range of experiences; having a variety of other trainees within your cohort ensures diversity within your training. This automatic access to ranging support might be more challenging to QSEP and SEPAR trainees, who may be required to be more self-motivated in sourcing alternative views if they wish to ensure a diverse training experience in which their opinions and experiences are supportively challenged by others. They may also meet more barriers in their attempts to do so, as they will probably have a smaller network of contacts.

iv. *Supportive relationships*. Our experience of undertaking a PD is that it engenders a strong sense of community. One of the most striking features of PD training is the vast number of supportive relationships that are formed along the way. The synergy between the supportive relationships we develop in training and the client-practitioner therapeutic relationship we strive to engender in our service delivery (Tod et al., 2019), including the important personal qualities (e.g., honesty, integrity, care and congruence) that positively influence the helping relationship (Chandler et al., 2016) is not lost on us! From supervisors to peers to placement providers to family and friends, we have encountered so many people who are giving of their time in their genuine desire to help our personal development. This network of supportive relationships serves to provide a protecting and reassuring space for us to listen to and share with others, and our PD experience affirms our belief that we are more confident and competent practitioners as a consequence.

Conclusion

To summarise the messages from this chapter, we return to the author narrative voices of Martin, Chris and Paul. Our PDs in Sport and Exercise Psychology provide a viable alternative for those who are interested in continuing their training in a university environment and we hope that reading this chapter will inspire other aspiring Sport and Exercise Psychologists to select this route to complete their own training. PDs are becoming increasingly popular as a training option, particularly for those who seek Chartered status, HCPC registration and a Doctorate award from one qualification. Compared to the independent routes outlined in the two preceding chapters, PD training has its unique features, particularly around the aspects of taught CPD, research and the scope of available resources and networks to support trainee development. Our trainees have provided candid and useful insights about their experiences of PD training, including their own perspectives on the USPs. We are grateful to these trainees for lending us their composite voice. There is good evidence in their accounts that the PDs we have developed and direct have begun to produce outstanding researcher-practitioners who are excellent ambassadors for their programmes and for the UK training system in Sport and Exercise Psychology. Going forward, we are confident that PDs will assume prominent positions within the field and contribute to a sustainable professional landscape through provision and the development of future professionals, and we encourage other education providers to consider the merits and benefits of establishing their own programmes alongside the three that currently exist. After reading this chapter, readers are encouraged to consider three key questions:

- Why is the professional doctorate the right training route for me?
- What are the USPs that attract me to want to study a PD?
- How can I best showcase my motivation, work-related learning and research interests/opportunities to study a PD in a 'stand-out' application?

Acknowledgements

We would like to extend our sincere thanks to the following Professional Doctorate trainees who contributed their reflections for this chapter: Sarah Findlay, Laura Kiemle-Gabbay, Heather Hunter, Daniel Martin, Leigh Ann McGeachy, Graham Mckenzie and Rich Sille.

References

Armsby, P., Costley, C., & Cranfield, S. (2017). The design of doctorate curricula for practising professionals. *Studies in Higher Education*, *43*, 1–12.

Chandler, C., Eubank, M., Nesti, M., Tod, D., & Cable, T. (2016). Personal qualities of effective sport psychologists: Coping with organisational demands in high performance sport. *International Journal of Sport Psychology*, *47*, 297–317.

Costley, C., & Armsby, P. (2007). Research influences on a professional doctorate. *Research in Post Compulsory Education*, *12*(3), 343–355.

Costley, C., & Lester, S. (2012). Work-based doctorates: Professional extension at the highest levels. *Studies in Higher Education*, *37*, 257–269.

Eubank, M., & Forshaw, M. (2018). Professional doctorates for practitioner psychologists: Understanding the territory and its impact on programme development. *Studies in Continuing Education*, *41*(2), 141–156.

Eubank, M., & Tod, D. (2018). *How to Become a Sport and Exercise Psychologist*. Routledge.

Hings, R. F., Wagstaff, C. R. D., Anderson, V., Gilmore, S., & Thelwell, R. C. (2020). Better preparing sports psychologists for the demands of applied practice: The emotional labor training gap. *Journal of Applied Sport Psychology*, *32*(4), 335–356.

Miller, G. E. (1990). The assessment of clinical skills/competence/performance. *Academic Medicine*, *65*(9), S63–S67.

Poczwardowski, A., Sherman, C. P., & Ravizza, K. (2004). Professional philosophy in the sport psychology service delivery: Building on theory and practice. *The Sport Psychologist*, *18*, 445–463.

Tod, D., Hardy, J., Lavallee, D., Eubank, M., & Ronkainen, N. (2019). Practitioners' narratives regarding active ingredients in service delivery: Collaboration-based problem solving. *Psychology of Sport and Exercise*, *43*, 350–358.

Tod, D., McEwan, H., Chandler, C., Eubank, M., & Lafferty, M. (2020). The gravitational pull of Identity: Professional growth in sport, exercise, and performance psychologists. *Journal of Sport Psychology in Action*, *11*(4), 233–242.

Quartiroli, A., Wagstaff, C. R. D., Hunter, H., & Martin, D. R. (2022). The identity of the sport psychology profession: A multinational perspective. *Psychology of Sport and Exercise*, *60*, 102140.

Wagstaff, C. R. D., & Quartiroli, A. (2020). Psychology and psychologists in search of an identity: What and who are we, and why does it matter? *Journal of Sport Psychology in Action*, *11*(4), 254–265.

Wellington, J., & Sikes, P. (2006) 'A doctorate in a tight compartment': Why do trainees choose a professional doctorate and what impact does it have on their personal and professional lives? *Studies in Higher Education*, *31*, 723–734.

4

INTERNATIONAL ROUTES TO SPORT AND EXERCISE PSYCHOLOGY

Eesha J. Shah, Nicholas de Cruz and Richard Keegan

International Routes to Sport and Exercise Psychology

Sometime in the late 2000s, in a noisy canteen at a British university, two students were talking between lectures, while hastily ordering some food for lunch. Unknown to them, a staff member from another university was visiting for the day, and looking for a caffeine-hit, using "popularity" as a heuristic for where to find the best coffee. That person, a registered Sport and Exercise Psychologist, listened with interest as the following words were spoken.

> Sport psychology is great isn't it! It's so obvious that elite teams in this country would benefit by engaging more with sport psych. I can't wait to get "out there" and start making bags of money by telling them how to think more clearly, and win more.

It sounded like the two students would be excellent company for a Sport Psychologist! But then, the tone changed.

> It's s*** we have to wait to be accredited before we can do that though. You know, I can't be bothered with all this ethics b*******! I reckon I'm already better than some of the folks out there in industry. I reckon we should just call ourselves "mind coaches" and get out there right now. It's time to make some money!

The listener no longer wanted to engage and instead found himself needing to pause and reflect on what the profession was really about. It could have been a teachable moment, but instead, the would-be teacher only later found the words to convey what he should have said that day. For there is important value in upholding accredited or registered status for a profession such as psychology.

Many years later, at an international conference in Europe, the same registered Psychologist was directly asked a different question after a conference talk.

> Thank you for your enjoyable talk. I wondered, if you don't mind, could you offer me any advice on how to compete with people calling themselves "mind coaches" or "mental skills coaches", when I am an accredited Psychologist? They can name-drop their famous clients, I cannot. They can make promises of guaranteed success, I cannot – as the research evidence does not support such a claim. But in a world where people want to know you have famous clients, and want to be told you will guarantee success, I find it very hard to compete with them!

So, it seemed, the two students may have had a point! *Just say you are great, and go make money, right? What could possibly go wrong?*

What *could* go wrong? Well – if there is no minimum standard of knowledge and competence to engage in professional practice – is that a problem? If there is no consequence to ineffective or unethical practices, and we just move onto the next client, is that a problem? If a psychologist may be using each client as leverage to make themselves rich and famous, not focusing on helping the specific client, is that a problem? What would be the consequences for a profession where these things are commonplace? Quality assurance, accountability, and ongoing regulation do have benefits: to the service-users, the practitioners, and indeed the wider profession (e.g., reputation). If sports organisations and athletes are not making informed choices, then they may continue to use faulty heuristics to pick their practitioners: fame, profile, sales pitch, glitzy products, and the like.

Where national accreditation and guidelines do exist, there can be some acceptance that they are necessary and some implicit understanding that it is better to use a regulated practitioner. We recognise, though, that such regulatory bodies often fail to convey the benefits of accreditation to the wider public. Often, however, there is almost no scope to prosecute someone doing the job of a Psychologist, but under a different and unprotected title. So, on the one hand, we need everyone in countries with accreditation systems to understand, value, and "sell" the benefits of being accredited. While, on the other hand, in countries without accreditation, we need to convince client groups, practitioners, and governments of the benefits of either accreditation – and the consequences of not having an accreditation framework – or at least how to select the most suitable practitioners. In this chapter, we hope to help you understand the accreditation requirements around the world – to navigate and compare them – and to, ultimately, be able to articulate the benefits of regulation/accreditation systems as well as chart your own accreditation journey. We will also consider the benefits of cross-national accreditations such as those offered by the International Society of Sport Psychology (ISSP) and the European Federation of Sport Psychology (FEPSAC).

In the following text, we provide an overview of the typical requirements for accreditation in countries where it does exist. Going beyond what other writing on this topic has done, we hear from practitioners in Europe, Asia, Africa, and Oceania, and present the challenges of not having an accreditation system and the experiences of cultivating one. We map these diverse experiences against existing guidelines and reflect on the areas of overlap and divergence.

Typical Requirements to Become and Remain Accredited

Globally, the field is working towards establishing national, regional, and cross-national accreditation frameworks because this step is paramount to developing, assessing, and fostering the professional identity and integrity required to practice effectively (Schinke et al., 2018). Before we dive into the different requirements to become accredited, take a moment to reflect on your journey to becoming a practitioner. Which country did you do your postgraduate training in or hope to pursue it in? Where do you wish to practise? These orienting questions can narrow your focus on the requirements of certain countries or regions of interest, as well as broaden it to consider other pathways to becoming the practitioner you envision to be. All national and cross-national accreditation frameworks assess and assure competence in three areas: (i) technical knowledge; (ii) practical skills and application; and (iii) current fitness to practice (Keegan & Cotterill, 2020).

Technical competence concerns your university education. If you intend to complete your education as well as practise in the United Kingdom (UK), you will minimally need to read an accredited, undergraduate degree or a conversion course in psychology as well as a postgraduate degree in sport and exercise psychology (British Psychological Society, 2022), as elaborated on in earlier chapters. Likewise, in Australia, there are a variety of other study pathways that involve internships and graduate diplomas in place of a postgraduate degree (Australian Psychological Society, 2022). Whereas in other parts of the world, such as China and South Korea, there are tiered systems of accreditation with entry-level requirements being a bachelor's degree in psychology, physical education, or related fields, as well as an entrance exam (Schinke et al., 2018). In the United States of America (USA) and Canada, there are no federal regulations; instead, state regulations determine the requirements. Minimally though, one must possess a doctoral degree to be a psychologist in the USA. Given the greater international mobility of sportspeople and practitioners these days, cross-national professional bodies such as ISSP and FEPSAC have broader definitions of technical competence that accommodate these inter-nation differences.[1]

The great diversity around the world in not only the academic rigour of educational pathways that prepares students for a career in applied sport psychology, but also their (un)availability in all countries, created the need for unifying platforms that legitimised the profession internationally (Schinke et al., 2018). These unifying platforms enabled practitioners of various training backgrounds to adopt common best practices and build competence-based trust with one another. In the spirit of internalisation, inclusion, and collaboration, both ISSP and FEPSAC define the minimum standards of competence that practitioners must demonstrate to qualify for independent practice in the field of applied sport psychology (FEPSAC, 2022; ISSP, 2022). If your country of practice has federal or state regulations or national accreditation frameworks that guide your development into a practising psychologist in sport, then the main benefits of ISSP or FEPSAC certification serve to augment your visibility, credibility, and professional network beyond your country of practice. If your country of practice has no accreditation frameworks or regulations, then the primary benefits of ISSP or FEPSAC certification are to "quality assure your ethical and professional provision of [psychological services] to athletes" and other stakeholders in sport, wherever you are based (ISSP, 2022) and "distinguish [this provision of services] from others in the marketplace" such as mental skills coaches (FEPSAC, 2022).

Navigating this information as a fresh graduate or perhaps as someone just considering this field can be overwhelming – we encourage you to anchor on the "Where?" questions asked at the start of this section and explore the educational requirements required by the accrediting bodies of your chosen country or region in the first instance. We also refer you to the work of Schinke et al. (2018), which summarises the accreditation requirements of ISSP and FEPSAC as well as the Association for Applied Sport Psychology (AASP) and the Asian South-Pacific Association of Sport Psychology (ASPASP). It is important to note that having ISSP, FEPSAC, or AASP certification does not entitle you as a psychologist and you must still fulfil the requirements of your country or territory of practice to be identified as one.

The next question to consider is what professional identity do you aspire towards? There are two interrelated but distinct aspects to consider. Firstly, an aspiring practitioner must build on their technical competence by acquiring practical skills in applied contexts by way of supervised training from a more senior and, preferably, registered supervisor. Through iterative rounds of independent practice and feedback from this chosen supervisor, aspiring practitioners develop an ethical, reflexive, and reflective practice; assessment skills and intervention techniques; interpersonal and self-regulatory skills; as well as a sensitivity and understanding of cultural nuances and diverse needs; all undergirded by their consulting philosophy and chosen model of practice (see Keegan, 2016; Poczwardowski et al., 2004). To acquire the aforementioned skills to practice ably and independently as a sport psychologist, some countries have established formal training pathways. In the UK, for instance, there are three training routes available: the Qualification in Sport and Exercise Psychology (QSEP Stage 2) by the British Psychological Society; the Sport and Exercise Psychology Accreditation Route (SEPAR) by the British Association of Sport and Exercise Sciences; and the professional doctorate in sport and exercise psychology.[2]

Secondly, upon satisfactory completion of your practical training, you can seek endorsement of your practical competence from an accrediting body relevant to your country of practice. Though only a handful of countries have legislated the titles of "psychologist" (e.g., Australia, South Africa, and the USA) or "sport and exercise psychologist" (e.g., UK), recent scientific literature on professional standards by Schinke et al. (2018) and Zizzi et al. (2014) recommends endorsement as a means to maintain and communicate professional integrity. Endorsement communicates to the public, as well as our fellow professionals, our undertaking of the "privileges and responsibilities of [our] profession... [especially] to do no harm, and to govern [ourselves] to ensure the dignity and welfare of individuals we serve and the public" (AASP, 2022). In the UK, you can seek registration as a sport and exercise psychologist with the Health and Care Professions Council once you have completed one of the aforementioned training routes or via a separate assessment track if you are an international practitioner wishing to practice in the UK. In the USA, while you need a doctoral degree to practise as a psychologist, you can work in sport and exercise psychology as a non-psychologist as long as you are registered with AASP as a Certified Mental Performance Consultant. This status is achieved by acquiring, minimally, a relevant master's degree and undertaking supervised training. Therefore, each practitioner needs to decide: what professional identity do you aspire towards? Use this question to identify the training routes and the professional accrediting bodies that are aligned with your aspirations.

You have arrived: after acquiring technical and practical competence, it might feel like there is finally nothing more to do but to get out there and start "psychologising"! However, to maintain our fitness to practise as well as remain relevant to the needs of our clients, we must continue our professional development for as long as we aspire to practise and, in some cases, be endorsed. We can keep our skills and knowledge current by attending practitioner training courses such as those on certain therapy modalities (i.e., Cognitive Behavioural Therapy, Rational Emotive Behaviour Therapy, etc.); workshops such as those on working in certain environments (i.e., school sport, para-sport, etc.) or developing skills (i.e., motivational interviewing, cultural competence, etc.); webinars, conferences, and other contexts that allow networking and learning from fellow professionals; as well as, by other self-directed means such as reading and engaging in peer supervision (Health and Care Professions Council, 2015). Readers are referred to Chapter 13 of this book for further details on the importance of engaging in Continued Professional Practice.

By acquiring, assuring, and continually developing our technical and practical competence to practise psychology in sport and exercise settings as autonomous professionals, we act in the best interests of our service-users, as well as uphold the good name of our fraternity. In the next section, we delve deeper into the accreditation trends in countries without a clear route to accreditation, paying particular attention to the challenges faced by practitioners in those environments.

Realities of Accreditation around the World

With the goal to better understand the journey to become a Sport and Exercise Psychologist, we emailed our professional networks as well as posted on social media, seeking from practitioners around the world their experiences of the pathway towards professional accreditation in their countries, and what the practice of sport and exercise psychology is like in their environments. We are grateful to have received comments from practitioners in Ghana, Hong Kong, Hungary, Iceland, India, Japan, Malaysia, New Zealand, Pakistan, Poland, Romania, Saudi Arabia, Singapore, South Africa, and Uganda. To effectively illustrate the diverse experiences of sport psychology practitioners, we used the principles of thematic analysis to understand and categorise this web of complexity, and provide a systematic framework to inform our discussion (Braun & Clarke, 2006; Clarke & Braun, 2017). From the comments provided, we developed common codes and themes across the diverse responses; divided them into two levels (i.e., refined themes and sub-themes); and, allocated names to represent their thematic content with attention to what had been said in relation to the reported experiences and practice of sport and exercise psychology.

The analysis identified three refined themes: (i) *current global trends*; (ii) *professionalism of sport psychology*; and (iii) *building and/or sustaining expertise*, communicated through our voices and those of our international colleagues, who share our passion for the field. We expound and reflect on these refined themes and sub-themes, illustrated in Figure 4.1 and in the following section.

Current Global Trends

Ascertaining a Requisite Level of Knowledge to Practice. The years dedicated to the learning, training, and development of psychological inquiry and its application are not without purpose. Bridging the gap between theory and practice, this acquired knowledge base will equip you with the confidence and competence to draw on a repository of relevant vocabulary and context-specific knowledge to effectively work alongside other professionals within the domain of sport science and human performance (Keegan & Cotterill, 2020). A strong and firmly established theoretical knowledge base of psychological expertise is just the beginning, if your goal is to provide a more comprehensive service:

> Many complete a postgraduate degree in psychology in clinical, counselling, or health settings, as well as 1,500 hours of supervised practicum to become registered as psychologists, and then they go on to practice in sport or exercise contexts.
>
> – *New Zealand*

In some countries, a clinical psychology qualification may be a pre-requisite for becoming a Psychologist in any applied setting. However, clinical competencies, alone, may not be sufficient, and *sport* and sport psychology knowledge and skills are necessary to ethically and competently practice sport psychology (Lesyk, 2005). According to Tod et al. (2007), the multidimensional constellation of knowledge, skills, and processes that encapsulate service delivery competence necessitate the mastery of human or soft skills (e.g., empathising and establishing meaningful therapeutic relationships with clients) in tandem with empirically grounded evidence-based

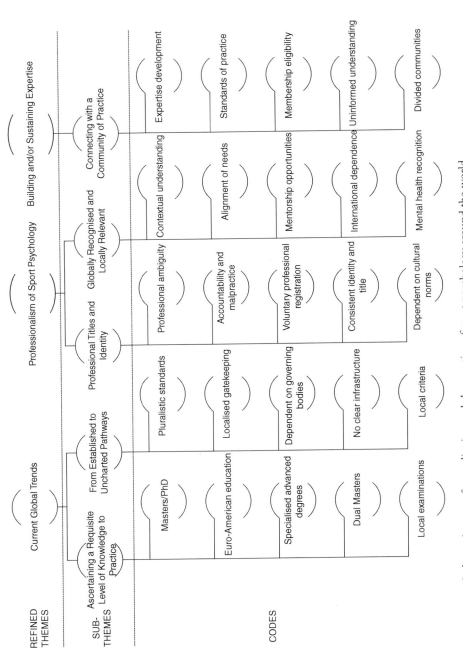

FIGURE 4.1 A thematic map of accreditation and the practice of sport psychology around the world.

practice (e.g., use of suitable theories to inform the design of relevant interventions and their implementation). It is important to clarify that sport psychology is focused on the "application of psychological principles of human performance to help people consistently perform in the upper range of their capabilities and more thoroughly enjoy the performance process" (Portenga et al., 2017, p. 52).

From Established to Uncharted Pathways. Sport psychology is still a relatively young profession and continues to navigate the various academic standards and professional competencies expected of any developing profession (Portenga et al., 2017). While some countries may have more established and structured pathways to becoming a sport psychologist (e.g., Australia, Canada, the UK, and the USA; Euro-American), this may not be so for other countries (e.g., Hong Kong, India, Poland, and Singapore; de Cruz, 2022). Dependent on the power and authority of local governing bodies, who define sport psychology and its associated training requirements in their environments, the profession is faced with the challenge of diverse understandings and interpretations of what the practice of sport psychology entails (Watson II et al., 2017). This is especially so for countries that do not regulate the practice of any field of psychology, allowing it to be defined by each researcher, author, and practitioner based on personal standards, experiences, and biases (Lesyk, 2005):

> Sport psychology in India is in its infancy. It is a blank slate. We can do anything at the moment... Lack of awareness, weak finances, and no specific system to accredit professionals... Many have gone to UK universities to further their studies. However, cost is a barrier so others have done modules offered by local institutes.
>
> – *India*

A working definition of sport psychology has been established by Portenga et al. (2017) to provide a shared understanding of what the practice of sport psychology entails. However, this shared understanding may not be readily accepted by local governing bodies or professional communities, especially if it goes against the prevailing status quo associated with ambiguous definitions and subjective standards of applied psychology. While all forms of accreditation are voluntary, they are specifically designed to communicate that a reasonable standard of theoretical and practical competence has been achieved, benefitting both you and your stakeholders (Keegan & Cotterill, 2020). Where established pathways to accreditation are not readily accessible or available, the responsibility to practise sport psychology ethically and competently falls on you, the practitioner.

Professionalism of Sport Psychology

Professional Titles and Identity. As mentioned previously, the titles of "Psychologist" or "Sport and Exercise Psychologist" are legally protected in a handful of countries (Watson II et al., 2017). Though this has precluded non-accredited individuals from identifying themselves as Sport Psychologists or Sport and Exercise Psychologists, it has not deterred some from using alternative titles such as, "mental skills trainer", "mental coach", or "sport and performance consultant" to gain entry and elevate their position in the sporting arena. This may be particularly prevalent in countries where ambiguity and subjectivity pervade the practice of sport psychology, perpetuating the fog of uncertainty surrounding the profession:

> Since there are many kinds of certifications from many private organisations, it is difficult for athletes to understand how to choose the right mental trainer for themselves. A fake mental trainer can promote themselves by selling books with consulted athletes' names on them. However, a real certified mental trainer is not promoting themselves like this. So, it is difficult for society to know who is the right trainer, who has [an] academic background.
>
> – *Japan*

Even though titles may not be protected in some countries, it is our scientific and professional responsibility to adhere to clearly stated boundaries, as defined by broader cross-national professional bodies (e.g., ISSP and FEPSAC), so as to provide an acceptable standard of care and only practise within our scope of competence (Winter & Collins, 2016). Clearly articulating your professional identity and adopting its associated title, in line with the typical accreditation requirements outlined earlier in this chapter, can distinguish you from other professionals who purportedly offer psychology-oriented services in the sporting arena (Tod et al., 2017).

Globally Recognised and Locally Relevant. The increase in globalisation has inspired the emphasis on cultural competence, which is the ability to recognise different identities, experiences, and behaviours, and interact in a manner that demonstrates: (i) cultural awareness – the understanding of one's own culturally constituted beliefs, values, and attitudes; (ii) cultural knowledge – the understanding and knowledge of other world views; and (iii) cultural skills – the use of culturally appropriate communication and interventions (Ryba et al., 2013). Nevertheless, countries with a nascent sport psychology industry, who are frequently non-WEIRD (i.e., Western, Educated, Industrialised, Rich, and Democratic) and still developing their sporting ecosystems, are often subject to dominant Euro-American cultural assumptions and standards, as psychological inquiry continues to be mainly located within the context of the Western world (Schinke et al., 2016):

> As there are no local degrees available and the profession must rely on individuals and their resources to complete degrees overseas, the number of practitioners is limited in Ghana. Those of us who are accredited to practice then have difficulty relying on a supportive network of professionals. It also means that our country does not have its own specifications as to how practitioners should carry out their work in this field, making it difficult to adapt to the cultural needs of Ghana and its people.
>
> – *Ghana*

A culturally competent practitioner will be equipped with the necessary skills to work with racially, ethnically, and culturally diverse clients. Unfortunately, there is currently little emphasis placed on multicultural competence within many applied sport psychology training programmes (Foltz et al., 2015). As such, seeking guidance from supervisors who have made multiculturalism a core tenet of their professional philosophy may support the development of culturally competent consulting skills, empowering you to become a relevant and effective practitioner in your working environment, society, and country. Every national accreditation system will represent its unique historical and cultural origins. You are therefore encouraged to study the surrounding sporting environment you choose to establish yourself in, and continually "sense-make" and reflect on the half-life of your knowledge in this dynamic field (i.e., rate of decline – in either veracity or relevance, or both).

Building and/or Sustaining Expertise

Connecting with a Community of Practice. On your journey to becoming a Sport and Exercise Psychologist, it is normal to experience anxiety, self-doubt, and insecurities (Tod et al., 2009). There will likely be a great deal of pressure, either from external parties or yourself, to appear competent and credible (Fortin-Guichard et al., 2018). Rest assured, as you gain experience, you will develop the confidence to handle the issues and challenges that you will encounter along the path to accreditation. When at the crossroads of challenging situations, established working relationships with supervisors, colleagues, and peers can provide the necessary insight, alternative perspectives, and emotional sustenance to support your ongoing professional development (Hutter et al., 2017; Tod et al., 2017). Actively receiving and sharing information is a hallmark of an effective and ethical practitioner (Keegan & Cotterill, 2020), and can contribute to a sporting ecosystem centred on contribution, cooperation, and reciprocity:

> There is no clear infrastructure at this time but there is a growing interest and recognition of the importance of the profession and the work that is being done...A clear structure, a clear level of expertise and ability to consult with peers all over the world, where ideas can be shared.
>
> *– Malaysia*

Working towards a meaningful convergence amongst regional, national, and international practitioners, researchers, and associated accrediting bodies can lead to the creation of a community of sport psychology professionals, increasing "accreditation literacy" and the provision of competent and credible psychological services in sport and exercise. Also, exploring beyond the parameters of sport psychology and being open to input from other professionals within and outside sport (e.g., medicine, corporate business, etc.) makes for valuable learning too. After all, training and accreditation are perpetual processes, not unchanging, end results, as "learning leads to new application, then more learning, then more new application" (Lesyk, 2005, p. 181).

Guidance on Acquiring Accreditation

The diverse experiences of our international peers corroborate and resonate with the earlier sections on the value of accreditation as well as how it enables ethical and effective practice. Just as a practitioner's self-regulation benefits their client in therapeutic settings, the self-regulation of the profession benefits the fraternity as well as the wider public. Collating our international peers' perspectives, we found a shared consensus that being accredited *somewhere* was preferred to being accredited nowhere: even amongst practitioners in countries with no accreditation frameworks. Over the course of this chapter, we have put to you the purpose of accreditation and its practical value, as well as forewarning you of the challenges of practising in environments with no accreditation frameworks and how to cope with some of them. We hope that we have convinced you that seeking accreditation is a worthy pursuit; we have provided a flowchart in Figure 4.2 to support you in choosing the path most appropriate to your aspirations and circumstances. While Figure 4.2 consolidates the most frequented routes to accreditation around the world, it does not exhaustively cover all the possible choices you can make and we encourage you to consider your unique situation alongside the flowchart as you plan and chart your accreditation journey.

Before we conclude this chapter, let us explain how to use the flowchart in Figure 4.2. At the top of the flowchart, you will find the reflection questions we asked in a previous section; use these questions to envision your future as a practitioner and use that vision as a starting point to determine which route is most suitable for you. Next, move down the flowchart to the first choice point, represented by the question, "Does the country that you wish to practise in use legally protected titles in sport and exercise psychology?" Determine if your country of practice uses legally protected titles in sport and exercise psychology. This can be done via a Google search, asking psychology educators or current practitioners, checking in with your country's psychological society or association, or looking at the examples of countries we have listed, in the light grey boxes at the bottom of the flowchart. If you wish to practise in Australia, Canada, Ghana, the UK, or in other countries that, likewise, have established mandated routes to legal registration as a Psychologist in sport and exercise, then follow the training and accreditation pathway as stipulated by that country's accrediting body. If you wish to practise in the USA, first consider if you would like to be a psychologist or a non-psychologist practising in sport and exercise settings; thereafter, as a psychologist or a non-psychologist, apply to AASP to become a Certified Mental Performance Consultant.

Next, move down the flowchart to the second choice point, represented by the question, "Is there an accreditation framework (or further endorsement) for sport and exercise psychology in your country?" Curiously, in some countries, such as

International Routes to Sport and Exercise Psychology 65

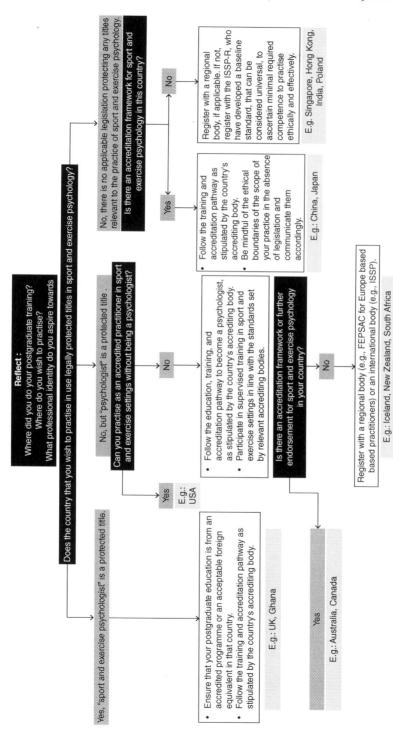

FIGURE 4.2 A flowchart of common routes to accreditation around the world.

China, Japan, and South Korea, there are accreditation frameworks guiding the practice of sport and exercise psychology, though there is no relevant legislation on professional titles. Whereas, in other countries, such as Iceland, New Zealand, and South Africa, there is legislation protecting the title of "Psychologist" but no accreditation frameworks with regard to sport and exercise psychology. If you find yourself in the latter situation or in a country with neither relevant legislation nor accreditation frameworks, such as India, Poland, and Singapore, look to cross-national frameworks such as those provided by the ISSP and FEPSAC. As covered in the abovementioned theme on professionalism of sport psychology, where there is ambiguity and subjectivity, lean on the guidance provided by these cross-national bodies who endeavour to anchor practitioners on globally recognised standards, while acknowledging locally relevant norms and challenges.

Conclusion

In this chapter, we sought to create a synthesised overview of the accreditation requirements around the world to support each reader as they navigate their own journey towards accreditation. We also included something unique amongst writings on this topic, by gathering and synthesising reflections from practitioners from diverse regions: those with highly specific and tightly enforced accreditation standards; those currently developing standards; and, also, those with no current desire to establish accreditation standards. From that reflective process, we identified clear benefits and difficulties of each situation and approach, as well as potential critiques of the dominant accreditation approaches (e.g., highly Euro-American-centric knowledge base, availability of education and training infrastructure, consistency of post-accreditation training, and continued professional development). In this way, as well as making a strong case in favour of accreditation, even where it is entirely voluntary or not well-regulated, we hope to at least balance that argument by acknowledging current challenges, and thus inform future progress with relevant considerations.

Knowing where you are based, and where you intend to operate as a practitioner, will be vital in informing decisions around training, accreditation, and continued professional development. Similarly, knowing the consistent elements and expectations may allow an aspiring practitioner to make informed decisions about what training to undertake next, where, and when. Thus, our newly proposed "map" is intended to help any future practitioner navigate towards either accreditation or an accreditation-ready profile of competencies and experience.

The strong arguments in favour of the existence of accreditation, with some caveats noted along the way, also lead us to recommend that even practitioners who require accreditation in their locale may still wish to seek regional or international accreditation, such as those offered by the ISSP or FEPSAC. Of course, in most cases, accreditation is only going to be added and refined, not removed – so even a region without current requirements may eventually see them introduced, as trends across other disciplines (e.g., Medicine, Clinical Psychology) illustrate that professions are only likely to become more regulated over time. Likewise, pursuing international accreditation may enable greater mobility during one's career, and connect a practitioner to a community of accredited practitioners sharing reflections, insights, and training opportunities – so, there are indirect benefits beyond merely quality assurance.

Understanding where one sits within the typical and/or international accreditation standards may also help one to understand the limits of one's current capability, and so remain ethical in working within one's training and competence. Also, as noted in the introduction, being able to articulate the benefits of accreditation to potential clients may actually lead to improved outcomes for each client, for the practitioner, and for the wider profession, as a consistent understanding develops about how quality is best appraised in psychology practitioners. Overall, we hope the picture painted in this chapter demonstrates that while accreditation systems can contain flaws and quirks, accreditation is arguably the least bad way of promoting quality assurance in a profession such as ours: it defines core knowledge, core competencies, and ongoing commitments, *and* it creates accountability for any poor practice beyond mere word-of-mouth. In summary, therefore, we have argued herein that – wherever you are in the world – accreditation is important, worthwhile, and – even where it is not in place (yet) – can inform and inspire better practice and better outcomes. After reading this chapter, readers are encouraged to consider the following key questions:

- Where did you complete your postgraduate training and how does it align with where you wish to practise?
- What professional identity do you aspire towards?
- How can you be recognised and relevant as a sport and exercise psychology practitioner in your environment?
- How can you connect with local and/or international professional communities to support your development?

Acknowledgements

We thank Anum Urooj, Clinton Gähwiler, Edgar Kazibwe, Gudrun Carstensdottir, Kalna Shukla, Karen Lo, Krisztina Bóna, Kunaal Doshi, Maurelle D'Sa, Miyako Tanaka-Oulevey, Mohammad Aldosari, Nanaki J. Chadha, Phyllis Esinam Adzoa Bissaba, Razvan, Timothy Wyatt, Tomasz, and Yuto Yasuda for sharing with us the accreditation routes in their countries.

Notes

1 For the most current information on the application process, we refer you to the webpages of FEPSAC Certification and ISSP-Registry.
2 At the time of writing, three UK universities offered this route – Glasgow Caledonian University, University of Portsmouth, and Liverpool John Moores University.

References

Association for Applied Sport Psychology. (2022). Ethics code: AASP ethical principles and standards. Retrieved May 29, 2022, from https://appliedsportpsych.org/about-the-association-for-applied-sport-psychology/ethics/ethics-code/

Australian Psychological Society. (2022). Study pathways. Retrieved May 29, 2022, from https://psychology.org.au/training-and-careers/careers-and-studying-psychology/studying-psychology/study-pathways

Braun, V., & Clarke, V. (2006). Using thematic analysis in psychology. *Qualitative Research in Psychology*, 3(2), 77–101. https://doi.org/10.1191/1478088706qp063oa.

British Psychological Society. (2022). Getting started. Retrieved May 29, 2022, from https://www.bps.org.uk/public/become-psychologist/getting-started

Clarke, V., & Braun, V. (2017). Thematic analysis. *The Journal of Positive Psychology*, 12(3), 297–298. https://doi.org/10.1080/17439760.2016.1262613.

de Cruz, N. (2022). *Cultural sport psychology and elite sport in Singapore: An exploration of identity and practice*. Routledge.

European Federation of Sport Psychology. (2022). Certification: The FEPSAC MC has established the European certification. Retrieved May 29, 2022, from https://fepsac.com/certification/

Foltz, B. D., Fisher, A. R., Denton, L. K., Campbell, W. L., Speight, Q. L., Steinfeldt, J., & Latorre, C. (2015). Applied sport psychology supervision experience: A qualitative analysis. *Journal of Applied Sport Psychology*, 27(4), 449–463. https://doi.org/10.1080/10413200.2015.1043162.

Fortin-Guichard, D., Boudreault, V., Gagnon, S., & Trottier, C. (2018). Experience, effectiveness, and perceptions toward sport psychology consultants: A critical review of peer-reviewed articles. *Journal of Applied Sport Psychology*, 30(1), 3–22. https://doi.org/10.1080/10413200.2017.1318416.

Health and Care Professions Council. (2015). *Standards of proficiency: Practitioner psychologists*.

Hutter, R. I., Oldenhof-Veldman, T., Pijpers, J. R., & Oudejans, R. R. (2017). Professional development in sport psychology: Relating learning experiences to learning outcomes. *Journal of Applied Sport Psychology*, 29(1), 1–16. https://doi.org/10.1080/10413200.2016.1183152.

International Society of Sport Psychology. (2022). ISSP-Registry. Retrieved May 29, 2022, from https://www.issponline.org/index.php/registry/issp-registry

Keegan, R. J. (2016). *Being a Sport Psychologist*. Palgrave Macmillan.

Keegan, R., & Cotterill, S. (2020). Accreditation. In D. Hackfort, & R. J. Schinke (Eds.), *The Routledge international encyclopedia of sport and exercise psychology volume 2: Applied and practical measures* (pp. 9–20). Routledge.

Lesyk, J. J. (2005). A school psychologist's self-study guide to sport psychology. *Journal of Applied School Psychology*, 21(2), 169–185. https://doi.org/10.1300/J370v21n02_09

Poczwardowski, A., Sherman, C. P., & Ravizza, K. (2004). Professional philosophy in the sport psychology service delivery: Building on theory and practice. *The Sport Psychologist*, 18(4), 445–463.

Portenga, S. T., Aoyagi, M. W., & Cohen, A. B. (2017). Helping to build a profession: A working definition of sport and performance psychology. *Journal of Sport Psychology in Action*, 8(1), 47–59. https://doi.org/10.1080/21520704.2016.1227413.

Ryba, T. V., Stambulova, N. B., Si, G., & Schinke, R. J. (2013). ISSP position stand: culturally competent research and practice in sport and exercise psychology. *International Journal of Sport and Exercise Psychology*, 11(2), 123–142. https://doi.org/10.1080/1612197X.2013.779812.

Schinke, R. J., Papaioannou, A. G., & Schack, T. (2016). Sport psychology in emerging countries: An introduction. *International Journal of Sport and Exercise Psychology*, 14(2), 103–109. https://doi.org/10.1080/1612197X.2016.1155828.

Schinke, R. J., Si, G., Zhang, L., Elbe, A. M., Watson, J., Harwood, C., & Terry, P. C. (2018). Joint position stand of the ISSP, FEPSAC, ASPASP, and AASP on professional accreditation. *Psychology of Sport and Exercise*, 38, 107–115. https://doi.org/10.1016/j.psychsport.2018.06.005.

Tod, D., Andersen, M. B., & Marchant, D. B. (2009). A longitudinal examination of neophyte applied sport psychologists' development. *Journal of Applied Sport Psychology*, 21(S1), S1–S16. https://doi.org/10.1080/10413200802593604.

Tod, D., Hutter, R. V., & Eubank, M. (2017). Professional development for sport psychology practice. *Current Opinion in Psychology*, 16, 134–137. https://doi.org/10.1016/j.copsyc.2017.05.007.

Tod, D., Marchant, D., & Andersen, M. B. (2007). Learning experiences contributing to service delivery competence. *The Sport Psychologist*, 21(3), 317–334. https://doi.org/10.1123/tsp.21.3.317.

Watson II, J. C., Way, W. C., & Hilliard, R. C. (2017). Ethical issues in sport psychology. *Current Opinion in Psychology*, 16, 143–147. https://doi.org/10.1016/j.copsyc.2017.05.008.

Winter, S., & Collins, D. J. (2016). Applied sport psychology: A profession? *The Sport Psychologist*, 30(1), 89–96. https://doi.org/10.1123/tsp.2014-0132.

Zizzi, S., Zaichkowski, L., & Perna, F. (2014). Certification in sport and exercise psychology. In J. L. Van Raalte, & B. W. Brewer (Eds.), *Exploring sport and exercise psychology* (2nd ed., pp. 439–458). American Psychological Association.

5
THE SUPERVISOR–TRAINEE RELATIONSHIP

Stacy Winter and Tim Holder

The Supervisor–Trainee Relationship

Supervision is a formal arrangement for trainees to regularly discuss their applied practice and be supported in their professional development. This process is facilitated by the supervisor, an individual experienced in both the intended domain of psychology consultancy and supervision. The supervisor and trainee work together to fulfil the purpose of supervision (Despenser, 2009). In the domain of sport and exercise psychology, the purpose of supervision is to successfully guide and support candidates during their training, so they are fit to practice in a safe, competent, and autonomous manner. As outlined in the previous chapters, there are three professional training routes within the UK: The British Psychological Society (BPS) Qualification in Sport and Exercise Psychology Stage 2 (QSEP Stage 2); The British Association of Sport and Exercise Sciences (BASES) Sport and Exercise Psychology Accreditation Route (SEPAR); and Professional Doctorates in Sport and Exercise Psychology. Successful completion of each of these routes confers eligibility to apply for registration with the Health and Care Professions Council (HCPC), the statutory regulator for Practitioner Psychologists in the UK. The HCPC (2015) standards of proficiency for Practitioner Psychologists include several elements relating to supervision, identified as an integral component of professional practice. Similarly, the standards of Continuing Professional Development (CPD) recognise supervision as an important feature of how "registrants continue to learn and develop throughout their career, keep their skills and knowledge up-dated, and ensure they work safely, legally, and effectively" (HCPC, 2018).

Regardless of the chosen professional training route, the supervisor–trainee relationship is at the heart of effective supervision (Millar, 2007; Stafford, 2008). Supervision is a commitment for both parties, with QSEP Stage 2 and SEPAR taking between two and four years and Professional Doctorates up to six years

DOI: 10.4324/9781003196280-6

to complete. As such, supervision can be described as a long-term interpersonal relationship designed to foster the growth and development of a trainee's skills as a helping professional (Bernard & Goodyear, 2009; Van Raalte & Andersen, 2000). The support, encouragement, and understanding provided by supervisors is fundamental to the development of the trainees (Feasey, 2002). In essence, supervisors are encouraged to foster a nurturing, positive relationship with their trainees that serves as a safe yet challenging forum (Andersen, 1994). Thus, the supervisor–trainee relationship can be seen as a powerful variable in itself (Flotz et al., 2015; Watson et al., 2004). If an effective supervisor–trainee relationship is to be initiated, developed, and maintained throughout the supervision process, several factors need to be considered. Subsequently, we have structured this chapter into the following four key areas: (1) Selecting the most appropriate supervisor; (2) How supervisors operate; (3) What supervisors are looking for in potential trainees; and (4) Managing the supervisor–trainee relationship. Guidance within each key area is supplemented with reflections from current QSEP Stage 2 and SEPAR supervisors and trainees, drawing upon their advice and first-hand experience.

Selecting the Most Appropriate Supervisor

Before applying to enrol on either the QSEP Stage 2 or SEPAR pathway, candidates will need to engage the support of an appropriate supervisor. Agreeing to act as a supervisor is a serious undertaking and a responsibility not to be taken lightly. Supervision is deemed central to professional development, competence, and quality assurance, and the supervisor can have a profound influence on an individual's future career (Watson et al., 2004). As such, it is an important initial process and key decision for the impending trainee to undertake.

The first place to look for a supervisor is directly through the professional organisations responsible for their respective training pathways. Candidates interested in QSEP Stage 2 can access the Register of Applied Psychology Practice Supervisors (RAPPS) via the BPS website.[1] RAPPS allows professional members to make themselves available to trainees for supervision, and for trainees to have a means of identifying and locating a supervisor. RAPPS covers all domains of psychology; therefore, in order to identify appropriate supervisors, candidates will need to search specifically for registrants with "Qualification in Sport and Exercise Psychology" listed in their training route. However, when speaking to trainees regarding their first-hand experience, some found going through this process to be more challenging than they had initially anticipated:

> When I first began thinking about BPS Stage 2, the enrolment process seemed relatively straight forward, complete a masters, find a supervisor, and start Stage 2. In reality it's a lot more challenging, particularly finding a supervisor to oversee your training. Firstly, there are only a limited number of potential supervisors to work from; with only 50 or so practitioners listed on the BPS RAPPS list. However, in my experience I found that it is likely that only a

> select few are based within a reasonable distance should you need to travel for meetings, group supervision etc. Soon the initial list of 50 becomes closer to 10. When I began working through this list, I found that two or three didn't have any availability to take on additional trainees and another two or three didn't even respond to my email. This then leaves you with just a handful of potential supervisors.
>
> *(QSEP Stage 2 trainee)*

Similarly, the BASES website permits potential trainees to search for approved supervisors on the SEPAR directory.[2] The advanced search in the directory allows candidates to filter by specialism (e.g., whether supervisors are proficient in sport, exercise, or both sport and exercise psychology). Table 5.1 outlines the requirements for QSEP Stage 2 and SEPAR supervisors.

As can be seen in Table 5.1, both the BPS and BASES require their supervisors to have completed training prior to being included in the RAPPS or SEPAR Directory (see Chapter 3 for Professional Doctorate Supervisory Arrangements) and attend refresher training either annually or bi-annually. This ensures supervisors are best-placed and prepared to be able to successfully support candidates through their respective training pathways. Given the importance of the working relationship between the trainee and supervisor, it is recommended candidates contact more than one potential supervisor before carefully considering who they wish to work within this role. This advice was reiterated by a current SEPAR trainee:

> When looking for a supervisor I was encouraged to "shop around" and speak to various people. This included not only the supervisor themselves, but also their trainees, to ensure that I had a well-informed understanding of the different offerings and experiences that were available. This helped me to find a supervisor that I felt suited my needs as a learner and developing professional.

TABLE 5.1 Supervisor Requirements for QSEP Stage 2 and SEPAR

QSEP Stage 2 Supervisors	*SEPAR Supervisors*
BPS Chartered Psychologist	BASES Professional Member
Full Member of the Division of Sport and Exercise Psychology	Registered with the HCPC as a Sport and Exercise Psychologist
Entered on the Society's RAPPS	Completed all the mandatory SEPAR supervisor training
Registered with the HCPC as a Sport and Exercise Psychologist	Attended the annual supervisor training workshop
Undertaken the Board's supervisor training	Have relevant insurance in place
Attended the Board's refresher training at least once every two years (annual attendance is encouraged)	Where relevant, procedures for HMRC requirements of tax and National Insurance, including all self-assessment completion

When contacting potential supervisors, it is advisable for candidates to prepare the questions they wish to ask, so the most important information can be gleaned to aid in their decision-making. Candidates may also wish to discuss potential supervisors with their lecturers, peers, or professional contacts as they might have personal insight, can advise on suitability, or purely act as a sounding board. For example, "Validation of my selection from my university tutor who was a well-established Sport Psychologist and colleague of the chosen supervisor, made me feel confident it was a good match" (SEPAR trainee).

The following is a checklist of areas to consider when choosing (or meeting a new) potential supervisor:

- Proposed mode of operating (e.g., individual, group supervision)
- Method of interfacing (e.g., face-to-face, remotely)
- Current availability to take on a new trainee
- Theoretical orientation to applied practice
- Access to any placement opportunities
- Details of fees charged for supervision and payment options
- The level of support and contact/minimum time commitments they will provide
- Their training and applied experience within the domain to be supervised
- Expertise in particular types of sports or demographics
- Specific research interests
- Experience in supervising other candidates through QSEP Stage 2 or SEPAR
- Are they suitable/compatible for me at this stage in my professional development?
- Do I think we will be able to establish an effective working relationship (e.g., personality fit, characteristics)?

It should be noted at this point, that neither the BPS nor BASES advises on supervisor fees. Both organisations recognise that in many circumstances individuals or institutions will charge trainees for acting as a supervisor and is, therefore, an important detail for potential candidates to enquire:

> Don't be afraid to ask about the cost of supervision. From personal experience, I found the prices ranged between £1200–£1500 per annum but some practitioners have been known to charge more. Deciding what you want from a potential supervisor and whether what they offer is worth the amount they are charging is a key consideration when choosing a supervisor.
>
> *(QSEP Stage 2 trainee)*

Fees will vary considerably, since supervisors may be independent, or their services may in full or in part be bound up with an educational course (and provided as part of that course such as the Professional Doctorate in sport and exercise psychology) or an employee contract position. When the arrangement is negotiated with the individual supervisor, the candidate should consider their financial position, the cost of the training pathway, additional costs that may be incurred (e.g., travel, CPD activities, insurance), and the supervision support and practices they will receive, in order to make an appropriate assessment of the proposed fee. Some of the key decisions for selecting a potential supervisor were highlighted by a current SEPAR trainee:

> The key decision for selection was who I felt I would have the best relationship with and the most experience and philosophical approach to myself. Another key factor was the opportunities for applied observations/work opportunities that my supervisor was able to provide. Consideration of logistical aspects, such as cost, and location of your supervisor were also important.

How Supervisors Operate

Effective supervision has so many benefits for the aspiring trainee along their developmental journey. A supervisor who provides a safe and positive learning environment will help to encourage the trainee/s they are supporting to reach their full potential and if successful be eligible to apply for registration with the HCPC. Therefore, it is important to understand how supervisors operate and the most effective means to support the individual trainee and encourage their development.

Supervisors will have different modes of operating between individual and group supervision or a combination of the two: "Very much a mixture between individual and group support, with regular/flexible one to ones and group meetings with other trainees, which are invaluable to sharing best practice, discussing research, and applied case studies" (SEPAR trainee). Traditionally, individual supervision was perceived as the most effective mode, but there are now many benefits recognised of group-based supervision (e.g., Hawkins & McMahon, 2020; Lane et al., 2016) as reflected by this current SEPAR trainee:

> An aspect of working with my supervisor which I find hugely beneficial are the group meetings. These are combined with another supervisor and her group of supervisees which gives a space for like-minded individuals to share experiences, normalise any fears or challenges faced as a training professional, as well as offer support and guidance to each other. Group meetings are often themed around a specific topic and is an opportunity to learn new skills. Besides this, it is a brilliant way to get to know other trainees and to develop a network of friends within the profession.

Operating in this manner provides a setting for giving and receiving support and challenge, sharing good practice/case reflections, and group-based supervision of ongoing practice:

> Practical and group-based sessions to compliment the individual sessions are really good. Setting challenges/discussion points and real-life practical cases is excellent, which is always done in a relaxed setting. Having a group with

BASES and BPS trainees is helpful not only for sharing experiences, but also feeling a sense of connectedness to a profession. It is especially helpful to connect outside of the group sessions, ask for advice, or just share similar experiences with other group members.

(SEPAR trainee)

Group-based supervision could be achieved through an individual supervisor creating a supervision group, linking to another supervisor/s, or geographically establishing regional supervisory groups: "My supervisor works with another supervisor; through this we are able to carry out fairly big group CPD sessions either remotely or in person" (QSEP Stage 2 trainee). There are also benefits for the supervisor in terms of not working in isolation, gaining peer support, and developing a supervisor network: "I value co-supervising and these experiences I find so enriching and reassuring. We also have a peer group system with regular meetings, and I find that my trainees gain so much from this set up" (QSEP Stage 2 supervisor).

Supervisors are expected to fulfil similar duties (regardless of the professional training pathway), and these may determine whether they are best accomplished within an individual or group scenario. Examples of duties supervisors are expected to perform:

- Help the candidate in undertaking a needs analysis at the outset of their training
- Challenge candidates on their developing professional philosophy as a practitioner
- Support the development of professional and personal knowledge and technical skills
- Guide the candidate in the identification and development of areas of best practice
- Recommend relevant CPD opportunities to development needs
- Monitor candidate progress of effective sport psychology consultancy processes
- Encourage reflection on learning, practice, and integration of theory into practice
- Assist the candidate to understand themselves as a practitioner and their values/beliefs
- Facilitate self-development through case study discussions
- Be a professional and ethical role model for candidates
- Develop candidates' method of working to maintain legal and ethical requirements
- Offer timely feedback and guidance on documentation prior to submission
- Engage in observation of practice as part of ongoing professional development

Irrespective of whether group or individual supervision is being offered, supervisors can differ in their method of interfacing, for example, whether face-to-face or remotely. For this current SEPAR trainee, they had a clear preference for interfacing with their potential supervisor: "When selecting a supervisor, it was important that the supervisor was located in a geographically convenient place, to allow for face-to-face sessions". Supervision conducted remotely, however, has the potential to support distant candidates when they are based in different geographical contexts to their supervisor (Townend & Wood, 2007). With advancements in digital technologies, it is possible for candidates to engage with remote supervision through virtual means:

> We have group supervision sessions every couple of months where we get together online and discuss a specific topic (e.g., how to plan a workshop). We also have a WhatsApp group where we share job vacancies and opportunities within the field.
>
> *(QSEP Stage 2 trainee)*

The use of technology-enhanced methods of supervision where discussions can take place remotely is a feasible and equally effective method of support (Stokes, 2018). In addition, candidates and supervisors can benefit from time and cost savings: "I can contact my supervisor whenever I feel the need either via email or phone. This has been extremely beneficial when something came up that I needed support with, in a quick timeframe, e.g., safeguarding" (QSEP Stage 2 trainee). It is worth considering if a working relationship has already been established between the supervisor and candidate and if remote supervision will be used solely or to augment face-to-face. Although remote supervision is not necessarily a barrier, both parties may wish to consider the implication that a face-to-face meeting early in the process may serve to facilitate the supervisory relationship. For example, online interactions might require a different communication style and limit access to micro-facial expressions and non-verbal cues which may influence the development of the supervisory alliance (Lloyd & Trudel, 1999). A final consideration with remote supervision would be the confidentiality and sensitive nature of some resources, such as client notes and videos, which would require the implementation of appropriate security measures.

As noted above, supervisors are to observe their trainee/s in practice, with both QSEP Stage 2 and SEPAR stipulating minimum hours for this requirement. QSEP Stage 2, as a guide, suggests observation should be done at least once in each year of the trainee's enrolment period, whereas SEPAR requires a minimum of 20 hours of observation over the duration of the trainee's supervised pathway. Observation forms a significant part of all training pathways and both formal and informal observation (Holder & Winter, 2017) can be used in supporting the growth and development of the trainee. It is the supervisor's role and responsibility to ensure that in taking on a trainee, they can dedicate sufficient time to this responsibility. Both supervisors and trainees identified significant advantages of being able to observe and be observed in the training process:

> There is a significant contribution that can be made to the supervisee's development through observing them and feeding back to them – asking questions

about the decisions they made. This is essential to supervisory effectiveness and quality. It is not about them becoming the same as you as a supervisor but about developing them towards their goals as a practitioner.

(QSEP Stage 2 supervisor)

Similarly, the benefits of observation were outlined by a current SEPAR trainee: "It offers a new perspective of my clients that I wouldn't have otherwise had the opportunity to see. Witnessing instinctual reactions to training and competition demands from both athletes and coaches provides a gateway into meaningful conversations". Observation may be done through direct "real-time" of delivery, indirectly via recording of a session, or through role-play/simulated practice. Therefore, an important aspect to consider when observing the trainee's practice is based on the supervisor's mode of operating and method of interfacing. For example, if engaging with individual and remote supervision, then the trainee would need to ensure they obtain the client/s consent to record the session and ensure appropriate data protection is in place for the supervisor to access the recording. Whereas, if direct "real-time" observation was to be conducted with face-to-face supervision, then the trainee would need to communicate potential dates/times and geographical location with their supervisor to confirm availability and ensure permission has been granted from the organisation, coaching staff, parents (if under the age of 18) and/or client/s depending on the sporting context being observed.

What Supervisors Are Looking for in Potential Trainees

While enrolled on either QSEP Stage 2, SEPAR, or a Professional Doctorate, candidates will be engaged in training aimed at furthering their career as a Practitioner Psychologist. As meeting the required competencies to become a registered Sport and Exercise Psychologist comes under the guidance of a supervisor, their professional reputation is potentially at stake based on how their trainee/s conduct themselves. It is, therefore, integral that potential trainees act in accordance with the standards of conduct stipulated by the respective professional organisation (e.g., BASES, BPS, HCPC). Thus, supervisors will expect their trainee/s to behave in a professional manner throughout the training pathway and familiarise themselves with the appropriate guidelines and regulations:

> During initial contact with a potential trainee, I always want them to demonstrate that they know about the processes (and associated available handbooks) for the qualification they will be working towards. With such a significant set of challenges in the qualification, ignorance of this strikes me as evidence that they don't really understand it and I would be unlikely to take them on.
>
> *(SEPAR supervisor)*

For example, QSEP Stage 2 trainees would need to abide by the BPS practice guidelines (2017) and code of ethics and conduct (2021); SEPAR trainees would need to adhere to the BASES code of conduct (2021) and specific guidelines within the SEPAR candidate handbook (2021); whereas all training routes including Professional Doctorates should follow the HCPC (2015) standards of conduct, performance, and ethics. Full details of this professional conduct are outlined within the respective regulations and guidelines. In brief, supervisors look for potential trainees who:

- Communicate professionally and respectfully with all relevant personnel
- Demonstrate organisational skills and manage their time effectively
- Seek suitable applied experiences that provide opportunities for the development of competencies with a range of clients
- Act in accordance with their respective training pathway code of conduct
- Ensure compliance with legal requirements regarding the title and status of a Trainee Sport and Exercise Psychologist
- Maintain awareness and developed understanding of ethical conduct and guidelines
- Avoid all practices of professional misconduct
- Arrange for indemnity insurance cover to be in place for all areas of work they may undertake
- Develop a comprehensive portfolio and keep up to date with all the required documentation related to the stage of the training pathway
- Make every attempt to meet agreed deadlines and provide advanced notice of any changes that could impact achieving these
- Undertake appropriate internal and external CPD activities
- Take responsibility for knowing when fees become due and make the necessary payment arrangements

Drawing upon first-hand experience from a current QSEP Stage 2 and SEPAR supervisor, they reflected when first meeting potential candidates:

> I guess you're looking for someone who has organisational qualities and a professional but relaxed approach to their conversation. This helps to establish whether you have a potential rapport and ability to develop an effective and collaborative working relationship with the candidate.

In addition to these, supervisors are looking for potential trainees who are going to be reflective throughout their training pathway (Scaife, 2010): "One of the most important earlier indicators that help establish whether I would be interested supervising a potential candidate is their overall attitude to the demands of the process and an openness to learn and develop through it" (QSEP Stage 2 and SEPAR supervisor).

Reflective practice is a requirement by all the organisational bodies, providing a useful and appropriate framework for the professional training and development of sport and/or exercise psychologists (Anderson et al., 2004). The supervision process involves the development of the trainee's self-knowledge and understanding of practice: "I would look for a trainee to be reflective and aware of their own limitations/competencies rather than be over-confident, have a desire to learn, pursue opportunities, and willing to acknowledge their own vulnerabilities" (QSEP Stage 2 supervisor). Reflective practice offers a suitable mechanism for sharing experiences and monitoring and documenting this development (Knowles et al., 2007). To facilitate the development of trainee's reflection skills, BASES, as an example, runs a reflective practice workshop that all SEPAR candidates attend within the first six months of their registration. The SEPAR supervisor will then play a key role in facilitating the development of their trainee's reflective practice, prior to and following on from this initial workshop. Throughout both training pathways, it is important that trainees develop their reflective practice skills and use established models (e.g., Driscoll, 2007; Gibbs, 1988; Johns, 1994) in which to structure their reflections. Supervisors will look for trainees who can be reflective of their applied experiences, the completion of CPD activities, and integrating theory and research into their practice. Written reflections form an integral part of the QSEP Stage 2, SEPAR, and Professional Doctorate portfolios, that trainees are required to submit to document their professional development journey.

Managing the Supervisor–Trainee Relationship

The supervisory relationship will take patience, approachability, and trust between the supervisor and trainee as it progresses along the developmental pathway: "I feel that the supervision relationship is enhanced by having a mutual trust and respect for one another" (SEPAR trainee). There is no "one size fits all" approach to supervision. Instead, it means being aware and willing to learn about individual preferences and potentially modifying the approach of working for each supervisor–trainee relationship: "I drive my own development. I like the flexibility from my supervisor around this, moving at my pace, giving more when I need and pausing/changing pace when I need it too" (SEPAR trainee).

In the previous sections, we outlined expectations from both the supervisor and trainee. For example, supervisors would expect to see positive developments over time in their trainee's performance, willingness to take on board constructive feedback, and awareness of the limitations of their knowledge and skill base. Whereas the trainee expects their supervisor to provide appropriate levels of contact time, have sufficient expertise and experience relevant to their domain, and support their growth and development. A current QSEP Stage 2 trainee reflected on their changing expectations of the supervisor–trainee relationship:

> The biggest challenge, coming out of university is to reset your expectations around professional relationships. I found I got a bit into the mindset of the teacher-student relationship in which they could only devote a certain amount of time. Clearly this is still true, but I found that the lines of communication are more open, and this was something which I had to adapt to.

> In this sense it is realising that you can make more contact and have a more advanced relationship with your supervisor than you would have done. This is something which a trainee needs to establish before starting their qualification as will make it a better experience on their part.

It is recommended that clarifying expectations and initial roles with the dyad is conducted from the outset of the relationship. Indeed, the importance of role clarity and managing expectations in supervisory relationships has been highlighted in several professions (e.g., Cutcliffe et al., 2011; Davys & Beddoe, 2010).

As trainees develop along their professional pathway, it is quite natural that the supervisory relationship shifts over time:

> I found that during the first few months the contact time with the supervisor was higher, which was really helpful when starting out. As I have progressed this has not been as frequent, but that is due to person preference. I have found my supervisor to always be on hand and able to answer my phone call or reply to an email when I have needed it.
>
> *(QSEP Stage 2 trainee)*

This may entail a trainee becoming competent in their respective field and the supervisor respecting their developed expertise and becoming more like colleagues within the relationship. Roles within the supervisory relationship will require regular reviews and thus adjustments communicated throughout the training pathway. It is therefore advisable to understand the changing nature of the supervisory relationship and continually clarify both the supervisor's and trainee's role to support the management of expectations:

As outlined in the first section (Selecting the Most Appropriate Supervisor) of this chapter, supervisors will have different modes of operating between individual and group supervision, or a combination of the two. All the Professional Bodies guide supervisors on the responsibilities expected within this role in providing a high-quality experience for candidates. Supervisors should consider whether they have the capacity and appropriate levels of time to support the growth and development of each candidate within their preferred mode of operation. Conversely, it is important for candidates to acknowledge that they are not the supervisor's sole trainee or professional work commitment, in being realistic with their expectations:

> Sometimes it's easy to forget that my supervisor has a full-time job, so when I want work looked at as soon as possible this isn't possible sometimes, but I think this is just about being honest about the constraints. My supervisor has been very good at organising any extra support if I need it and keeping me up to date with any changes in her life/schedule which might cause problems for supervision. If she had not done this, I might have found the process frustrating.
>
> *(Current QSEP Stage 2 trainee)*

While entering into a supervisory relationship is voluntary, the professional organisations responsible for the training pathways recommend that supervisors enter into a formal agreement with candidates that will specify objectives, goals, expectations, and any restrictions and financial implications. BASES strongly advises that an agreement is made on paper to reflect this and to protect both parties. With the BPS, potential candidates are required to agree to a contract with their supervisor and submit it as part of their enrolment supplication. Sample contracts are available to view on the BASES and BPS websites, but similar to supervisor fees, both organisations will not advise or become involved in the contractual process. In most circumstances, the supervisor–trainee relationship will last for the duration of the contract: until all qualification requirements have been met. However, in some instances, the relationship may start to break down, for example, a change in circumstances for one or both parties. In the first instance, it is expected all reasonable steps are taken to resolve any challenges. If the issue cannot be resolved, either party has the right to withdraw from the supervisory contract if the relationship is not satisfactory or workable. Termination of this agreement should be given in writing to the other person no less than twenty-eight days in advance. A current QSEP Stage 2 and SEPAR supervisor noted how they have found an annual review process to be useful in monitoring the supervisor–trainee relationship:

> Managing the relationship with a trainee requires regular open conversations to gain feedback on the experiences of both parties in relation to how it is working. Any agreement in place is best left open to annual review to enable both parties to monitor effectiveness. Candidates should feel comfortable to adapt any agreement in-line with their development, including terminating the agreement in order to find a more appropriate supervisory arrangement for their future development. Under such rare circumstances it would be optimal practice to assist the candidate in the transition to alternative supervisory arrangements.

In the event that a change in supervisor is required, the trainee will need to inform their respective professional body. With BASES, either the trainee or supervisor should refer the matter to the Chair of the SEPAR Advisory Group for approval. With QSEP Stage 2, a Change of Supervisor form must be completed, submitted to the Qualifications Team, and is subject to the Chief Supervisor's approval. The original supervisor will also be required to complete an Evaluation of Professional Competence form and send this to the Delivery Team Administrator, who will forward it to the Chief Supervisor. Once reviewed the administrator will send a copy to the newly approved supervisor.

It is advisable that trainees maintain regular contact with their supervisor to keep them informed of progress and any queries or concerns regarding their training and/or supervisory relationship:

> To manage the supervision relationship, I have found being open and honest is key. If something has not gone to plan or I have concerns, then sharing these has been key to my learning and development. Having a fast line of

communication has also been really important. Getting a response from the supervisor promptly is important in maintaining the relationship. Responding to the supervisor promptly as the trainee is also important in keeping the relationship open.

(QSEP Stage 2 trainee)

Indeed, the Professional Bodies suggest formal records should be kept of meetings and communications throughout the process, to help manage the supervisor–trainee relationship.

Conclusion

Effective supervision has so many benefits for the aspiring sport and/or exercise psychologist in their quest to practice in a safe, competent, and autonomous manner. At the heart of effective supervision is the supervisor–trainee relationship, deemed central to professional development, competence, and quality assurance. This chapter was structured into four key areas, reflecting the initiation, development, and maintenance of the supervisor–trainee relationship. The different ways supervisors operated, geographical locations, and how much they charged, were some of the key logistical deliberations for potential candidates before commencing their trainee journey. Whereas, at an interpersonal level, trainees favoured potential supervisors who were open, friendly, approachable, supportive, understanding, encouraging, flexible, and provided appropriate guidance, direction, and challenge. Drawing upon both parties' viewpoints provided a valuable and additional perspective to hear established supervisors' and trainees' advice, reflections, and first-hand experiences. In this regard, the chapter offered a unique insight to also hear what supervisors are looking for in potential candidates and what might influence them when agreeing to enter into a new supervisory relationship. We would thoroughly recommend potential candidates take this information on board when embarking on a professional training pathway and contacting respective supervisors. With the training pathways taking up to six years to complete, supervision is a long-term mutual commitment and interpersonal relationship. The importance of managing the supervisor–trainee relationship through entering into formal agreements, clarifying roles and expectations, being open and honest in communications, having mutual trust and respect for each other, and scheduling annual reviews were therefore highlighted within this chapter. We hope the information presented is useful for anyone contemplating a recognised training pathway in sport and/or exercise psychology, in addition to current trainees and supervisors, and those practitioners who may be considering becoming a registered supervisor with one of the professional bodies. Finally, we would like to close the chapter by offering the reader the following three questions to consider:

- What do you feel are the key messages from this chapter you could take on board as a supervisor or trainee?

- On reflection, what do you value most in establishing an effective supervisor–trainee relationship?
- Have you encountered any challenges in the supervisor–trainee relationship and how did you go about resolving these?

Notes

1 www.bps.org.uk/rapps
2 https://www.bases.org.uk/separ_directory.php

References

Andersen, M. B. (1994). Ethical considerations in the supervision of applied sport psychology graduate students. *Journal of Applied Sport Psychology, 6*, 152–167. https://doi.org/10.1080/10413209408406291.

Anderson, A. G., Knowles, Z., & Gilbourne, D. (2004). Reflective practice for sport psychologists: Concepts, methods, practical implications and thoughts on dissemination. *The Sport Psychologist, 18*, 188–203. https://doi.org/10.1123/tsp.18.2.188.

Bernard, J. M., & Goodyear, R. K. (2009). *Fundamentals of clinical supervision* (4th ed.). Pearson.

British Association of Sport and Exercise Sciences (2021). Code of conduct. Retrieved from: https://www.bases.org.uk/imgs/code_of_conduct202.pdf

British Psychological Society (2017). Practice guidelines. Retrieved from: https://www.bps.org.uk/news-and-policy/practice-guidelines

British Psychological Society (2021). Code of ethics and conduct. Retrieved from: https://www.bps.org.uk/news-and-policy/bps-code-ethics-and-conduct

Cutcliffe, J. R., Hyrkäs, K., & Fowler, J. (2011). *Routledge handbook of clinical supervision: Fundamental international themes*. Routledge.

Davys, A., & Beddoe, L. (2010). *Best practice in professional supervision: A guide for the helping professions*. JKP.

Despenser, S. (2009). Getting the most from supervision. *Therapy Today, 20*, 28–31.

Driscoll, J. (2007). *Practising clinical supervision: A reflective approach*. Bailliere Tindall.

Feasey, D. (2002). *Good practices in supervision with psychotherapists and counselors*. Whirr Publishers.

Flotz, B. D., Fisher, A. R., Denton, L. K., Campbell, W. L., Speight, Q. L., Steinfeldt, J., & Latorre, C. (2015). Applied sport psychology supervision experience: A qualitative analysis. *Journal of Applied Sport Psychology, 27*, 449–463. https://doi.org/10.1080/10413200.2015.1043162.

Gibbs, G. (1988). *Learning by doing: A guide to teaching and learning methods*. Oxford Polytechnic.

Hawkins, P., & McMahon, A. (2020). *Supervision in the helping professions* (5th ed.). Open University Press.

Health Care and Professions Council (2015). Standards of conduct, performance, and ethics. Retrieved from: https://www.hcpc-uk.org/standards/standards-of-conduct-performance-and-ethics/

Health Care and Professions Council (2018). Standards of continuing professional development. Retrieved from: https://www.hcpc-uk.org/aboutregistration/standards/cpd/

Holder, T., & Winter, S. (2017). Experienced practitioners use of observation in applied sport psychology. *Sport, Exercise, and Performance Psychology, 6*, 6–19. https://doi.org/10.1037/spy0000072.

Johns, C. (1994). Nuances of reflection. *Journal of Clinical Nursing, 3,* 71–75. https://doi.org/10.1111/j.1365-2702.1994.tb00364.x.

Knowles, Z., Gilbourne, D., Tomlinson, V., & Anderson, A. (2007). Reflections on the application of reflective practice for supervision in applied sport psychology. *The Sport Psychologist, 21,* 109–122. https://doi.org/10.1123/tsp.21.1.109.

Lane, D., Watts, M., & Corrie, S. (2016). *Supervision in the psychology professions. Building your own personalized model.* Open University Press.

Lloyd, R. J., & Trudel, P. (1999). Verbal interactions between an eminent mental training consultant and elite level athletes: A case study. *The Sport Psychologist, 13,* 418–443. https://doi.org/10.1123/tsp.13.4.418.

Millar, A. (2007). Encouragement and other Es. *Therapy Today, 18,* 40–42.

Scaife, J. (2010) *Supervising the reflective practitioner: An essential guide to theory and practice.* Routledge.

Sport and Exercise Psychology Accreditation Route (2021). Candidate handbook. Retrieved from: https://www.bases.org.uk/imgs/4__v4_separ_candidate_handbook___rt___jan_2021123.pdf

Stafford, D. E. (2008). Supervision – The grown-up relationship? *Therapy Today, 19,* 38–40.

Stokes, A. (2018). *Online supervision: A handbook for practitioners.* Routledge.

Townend, M., & Wood, W. (2007). E-learning the art of supervision. *Therapy Today, 18,* 42–44.

Van Raalte, J. L., & Andersen, M. B. (2000). Supervision I: From models to doing. In M. B. Andersen (Ed.), *Doing sport psychology* (pp. 153–165). Human Kinetics.

Watson II, J. C., Zizzi, S. J., Etzel, E. F., & Lubker, J. R. (2004). Applied sport psychology supervision: A survey of students and professionals. *The Sport Psychologist, 18,* 415–429. https://doi.org/10.1123/tsp.18.4.415.

PART II

Developing a Sport Psychology Consultancy

Stephen Smith

I am one of the very few psychologists in the UK that are formally registered as BOTH an Occupational AND a Sport and Exercise Psychologist. I have operated in both spheres for over 30 years and have always found the siloed thinking from both communities completely bewildering. As a human, I understand that we like to think that what we do with our lives is special and unique. But the real truth is that there are far more similarities than differences between the two areas of psychology.

Interestingly this section really looks at your ability to run a successful venture – which just happens to be a sport and exercise psychology business. However, the key messages could, actually, apply to anyone setting up any kind of consulting business. Thus, it is apparent to me that anyone setting up in business should be looking at what occupational psychology has to say – if only to save cost and time in not reinventing wheels or making the same old mistakes that others have learned from years ago. This section looks at key learnings from colleagues in terms of setting up, marketing and taking your business forward. It won't have all of the answers, but it will cover the key challenges that each of the contributors has faced.

I have also added these little thoughts here in terms of what you should be observing when you look in the mirror each morning.

Physician Know Thyself

In my occupational psychology career, I have travelled the world consulting to some of the biggest brands or delivering the leadership pipeline internally when I was Chief Psychologist at one of the world's biggest oil and gas companies. In that time, I have met the good, the bad and the ugly in talent and it has become apparent to me that there are some core things about the good that really make them stand out from the rest.

I have yet to meet a leader or entrepreneur who wears a big red S on their spandex-covered chest, wears their underpants outside their trousers and can move faster than a speeding bullet. No one on this planet is the finished article as the vagaries of running a business mean that you always have to learn and develop. The one thing I can be sure of is that those who go on to be successful challenge themselves through self-reflection and feedback and are brutally honest about themselves and their weaknesses – those who do not and think they have little to learn are the ones who derail.

I have never forgotten the example of one of the world's most iconic and successful business leaders who completed a personality inventory for my then-employer in occupational psychology. When it was scored up, it became apparent that this individual had described themselves as woefully inept in the area of planning, organising and operational delivery. As our Chief Psychologist put it, "This looks like he could not organise anything – how am I going to feed this profile back?"

The day for the feedback came and it came to the point in the discussion where this section in the report could not be ignored. "That is fantastic!" roared the famous business name "That captures me perfectly…do you know I could not organise anything". He quickly went on to add "But I have always known that, which is why my first employee was the exact opposite of me – I chose them because they covered my blindspots".

This level of self-awareness is key to business success. You do not have to be great at everything, but you do need to be very honest with yourself and identify where your strengths and development needs are – if you do not address them, they will jump up and bite you.

Global Competency Model

There are many competency models for business success but, when you look at all the leading personality inventories and competence models used in commercial organisations, the same three factors come up time and again: Intellect – how bright is the person; resilience – how driven are they to cope with challenges; interpersonal skill – how well do they lead and work with others. Not only do these work across all industries but they are recognised on a global scale. I have rolled out many similar versions of this model in both the UK and the whole of the world – no one ever said they did not apply to their culture, role or region.

The first key message here is that your technical knowledge as a Psychologist is completely irrelevant. These factors underpin behavioural success in any role. This is my top line version of those factors – and I am happy to share it (Figure PII.1).

The exact weighting, detail and level required for any role may vary but this model is like a three-legged stool. If any of the three legs is not as well developed as the others it won't work very well as a stool at all.

The challenge that faces everyone is to be able to look at themselves honestly and that is much easier said than done.

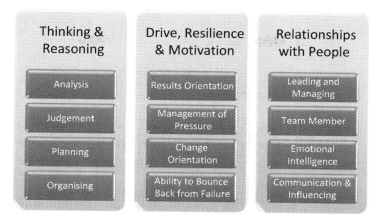

FIGURE PII.1 Global Competency Model.

Once you have identified where your weaknesses are – and everyone has them – you now need to decide on what you are going to do about them which gives you the following options:

i. Ignore Them: If you are exceptionally lucky, they will never trip you up as you merrily dance your way to a land of milk and honey.
ii. Develop Them: Maybe you can develop them. Some business competencies are skills-based and others are experience–based; so, with the right approach you may certainly find you get better…over time, let's hope your business succeeds to give you that time.
iii. Use the Talent of Others: You may not be able to develop certain things or simply do not have the motivation or time to invest in that development. If so, it would be a good idea to follow the example of our business icon and recruit others who have the competencies you lack. But, as Shakespeare once said, "Aye, there's the rub". It is hard work leading those who are very different to ourselves – which is why most managers recruit in their own likeness and do not understand why the team fails. This is the schoolboy error that most poor leaders make, so be warned.

Been There, Seen It…Got the Scars

It can be exciting to launch out on your own…but being on your own is a very lonely place when times get tough. So, get a coach or mentor who has been around the block before you. A good one will save you immense amounts of time and money and will see the bear traps long before you do. Good luck, I hope this section sets you up for success.

6
SETTING UP AND OPERATING A SPORT AND EXERCISE PSYCHOLOGY CONSULTANCY PRACTICE

Hannah Stoyel and Paul McCarthy

Getting Started

When I (Hannah) thought about becoming, and eventually became a Sport and Exercise Psychologist (from now on, I will refer to my job as a Sport Psychologist), I knew I wanted to be a Psychologist, and I knew I wanted to work with a population that I would understand – athletes.

What I did not know was how I was going to work. I assumed, perhaps naively, that I would become employed by a large organisation or team and work as an employee. However, there are few full-time applied roles and so it became apparent to me quickly that I would need to set up my consultancy. What I also learned is that I did not want to do it on my own. I wanted to create a group of practitioners that I could trust and that would allow me to build a brand and offer a service to athletes I was proud of. When training to become a Sport Psychologist, no one told me I would need a knowledge of the business world, and so this chapter aims to explore how I started my consultancy, Optimise Potential, and how I made it into a group consultancy that thrives financially and allows me to be the boss.

People will often say that they love the idea of being their own boss. And I get it. It seems, on the face of it, really enticing, with flexible hours, flexible responsibility, flexible holiday. However, starting your own business, being your own boss, is incredibly hard. It is hard logistically and financially. Having no one to answer to means that it is all down to you. If you don't work hard, the business does not progress. For many years, I worked all weekends, and no phone call went unanswered, even on a Sunday evening. There is stiff competition, and you have to stand out, and doing that means working harder and smarter than your competitors. If a new/potential client contacts me, they never wait over 24 hours for a reply. They have rewarded me for my promptness and organisation, and I would encourage that attention to detail for others starting out.

I will pause here to say that often those of us in a helping profession can feel daunted or ashamed in talking about money and financial gain. You cannot, however, do your job well without being paid to do it. Under-charging undervalues and undermines your work, all the training you did to get to this point and the profession. You cannot pour from an empty cup, and sometimes that proverbial cup needs to be filled with financial security. Being paid well to do what you have trained for also means that when a client or team comes along that cannot afford you, you can offer your services for discount or pro bono. But you cannot offer a discount or pro bono work if you cannot make ends meet.

Why Private Practice?

As I already mentioned, my foray into private practice stemmed from necessity, but looking back and actively working in private practice to this day, I can comfortably list a huge number of pros. Working in private practice allows you to gain experience, and it allows you to do so in a vast range of sports. In my time, I have had runners, swimmers, divers, equestrian athletes, gymnasts and boccia players, come through my doors, just to name a few! I have delivered workshops to lacrosse players, tennis players, triathletes, footballers and so many more. The breadth of sport type and client type that I have got to work with would have been impossible in a role with a single team or organisation. This proficiency in a range of sports has allowed me to gain experience that is useful for my CV and career progression, but also private consultancy work also pays better. While not without its own overhead, the money I can make with a single private session is often more than what I can make seeing a player as part of a scholarship scheme or National Governing Body.

Setting Up for and Securing Your First Clients

After my MSc and starting on my supervision journey meant it was time for me to find work. It takes time to build experience and build connections within this world, and it is important to know that your supervisor will (most likely) not provide you with clients or work. That is your responsibility. I have outlined my personal journey to working full time in sport psychology in Figure 6.1. You can see that I coached gymnastics to help subsidise my supervision while I gained a client base. But the question everyone has is how did I secure that first client? How did I get started?

The first thing to know is that I didn't necessarily do it all "right." I didn't set out a business plan to start, but perhaps if you are reading this ahead of starting your work, your foresight and organisation out-matches mine and you will be in a better place than I was and create a plan. That being said, what I did (what we outline below) worked for me to get those first clients despite being rather ad hoc in creation. Before we dive into the logistics, I will add that when reaching out to your potential first clients you need to know how to describe sport psychology quickly and clearly and what you can offer to potential clients. Figure out a way to market your work that is truthful and exciting both in written format and when networking in person (readers are referred to Chapter 7 of this book for guidance on marketing yourself) (Figure 6.2).

Operating a Sport and Exercise Psychology Consultancy Practice **91**

FIGURE 6.1   My personal timeline from undergrad graduation to moving Optimise Potential to a group consultancy. OP = Optimise Potential.

GETTING STARTED: YOUR CHECKLIST

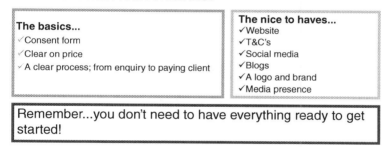

FIGURE 6.2   Checklist for your first client.

To start consulting you need "the basics": you need to have a consent form that will keep you and your potential clients safe, you need to be clear on prices and cancellation fees and you need to know how you will work. You need a clear process when a client comes to you, engages in your services and how they will pay (aspects of these basics to consider can be found in Figures 6.3–6.5). I can recommend contacting other therapists, counsellors or Psychologists and asking about sessions or visiting their websites to see real-life examples of the aforementioned.

Once you have a few clients engaged in your services (more on finding those below), you can grow the "nice to haves" (see Figure 6.2). You don't need everything in place to get started, and you will adjust many aspects of your consent form, prices and website as you move forward, but it is important to get a few key things in place. As I discuss how I got my first clients, you will see that my order and method may not have been the "right order" upon reflection, but it is an honest account of my experience so you can learn from me and what I did right… and wrong!

Despite now feeling like it is a "nice to have," the first thing I did was set up my website and had a logo designed. I think a website is not essential, but it is helpful,

> **Consent form items for consideration**
>
> - Under 18 and over 18
> - Name, age, contact details, emergency contact details (if remote, location of client)
> - Confidentiality
> - Competency
> - Other information – e.g. GP, occupation, reasons for seeking support, release of information
> - Where will you save data? Remember to adhere to data protection and storage rules

FIGURE 6.3 Items to consider for inclusion in a client intake form.

> **Pricing factors to consider**
>
> - Travel/expenses
> - Preparation time
> - Initial discovery call
> - Is the first session free?
> - Is this a long-term opportunity?
> - Sliding scale (e.g., student discounts)
> - Bulk buy/returning costumer discounts

FIGURE 6.4 Items to consider when establishing prices.

> **How will you work?**
>
> - Will you offer an initial free call or calls with parents/coaches between sessions?
> - When will clients pay? (before or after sessions).
> - How will clients pay? Invoices need creating
> - What email will you use?
> - Online consultancy: what service will you use? What if there are connectivety issues?
> - How many clients per day is realistic?
> - Will you have a client evaluation form?

FIGURE 6.5 Aspects to consider when establishing how you will work and run your private practice.

and I would suggest it should be your priority after setting up "the basics" (see Figure 6.2). For the website, I used Wix,[1] but there are various platforms that can help you set up a professional-looking website. But be aware that there are fees. Paying for domain names, email addresses and website upgrades can cost about £100–£200 a year depending on the number of domains. The website needs to be the first point of information about what you can offer to clients and so information should be accurate. When starting my website, I decided to not name it after myself because I thought I may have the long-term goal of creating a business that was a group consultancy and a brand larger than me. Something for you to consider as renaming is often hurtful to brand success. To start a website, I also needed a logo, again something that can take financial investment. For a logo that will go on the website, business cards, shirts and more, taking the time and resources to have one that looks professional is key. It needs to be yours so that you can own the copyright. It needs to be of excellent quality so that you can blow it up as large as you may want from tiny business cards to banners!

Once I had my logo and website, I started making phone calls and sending emails. I emailed local physiotherapy clinics to see if I could be on their websites as someone they referred to and trusted. The more places my name was on the internet, the better. Starting grassroots with local clubs is also a great place to begin. Emailing local swim clubs, Sunday league rugby clubs, local gyms and so forth is much more likely to get you that first workshop experience than emailing all the Premier League academy clubs in the nation. It also will allow your confidence to grow as an applied practitioner. Most likely, coming out of your MSc, you will lack applied experience, and that is okay. But this is your time to get that experience and not worry about how elite or fancy the club is where you find that experience. Workshops are a great place to start, they can feel less intimating than a 1-2-1 meeting with an athlete and it also exposes your work to many more people in one go. It was doing workshops for local clubs that eventually got me enough experience to land a part-time role with Swim England, which is when my applied career really took off.

That First Workshop

Let's say you get that first workshop with a local club: there are a few things to think about when you give a workshop that you might not learn in your MSc, namely what are the logistics? I have shown up to rooms where I was promised a projector and there wasn't one (this has prompted me to buy a small cheap one). Or there was a projector, but no plug. Sometimes, athletes are sitting on the floor, and it is hard to write and therefore pay attention or get engaged (I now travel with clipboards). I have printed worksheets to increase engagement for the 30 attendees only to show up and find there are 50 athletes there. Knowing what to prepare and deciding what is your responsibility versus that of the clubs is important to nail down and to nail down in writing. Even if you are working for free, learning to draw up a short contract of what you will provide and what the client/club handles is key. What happens if training runs late and so your workshop starts late and you miss the last train home? What if your workshop needs tools or materials, you thought the coach was printing, and they thought you were printing? If online, who provides the Zoom link? In short, write a contract and spell it all out. You will look professional and save yourself from tons of mess.

Of course, smaller clubs have less budget and so you have to think about what you will do/can do for less money *and* gives you that experience in your early days. As mentioned before, you need to make money and working for free beyond your first workshop or two or first few clients will only devalue your work and the profession. It is very hard to ask for payment after working somewhere for free, so establish that if you will work for free or for a discount, it is a one-off. Get this in writing. Talking to clubs about each member paying £3 to attend a workshop is a great way for you to at least get some money for travel or any expenses. If you can offer free work as you gain confidence, that is an option, but work on increasing your fees as soon as possible. You can remain flexible and open to negotiation, but you can't work for free forever. People will pay for what they value, so make your service something of value. Also, something I learned long ago is that when clients pay for sessions, they also value the sessions more, will put more effort into your work together and won't cancel last minute!

Why Group Consultancy?

When I first set out to practise sport psychology, I did so on my own. However, a group consultancy, something I had only seen outside sport psychology in more clinical realms, quickly became of interest. In group consultancy, you have peers to learn from, colleagues to enjoy and the business can be bigger than you and therefore it can reach more people and you can make money while you yourself are not working. A group consultancy does not need to only be a group of psychologists. Some of the most successful consultancies are those that are set up across disciplines and Optimise Potential has partnered with some great sport nutritionists and strength and conditioning coaches over the years.

Expanding to Group Consultancy

About two-and-a-half years after first reaching out to a local swimming club, I felt my consultancy could expand to more practitioners. The reality of this work is that most clients want a session somewhere between 4 pm and 8 pm each evening or on the weekend. So even though I was not technically at full capacity, I was rapidly running out of 6 pm and 7 pm slots. I also wanted to expand as I knew it would offer me professionalism I currently didn't have, and I wanted to expand what I had created and remain in charge. This reality, coupled with two coffee shop chats I had with Serena MacLeod and Hannah Winter, meant that I considered how I could expand the consultancy.

When expanding to other practitioners, it can be nerve-wracking. It is your name, your reputation and your brand on the line. So a lot of thought needs to go into who you will hire and bring into your group; be picky. Before my coffee shop chats with Serena and Hannah, I don't think I knew what I was looking for in a fellow consultant, but once I met them, I learned a few things that I knew would make them great. The first thing was that they wanted to be part of a peer network and learn from me, and I wanted to learn from them. They were also slightly different to me in how they practised and where they saw their niche (e.g., Serena has expertise in para and disability sport). I knew that by having them on the team, it would expand Optimise Potential's expertise, not simply be a replica of my own. Finally, I could see myself wanting them to be my Psychologist if I was choosing one. I liked their mannerisms, their training and their style. Neither had a wealth of international experience working with famous athletes, but they were (and are!) good at what they do, eager to learn, self-aware of what they need to progress in their own careers, great team players and kind. In short, I could see their potential as practitioners and as colleagues and that is why I picked them. The same was true when, a few years later, I expanded the consultancy to include Louise Byrne and Alex Stoyel. Louise and Alex each had unique expertise in other therapy modalities

> "Having gained experience within an organisation and in solo private practice, the big draw for me of being part of a team is the ability to learn from other people's experiences and mistakes. It has allowed me to become more confident in my own level of practice when I am a bit more aware of what others are doing and seeing the quality of work expected. Most significantly though I really appreciate the support of a team around me, particularly when feeling unsure of a new technique or approach I am implementing. Having a knowing ear to listen helps me to continue to refine techniques and progress further than I would have pushed myself alone."
> —Louise Byrne

> "Working as part of Optimise Potential has been a key component in my development as a Trainee Sport and Exercise Psychologist. It's great to be a part of a team of practitioners from different backgrounds that I can turn to for advice and support regarding working with athletes, coaches, parents and relevant stakeholders. My director Hannah Stoyel, an HCPC registered Sport Psychologist, has contributed to my development, competency and confidence levels as a Trainee and has provided me with various applied opportunities working with clients. I would recommend to anyone that is a Trainee or accredited Sport Psychologist to be a part of a consultancy team to receive on-going support and advice as working independently can be quite isolating and difficult to build your own private practice." —Serena MacLeod

> "I have worked with Optimise Potential since 2019 and have thoroughly enjoyed working within a consultancy. I first met Hannah when I was starting out as a sport and exercise psychologist. Hannah and I instantly clicked from the first time we met and it was clear our values and ways of working aligned. Hannah at the time was completing her PhD and therefore we agreed that I would join Optimise Potential and she would refer clients on to me should she not have capacity. It was by far the best thing I did at the start of my career and I quickly had access to a number of clients without the challenge that many neophyte practitioners face of sending out cold emails with little response...However, by far the most impactful part of working with Optimise Potential has been working with a group of peers. After I joined Hannah had three more sport and exercise psychology trainees join the consultancy and it has been incredibly valuable to surround myself with peers who are at a similar stage of their careers. We share our challenges with each other and share resources with each other to develop our skills. When you are self-employed you can feel isolated and it has on numerous occasions been incredibly helpful to have a group of peers to work with." —Hannah Winter

> "As a trainee sport psychologist starting out in the industry I've found working for a consultancy to be invaluable. It has definitely helped me build my client-base far quicker than I think I would have on my own. It has also given me a chance to work with other sport psychology consultants. Those colleagues mean I have more experienced colleagues to call on for ideas and feedback and has given me a sense of camaraderie that I might have missed out on as a solo practitioner." —Alex Stoyel

FIGURE 6.6 Quotes from OP practitioners on why being part of a group consultancy is valuable to them.

and sports that expanded Optimise Potential and meant that we remain greater than the sum of our parts (see Figure 6.6 to read why Serena, Hannah, Alex and Louise find it valuable to be part of a group consultancy).

Legal and Logistics of Group Consultancy

When Serena and Hannah (and eventually Louise and Alex) joined my consultancy, I did not have enough work to promise them full-time employment. Some weeks, I would have enough work, and in others, I wouldn't. So we operate with everyone as self-employed, but we work as a group consultancy. I do not employ them, which means I do not pay sick leaves, holidays or pensions. I will next outline how we work.

- All the consultants in the group must have their own liability insurance and be part of a recognised training route in the UK or be accredited by governing bodies. They each have their own supervisors as part of their post-MSc qualifications, but I am there as a mentor as the most experienced practitioner in the group.
- By being part of Optimise Potential, I run the website, pay for the Google advertisement fees, and in the past, I have offered shared office space. When clients come to me either through the website or through word of mouth, I pass them along to one of my consultants. When I do, I do all the legwork of creating and sending an intake form, letting the potential client know about our Terms and Conditions (which include things such as how to pay, late fees and cancellation policies). I allow my practitioners to just do their jobs, which is to be a Sport Psychologist and minimise the administrative burden on them. I offer workshops and 1-2-1 work to whoever is the best fit for that client's needs and based on the capacity of the practitioners in the group. I know what type of client each of my practitioners is best at working with and what they enjoy most. I keep an updated account of everyone's current capacity so that I can pass along an incoming client with logistical ease and know that the support they are getting is top-notch.

In return for my work, and for being part of the brand which has a much larger reach than any single one of us alone, they pay me a referral fee of 10% on each session they do with a client for the first eight sessions, and they pay £25/month to be listed on the website. These fees are what I feel are right. It can be tempting, especially when working in a helping profession, to feel the need to justify them. However, I have learned that if someone does not want to be part of the consultancy because of the fees, then they will not join. While it is wonderful to work with colleagues that I now call friends, there is a business to run, and that business must come foremost for everyone's sake. You can be flexible or open to negotiation regarding your consultancy fees, but don't undervalue yourself by over-justifying why you do what you do.

I also require certain things from my consultants. For example, they must help with social media posts, creating them and promoting them. Each person must do two a year so that we have content every few weeks. They must promote the consultancy in the work that they do. When I send them an email, I expect a reply within 48 business hours, but if it is a new/potential client, then I expect them to reply within 24 hours. I have earned the reputation of being prompt and responsive and I want that same reputation for my entire consultancy. If a client writes to three sport psychology firms when searching for a Sport Psychologist, I want our group to be the one who replies first.

I write everything I expect from my consultants in a contract. Even though when starting out, it felt casual, not having things in writing only makes things more complicated in the long run. Even if you are setting up a consultancy with friends from your MSc, create a contract and make it professional. If you are running the consultancy, it is important that at least in part of your relationship you know that while you are friendly; you are the boss.

Operating as a Consultancy

The aim of any consultancy is to operate as one rather than a collection of individuals, and for everyone to rise to new career heights together because of the group. This took several years for Optimise Potential, but we have eventually got the entire group hired and have a retainer fee with a few organisations. As with the ethos, you want the work you can do to be greater than the sum of your parts. One of the hardest things as the Founder and Director of a consultancy in which everyone operates as freelance or self-employed is keeping your consultants engaged in being part of the group. This is key, as you do not legally require them to sign non-competes or to turn down other work. If your consultants can get work elsewhere and not have to pay a referral charge, what entices them to be part of your group? Offer them what they cannot get elsewhere. That can be things like mentorship, reduced admin for them to do, advertising, enjoyment of having colleagues, shared resources (such as workshop slides and worksheets for clients) and a consistent workload that shows them that the consultancy allows for more work to come in. At Optimise Potential, I offer these things to my practitioners and do things like holiday parties and organise speakers to come in for peer mentorship chats. Being part of my consultancy also means that I advocate for my practitioners. I set up the payment and fees policy, so they do not have to have those trickier conversations. I will be the one who says, "no we do not offer that type of work for free." I will chase up those people who have not paid my practitioners and so forth. I act as a buffer if needed with the business side of things.

Final Thoughts

The overall aim of group consultancy is for the group to be improved at offering great sport psychology services than a sole individual could ever do on their own. For you, as the Founder and Director, it means that you will end up doing more work as a small business owner rather than as a Sport Psychologist. Consider that. Being your own boss is hard, being others' bosses is also hard. It takes a lot of love and care to grow something from nothing, but in terms of career progression and potential financial gain, there are enormous benefits to reap.

Launching a Private Practice

Setting yourself up in private practice means dealing with two major themes: one is professional and the other is personal. I (Paul) shall open with the personal theme because it determines so much of our professional success or failure in the years that follow. When I opened my private practice, I did so for several reasons: independence, flexible working hours, working from home and time away from the upheaval of company politics and ways of working. Although I value financial income and a sense of achievement, these motives were, and remain, low on my list of primacies. I hold a mix of pure and shadow motives for being a Sport Psychologist. Through supervision, I learned that one of my pure motives is to help others and one of my shadow motives is to meet my needs through helping others. If I do not recognise my motives, I cannot be sure how they influence my actions when working with clients, so I continue to explore these motives under supervision. Four common shadow motives in helping professions like sport and exercise psychology are (1) the drive for power, (2) meeting our own needs through others, (3) the need for others to like and value us and (4) the wish to heal (Hawkins & McMahon, 2020). I raise these points here so that we can know ourselves, our motives, shadow and pure, and stop ourselves from using others inadvertently, for our purposes, or project parts of ourselves onto clients rather than facing those parts ourselves. In private practice, these motives ebb and flow, so it is our duty to make sense of these personal challenges running a private practice.

We might see one professional practice succeed while another falters, yet all the external factors (e.g., accessibility to clients, office space, consultancy support) appear similar. The differences between those businesses that succeed and those that fail usually lie at a business level with specifics such as an insufficient cash flow or capital to begin, a deficient business plan, a faltering advertising strategy and a scarce customer base. But if we add to this list (1) personal challenges, (2) few business skills and (3) motivation to address the business challenges and the encroaching demands (e.g., supporting a family, working from home), we might sink under their pressure. To begin, we need to address motivation, dependable business skills, planning and managing acceptable risks.

We can help ourselves by talking to others who run a successful private practice, read business books, watch tutorials for advertising ideas, for example, and seek a business advisor. I benefitted from setting up a trading company when I was 20 years old, which runs successfully to this day. One of the first steps to set up a business is to write a business plan.[2] A business plan helps you to clarify your idea, set goals, identify problems and measure progress. A business plan forecasts sales income, cost of sales, overheads and profit. I read several books available in most libraries to develop my business plan and my accountant assessed my business plan with me. The books offer step-by-step guides to follow. Because you are your business, your well-being is central to the success of your business plan. We need to take care of ourselves and part of this process is remaining agile personally and professionally. For example, professional agility might mean offering services by telephone, e-mail, online and face-to-face. But it might also mean diversifying your portfolio of work by lecturing, public speaking, book writing, course writing, contributing to local and national media and so forth. You might not enjoy all tasks associated with running a successful business, so I try to work with a 4:1 ratio. For every four engaging, enjoyable and enriching tasks (e.g., meeting clients, writing blogs, giving workshops and reading), I undertake one necessary but less enjoyable task (e.g., invoicing) for my business success. This ratio works well for me and keeps the scales tipped in favour of my intrinsic motivation.

Managing Our Time and Resources

My time matters to me, and I like to have psychological boundaries between my work and family life. I begin by addressing legal and business issues to erect this psychological boundary, offering peace of mind for me and my clients. At the outset, we have legal issues to manage for our safety and security and that of our clients. For example, we can address General Data Protection Regulation (GDPR) for the information your record about your clients by using an online system (e.g., https://www.writeupp.com) that also helps to organise a host of related issues (e.g., bookings, invoicing, contracts) that reduce your administrative burden and increase your time to work with your caseload. Many practitioners use their website to explain their services, fees, late appointments, insurance and affiliations for the client's benefit. You can help clients make the best decision for their needs by offering this information and assurance about your qualifications, approach, accreditations and fees.

While we offer the client confidence in us and our ability to work with them safely, we also need to stay safe; therefore, once qualified, we can develop our continuous professional development (CPD) by attending training events and conferences, auditing our practice and asking clients for their evaluation of our practice. Through ongoing supervision, we can practise self-care and perhaps offer supervision to fellow practitioners in sport and exercise psychology. Dealing nimbly with problems keeps problems in their place and in perspective. With a growing caseload, we need dependable professionals to whom we can refer clients (e.g., General Practitioner, Counselling Psychologist).

The benefits of working in private practice I wrote about above ought to be tempered with the costs of holidays, room rent (if you see clients in a practice), unpaid leave, telephone, Wi-Fi, marketing, computing, travel and parking. Some of these items are capital items (e.g., car, computer, phone, photocopier, furniture) depending on whether you have a rental practice space you would also have costs such as water, heating, electricity and business rates. To pay these expenses, we need clients – no clients, no money, no practice. Earning money means we need to consider our location, our competition and the services we offer. In our line of work, we offer our time for money; however, we might exchange our expertise for money with an online course (e.g., learning to focus) too. Today, we can offer services to a worldwide audience using Skype, FaceTime, Zoom or a host of other online systems. With this global audience, offering services online is sensible, efficient and exciting for service providers and service users. Imagine a swimmer in Sydney wishing to work privately with a Sport Psychologist in London whom she valued because of the psychologist's expertise, training, honesty, trust and sound practical support. Even with the distance and time difference, it's still possible for good service delivery to unfold online.

The greatest challenge after gaining our qualifications to practise is marketing and advertising our services to a local and worldwide audience. I have spent about one-fifth of my consultancy time developing all areas of my practice, especially for members of the community to find my services online, understand my credentials, get to know me and my ways of working and book my services using an online payment system. Many businesses offer goods and services for an e-mail address to build a portfolio of followers. These goods and services might include an e-book, workbook, resource manual, downloadable MP4 or access to a video series. These offerings take your time; however, they form part of your marketing and advertising investment, which flourishes cumulatively.

Being a good sport psychology consultant and establishing a flourishing private practice depends on your digital presence more now than ever because most people are searching and purchasing needs and wants online using their mobile phones (readers are referred to Chapter 8 for advice on using digital technology to enhance their consultancy). For this reason, we need to be accessible online (e.g., website, social media, directory listing) and mobile friendly with values and standards of service from our digital profile that exude responsiveness, efficiency, effectiveness and trustworthiness.

Many sport psychology consultants split their time between private practice and other employment (e.g., university teaching). When we work for an employer, we often miss the significance of what they offer until we set up a private practice, such as paid holidays, maternity pay, office space, equipment (e.g., computer, telephone), training, pension, colleagues and more. It is not always easy to secure employment and it's possible to be made redundant. While we become our own boss in private practice with our time and flexibility as options, we need to consider securing office space, equipment, insurance, pension and so on. Now in the 2020s, we can enjoy the best of both worlds with the security and flexibility of each option. The move towards online consultancy means we do not need office space or to rent rooms, pay business rates, heating and electricity if we are working from a home office (of course, we pay indirectly for these goods and services through our cost of living). You can set up a website in a few hours (e.g., the Wix platform) and be available for online customers thereafter. You can invest in paid advertising, search engine optimisation, list in an online directory and be ready to see clients at your availability. You can set up a limited company at Companies House[3] and complete your own accounts or seek the support of an accountant whose services you can secure for £350/per year depending on the time spent on your accounts. I have benefitted enormously from the expertise of an excellent accountant.

Along with a colleague, I set up another business – Sporting Bounce – an online directory for general professionals working in sport to connect local people with local service providers.[4] Professionals working in sport advertise their services in our directory through their profile page which details all their credentials, contacts, experience and so forth. Then, we promote their profile page to their local community through online advertising (e.g., Google Ads, social media outlets, e.g., Twitter, Instagram). This business demanded significant capital investment and time; the capital I gathered through my (1) trading company and (2) my private practice. My colleague and I believe in generating business services and security for other professionals who perhaps cannot help themselves easily at this point in time.

I enjoy the blend of researching, writing and teaching at university, working with clients in private practice and running my other companies to help others to generate an income to enjoy their lives. Although I enjoy this variety of challenges, I do so within time boundaries (i.e., 9–6 pm) and not working at evenings or weekends. My natural idleness and lack of ambition mean I work efficiently to enjoy time outside work, especially spending time with my children, my wife, my friends and myself. I enjoy a full life because I spend my time doing things I enjoy. What I feel is most important here is not just the practicalities shared but also that you can learn along the way and most, if not all issues, are practical or emotional. The good news is that you can help yourself solve these practical or emotional issues with the help of mentors, supervisors, family and friends. Though I hold no ambition for fame and fortune, I love mastering tasks. If you see a queue, you will probably find me at the back of it, but it's not an issue for me because I gain all my happiness and enjoyment in being with others, reading, writing and mastering tasks (e.g., baking a cake, woodworking).

In short, I love simple processes and I let outcomes take care of themselves. So if you wish to set up a successful private practice, enjoy the processes along the way (as a good Psychologist might suggest), bask in the small wins they offer you, and getting better is its own reward. I set the bar low and I keep it low; yet in there lies a wonderful success. My behaviours are simple yet cumulative, which means though I might only write 500 words in one working day, it grows to 50,000 words after 100 days. Let's finish this chapter by you choosing to do one simple, low-bar task, to help you start your private practice.

- Visit a website provider like Wix and see which business options suit you.
- Send an e-mail to a company specialising in SEO or PPC advertising to find out more about their services.
- Write one blog of 500 words about your favourite topic in applied sport psychology and share it on a social media platform.

Notes

1. www.wix.com
2. Santander provides a template for writing a business plan online which can be found at https://www.santander.co.uk/csgs/StaticBS?blobcol=urldata&blobheadername1=content-type&blobheadername2=Content-Disposition&blobheadervalue1=application%2Fpdf&blobheadervalue2=inline%3Bfilename%3D59%5C214%5CSuB1+Writing+a+business+plan.pdf&blobkey=id&blobtable=MungoBlobs&blobwhere=1314010759188&maxage=3600
3. https://www.gov.uk/government/organisations/companies-house
4. www.sportingbounce.com

References

Hawkins, P., & McMahon, A. (2020). *Supervision in the helping professions* (5th Ed.). McGraw-Hill Education. Kindle Edition.

7
MARKETING THE SPORT AND EXERCISE PSYCHOLOGY CONSULTANCY PRACTICE

Paul McCarthy

Fully Booked?

Many aspiring sport psychology consultants ask for guidance and advice when setting up their private practice and I am humbled to be asked for support because I feel what I know and do does not differ from what others working within the field also know and do. Perhaps those who search for support hunger for authenticity, which remains at the core of how I practice. I have worked in sport and exercise psychology for the past 20 years with a purposeful passion to do the greatest good I can do. With this intrinsic desire to help others, my work is a calling. Although this calling means I do not see service delivery as work, I am careful about my boundaries (e.g., practical, psychological, financial) to do what I do well, but not at the expense of family life and friendships.

The first challenge we encounter in private practice is encouraging clients through our doors. Regrettably, no clients mean no practice. Setting up one's private practice is a challenging undertaking for any sport psychology consultant, and I appreciate we cover that topic elsewhere in this book (see Chapter 10 for the Mental Health of the Consultant). The goal of this chapter is to explore how we bring our services to the notice of the public. In today's digital marketing world, we use social media platforms (e.g., Facebook, Twitter, Instagram), paid ads (e.g., Google ads) and search engine optimisation (i.e., SEO) to bring our services to those searching for them in a global market. These digital platforms encourage people to click on advertisements that might comprise a suggested service or benefit; however, most people searching for the services of a sport psychology consultant wish to know more about the person offering these services. Sport psychology consultants meet this demand by listing their services in an online directory or establishing a professional website to share information about their training and qualifications alongside their services and charges for these services. Social media platforms and websites allow us to offer services to the broad community of services users, so we are continually learning about their needs, wants and preferences in the services we offer.

Social media outlets (e.g., Facebook, Twitter, Instagram) are free to join and much of your marketing (e.g., posting offers of services) can exist on these sites without paying for your advertisement to be shared with a selected audience (e.g., people in London). You can, however, set up paid advertising on these platforms (e.g., £10 per day) to gain followers, develop brand awareness or increase visitors to your website, for instance. Once we have set up our digital marketing system, we can get started building our professional private practice. But we need to know who's buying what we're selling. And we need to know how we fit among other professionals offering psychological services to the public so our services match and exceed the current standard.

Building Trust and Credibility

A core principle of our work as sport psychology consultants is to build trust and credibility with clients for effective outcomes for them. As a private practice, we also build trust and credibility through the information we offer to the public, especially the details on our website.

Write to the Top

Much of the information that I share in this chapter weaves across your website, listing on directories and social media platforms. The one common denominator is writing because writing represents your content generation, and you require this content for your platforms. Learning to write for a consuming public combines two interrelated points – enticement and offers – so what you are writing is enticing people to learn about you and what you offer as a practising sport psychology consultant. This point feels contentious to some people because they feel they are trying to maintain a balance between marketing copy and sound guidance and advice for a consuming public. Copywriters will write content aimed toward the best public relations and with an intent for enticing the consumer, but it is possible to write content for your website and social media platforms and other media outlets that remain simple, authoritative and meaningful.

The first pitfall most people fall into is that they are eager to start their business and online presence, which is heartening; however, we can easily lose sight of the many commitments to maintaining a presence online that is coherent and up-to-date. My recommendation from the outset is to set aside 90 minutes per week for your commitments to your website and online presence. During this time, you could write some blog content and create content to roll out over the next week on Twitter, Facebook, Pinterest or Instagram. For example, you could write a blog about choking in sport or adherence to exercise. Writing the content is step one and step two is sharing your content. Step two requires much work because we need to share content far and wide to reach an audience interested in what we offer as a profession and what you offer as a professional.

We can give sport psychology to people with honesty, openness and trust. We can communicate these values and more through our writing, so it's sensible to keep the reader in mind and the type of article or blog that is accessible, understandable and a practical way forward for the reader. I encourage creativity here to whet the reader's appetite through titles, headings, subheadings and images. Some integrated website systems (e.g., Wix) allow you to write a blog and all the SEO data attached, such as URLs, meta tags, descriptions and related articles. You can also add buttons and links to contents you might wish a customer to purchase. For example, you might write a blog about learning to relax in stressful environments. At the end of the blog, you can add a button to link to the online course you created (e.g., learning to relax) which might be off-site (i.e., on another website like teachable.com). In this marketing funnel, you are bringing your customers from awareness at the top of the funnel to purchase at the bottom of the funnel. The top of the funnel represents marketing, while the bottom of the funnel represents sales. Once you gain the awareness and interest of a customer, the marketing funnel works towards consideration towards a decision about an intent to purchase. Off-site marketing (i.e., marketing to bring people to your website) might happen through videos on YouTube or contributions to podcasts. For instance, you might offer the public an education on topics in sport and exercise psychology with links to your website and services. Similarly, podcasts offer the public a popular and engaging way to know you, your services and how you might help them.

Although most sport psychology consultants will be less aware of the sales and marketing processes, web design companies now present integrated packages that include booking services, booking calendars, blogs, pricing plans and subscriptions. Behind these usual tools lie your inbox, customer relationship management systems, marketing and SEO, analytics and finance systems for raising invoices, sending pricing quotes and payment systems. The typical cost of this website system (e.g., Wix) is about £25 per month for all these business services. Your private practice and the whole management of your private practice are within your hands, but we must factor this time into your working week because it is how you run your business.

A commitment to writing is a central principle for our private practice, to which we tie a few more commitments; though you have a choice about how you wish to proceed. The extra commitments I mention here are learning about search engine optimisation, pay-per-click (PPC) advertising and ads on social media sites (e.g., Facebook, Instagram, Pinterest). There is a choice because you can do so much excellent marketing and sales work without spending much money if you have access to a computer and the web; however, these activities will cost you time. We could subcontract such work to a company specialising in these activities (e.g., blogs, advertising) and companies vary in the management fees to look after your SEO, PPC advertising, social media adverts and so on. When these systems work well, you find yourself on the first page of searches (e.g., Google, Bing) and a series of display advertisements that draw people to your website offerings.

Sport and exercise psychology is a small market globally. In the United Kingdom (UK), for example, there are about 300 registered Sport and Exercise Psychologists with the Health and Care Professions Council (HCPC). Some of these registered professionals will not be practising; however, the profession is growing in the UK. Average searches in the Google search platform in the UK for the term 'Sport Psychologist' remain around 3k per month at the time of writing. In comparison, personal trainers will have searches on Google of around 22k per month. In short, the demand for Sport Psychologists is about 15% of the personal trainer market. These figures mean some people are searching for the services of a sport psychology consultant, though these numbers are low, they do present exciting possibilities for growth.

Pricing

Though pricing is a sensitive subject in many professions, I include pricing early in the chapter because it influences so much of the work we do in private practice. Sport psychology consultants are free to charge whatever fees they deem right for their services, with typical charges in 2010 ranging from £80 to £200 per hour from a BPS survey. My rule of thumb is that each hour of professional practice, for instance, 1 hour (charged at £100) per day per working week across 50 weeks of the year, would return £25k of income. Every £25k represents 250 hours (50-minute hours) across the calendar year. This example is how I have worked in my private practice for many years with 50% of my work offered pro bono publico (i.e., for the public good). On average, I see clients for about 10 hours, so every 250 hours represents about 25 clients. Clients book my services online and pay for the sessions beforehand. Owing to COVID-19, I have seen most of my clients online (e.g., using Zoom, Skype, FaceTime) over the past two years and my online sessions have grown to about 70% of my client work. I work privately and confidentially in my home office for my online consultancy.

The focus of my argument here is about time rather than money. I value my time so I wish to spend it well on those commitments I must do and those interests that I choose for my health, well-being and entertainment. I divide my time among family, work, lifestyle and interests, which means I set my time boundaries to meet these choices. I hold my life in academia, within firm boundaries (typically 9–5 pm and I never work evenings or weekends), because though I enjoy lecturing and researching immensely, I have other interests and commitments outside academia. Within academia, I write 500 words per working day, which usually takes me about 90 minutes, including reading research articles to generate this content. Though 500 words are relatively few, it amounts to about 125k words per calendar year, which one can divide into a book, a book chapter and four peer-reviewed publications.

For my work purposes, I enjoy scholarly work, especially reading and writing (e.g., academic papers, book chapters, books) and I enjoy working with athletes, coaches and teams. Some words form weekly blogs with a blog content between 600 and 800 words targeting keywords for my search engine optimisation generating traffic for my website. I shall elaborate on SEO later in this chapter.

Charging for Services

There are several ways to charge for your services. We are most familiar with time for money in which we exchange an amount of time (e.g., 1 hour) for a set fee (e.g., £100). Occasionally, our exchange of time for money is open-ended in which an organisation pays for your services for their staff over a year and you bill them monthly for the hours, for example. Some organisations and professional clubs choose this payment structure to support their staff over a calendar year. Some clients pay a retainer or recurring fee which they pay you for your services monthly. A client might pay a retainer fee for your services to guarantee access and availability to you over a year. In golf, for example, some management companies will pay a retainer fee to cover expenses and a modest payment, but most of the earning potential depends on the golfer's earnings throughout the season. This back-end payment might be 3% of the total earnings in that season. For example, a golfer finishes the season with earnings of £1 million. You would receive your 3% (i.e., £30,000) at end of the season. Sliding scales or flexible pricing is common with many organisations because they are guaranteeing hours of work per week across the year. Sometimes, I sell products and services as bundles at a reduced rate. In these bundles, the purchaser might receive one-to-one training and online training (through teachable.com). Getting into some markets can challenge us so newcomers might use loss-leader pricing. Loss-leader pricing happens when we price a product lower than its production cost to attract customers to other, more expensive products. Though we often see loss-leader pricing on products in a supermarket, for example, it can be helpful for services too. You could offer one course free (e.g., building self-esteem) even though it cost you time and expertise to prepare the course offering. When customers can sample your course, they are more likely to trust your priced products. We counterbalance the loss made on one service with the gains on other services that are available to the client. You will be familiar with pricing for goods (e.g., grocery shops) that remain low and those that remain high, consistently. Some people fear low prices mean low value; however, it need not be this way and you can build a personal brand that grows over time with services positioned at different price points. At the other end of the pricing scale is premium or prestige pricing, in which you charge fees higher than is typical for the industry (e.g., £200 per hour).

Together, these pricing systems allow you to think about what might work best for you financially, ethically and morally. These are your choices and your prices and the marketplace will test your pricing strategies, which gives you guidance about which prices work for your goals. I have written about pricing and charging for your services here because it provides you with a marketing budget. Marketing in this digital age means a blend of finance and personal effort. You can do well without spending much money; however, the gains from a minor investment are worthwhile.

Finding Your Audience

Working in sport and exercise settings means that most of our audience associate with sport and exercise for products and services. Some argue that psychological services are a luxury item lying below other necessities like shoes, clothing, apparel, coaching and so on. Understanding these categories of need means at least two things: first, we need to establish the short- and long-term value of sport psychology services and second, break into existing and new markets. In private practice, you might choose to identify skills and abilities that fit with identified sports. While I have been involved with athletes from over 30 different sports, most of my clients are involved in golf, football, athletics, swimming and gymnastics. Over the past 20 years, 50% of my clients have been child- and adolescent athletes. For this reason, I tailor my services to the needs of this client group and their parents or guardians. Much of this work has a psychoeducational base, so I have written online learning programmes to meet these psychoeducation needs. I have also written guides and courses for parents of child and adolescent athletes.

Bringing Your Audience to Your Website

If we consider your website in a virtual space like a shop window on the high street, we need to pay particular attention to its layout, accessibility and orientation. We want people who pass by to notice what we are selling and be encouraged to walk into our store. With this picture in mind, you will understand how much a professional store matters to potential customers. We want customers to click on our website and for it to load quickly so that they do not bounce off to another faster-loading site. Once on the webpage, we need detail for the customer that tell them about you and what you offer with opportunities to read more or buy now. For example, you might tell them about you and the services you offer and how to purchase these services with the least friction possible. The personal nature of our service delivery as sport psychology consultants means we might wish for our potential customers to see professional pictures at different locations (e.g., office, athletics track, golf course). You can organise your content all on one page or on different pages. There are two chief considerations here: ease of use for the customer and search engine optimisation. Typically, we are using the URLs on each page for the search engine to find content that matches the content of the search and provide the best answer to the search. To optimise your page, you need accurate URLs that the search engine crawls to offer websites to the searcher (e.g., 'sport psychologist near me'). Many of the website providers (e.g., Wix) bring these requirements together for you to manage on your own. Most crawls by a search engine should provide the best responses to the searches from the searcher. For this reason, you need to optimise each page on your website by including relevant and authoritative content for the end user.

One mistake many people make is that they want their website to look good; however, while the site might look professional, many of them are missing the required details to be found by a search engine and to rank high in a search engine's results. Once you have written suitable content for your website targeting keywords for search engines to find you (e.g., 'sport psychologist near me'), you will also need to write blogs that reflect an active and vibrant website with helpful advice and guidance for people searching the net. Blogs are a wonderful opportunity for you to tell a worldwide audience about you and the work you do. You can also optimise blogs for search engines with the tags for the image(s) on the blog, the related URLs to other blogs on the website or links to purchase products and services. Through blogs, customers get to know you and establish a relationship with you. Where possible, you might create video introductions to you and your services that help to personalise and reduce the barriers to working with you. All websites offer links to prominent social media outlets (e.g., Instagram, Pinterest, Twitter) which means those who land on your website can follow you on these social media outlets and form a social connection and a widening social community. Likewise, those who land on your Twitter account or Facebook page can be redirected to your website. It will not have passed your attention that we offer free advertising to all these social media platforms on our websites; however, their reach and social following makes it worthwhile for us.

Memberships

Some websites offer the possibility of forming memberships for those who wish to pay a subscription for your services over a year, for example. Within these memberships, a member might receive personal e-mail support, exclusive content and promotions which are unavailable to non-members. Several companies work to develop large e-mail groups. One way to achieve this large group of e-mail contacts is to offer a free e-book for an e-mail address. Over time, you might establish an e-mail list of 10,000 people and an Instagram following of 40,000 followers. This following represents a section of the market who value what you offer. Later, you might wish to write a book or create an online learning programme. Instead of paying for marketing for your course or book, you might offer a deal to your followers for their support to access your book or online course for a reduced fee. For instance, you might create an online learning programme and offer it to your 40,000 followers on Instagram and your 10,000 e-mail list for a reduced fee of £35 reduced from £75. If 2% of this 50,000-strong following purchased your offering, you would generate £35,000 for your efforts. Maybe you make one offering per year to your following.

Memberships are common in many fields (e.g., coaching, physical fitness) and while some are free, some have minimum pricing while others charge a premium for access to content and support. Running membership programmes requires much commitment because the membership usually depends upon receiving fresh content each month for the benefit of the member. Running memberships, just like websites and social media accounts, means a time commitment; however, it's possible to share content on several platforms at once or schedule posts. Between search engines (e.g., Google, Bing), social media (e.g., Twitter and Instagram) and local marketing (e.g., listing in directories), you can create a comprehensive and coordinated presence for your digital marketing efforts. Today, each search engine can generate reports from Google, for example, about our website's performance and the contribution of all the social media accounts too. In Google Search Console, for instance, you can review your reports regarding performance, URL inspection, coverage, sitemaps, page experience and internal and external links on your website. You might find that some pages are generating all your traffic while others are not or people who find your website do not stay on your website for long because it is challenging to navigate, or it doesn't offer the information the searcher is seeking. These reports help us tailor our work to best need the needs of our target audience.

Paying for Promotion

There are several ways to promote your services digitally. One of these common ways is PPC advertising, in which you pay a price for each click that brings a customer to your website. The success of PPC depends upon the competition for the advertising space. In Google, for instance, you might wish to appear in the ads above the organic listings. To be listed here on the first or second pages on Google, you need to pay a competitive price. The competition determines this price as they compete to advertise in this space. Setting up a PPC campaign is relatively straightforward, however, to generate a return on your ad, spending often requires much learning or help from a dedicated PPC company. If you do not set up your adverts for PPC correctly, you might well be spending your money on broad searches that rarely generate the traffic you need for your site and services. Several commercial companies offer excellent management services to manage your PPC campaign for you; however, average management fees are about £350 per campaign per month (though you will find cheaper offerings). A good campaign for high-priority keywords related to the profession of sport psychology might range from £0.30 to £1.99 per click, but a good PPC campaign will maximise the return on your investment in AdWords. It's likely that you might spend £500–£750 per month running a PPC campaign that is managed by an external company (including their management fee). Of course, these prices vary and searching for value for your money is a worthwhile investment. Some of the PPC adverts also use display ads in various search engines and social media outlets in which your ad might appear for much less than you pay at the top of the page of Google. These display ads might be a few pence per click and offer much value in promoting your brand or service.

Many digital advertising companies also offer SEO for websites and PPC. The advice given is that PPC and SEO work well together because PPC brings clients to your website, but if the site does not work well for the end user, it might need an overhaul. The goal of SEO is to get your site ranking as high as possible on the first page of a search engine. Simply, if you type 'Sport Psychologist' into your Google search engine now, whom do you see? Who is on the paid ads at the top and bottom of the page and who is in the organic listings on the page between the paid ads? You might only be interested in offering services to those in your local area (e.g., York), so you can specify your local area. In short, the websites you see here are those with whom you will compete for the best listing in a search engine.

Is SEO Worth the Money?

The simple answer to this question is yes because if you have goods and services to trade, you will need to be found online and you will need to be listed at least on the first page of a search engine in your local area if you are targeting a local market. One of the most common queries I receive from trainees and those recently qualified as Sport and Exercise Psychologists is that they have so few clients. When I ask which directories they have listed in and where they are advertising, most show surprise because it had not occurred to them about how people will find them and avail of their services. Or if they have a website, they have not optimised the site for the search engines to find them quickly and easily. Having a website built for you is a positive first step; however, until it is optimised for search engines and listed on local and national directories, it cannot serve you.

You might wish to work on your own SEO following several helpful books or you might wish for a specialist SEO company to do the work for you. Because sport psychology and the services a Sport Psychologist offers are niche, you can make inroads quickly into this market. Some SEO packages will optimise your site for the local area and a company might manage that process for £150 per month to target three keywords. Adding up our costs as we go, we might spend £750 per month between SEO and PPC advertising, for instance, with specialist companies running our campaigns for us. You might feel that organic listings on search engines are enough so you can cut your costs dramatically and still feel you are moving forward with your private practice. After all, clicks on organic listings from SEO work do not cost us any money.

Directories

Listing on directories is a sensible move for several reasons. First, directories work to place themselves prominently on search engines so that people can find those listed quickly, easily and with trust. Second, directories are an inexpensive (typically £15 per month) advertising option if you cannot afford a website and other requirements (e.g., SEO, PPC). Third, most directories offer all the details to a prospective customer and details about you, your charges, contact, blogs, videos and more. Fourth, directories offer prospective customers a chance to read reviews about you and your services, which increases their trust in you and your services. Fifth, directories often offer access to goods and services to help your business to grow by optimising your profile or providing education and training at a reduced price or for free because you have invested in advertising space in the directory. Sixth, directories spend their time working on digital marketing so that you do not have to. Maybe over one year, you benefit from tens of thousands of pounds of advertising for just £200 per year. Finally, some directories offer limits to who can list in their directory like only those with insurance and qualifications from a reputable body (e.g., HCPC). These limits fill those who list in the directory and those who search the directory with confidence and trust in the services being offered and the homogeneity of the community. One helpful directory with a worldwide presence is Sporting Bounce. My colleague, Professor Marc Jones and I set up this company to help aspiring practitioners to be found online for their services.[1]

Getting Started

Getting started as a sport psychology consultant is challenging for the reasons listed above; however, there are tremendous opportunities as well. Practitioners wishing to establish and grow a private practice must invest in their practice, especially their online presence. This investment is often financial and temporal, which means we might need to spend money and our time to grow and sustain our business. We might decide that we will invest 15% of our income into our website hosting and digital marketing. If we were to generate £50k, then £7,500 would be our investment at £625 per month. To generate £50k income, we would need 2 client hours per day across the working week from Monday to Friday for 50 weeks of the year. It is possible to generate this income; however, it depends heavily on advertising (paid and unpaid). Working 2 hours per day seems like a welcome exchange of time for money; however, you might need to invest another hour to create content for blogs and social media accounts. Depending on your choices, you might also wish to pay an external company to write 4,000 words of content each month for a fee (e.g., £300/month) which means you spend 20% of your income from all such digital marketing without you having to do any work other than supporting your clients in service delivery. I addressed this option for practitioners because external companies cater to their digital marketing needs and they focus on the work for which they studied and trained for over several years. In short, the choices are yours based on your interests and inclinations.

Conclusion

In summary, I have painted a picture of the work you need to do to market your private practice. I have written about a digital presence using a website and all the social media outlets that link with it to offer your services to a local, national, or worldwide audience. You can do all the work on SEO, PPC, blogs and content generation for the social media, which means you can keep your costs low. You could also subcontract these tasks to a company that manages the campaigns and content for you while you concentrate on doing sport psychology consultancy. I have found immense benefits from learning about digital marketing but also, I have benefitted immensely from my other companies by subcontracting these services. Their reports each month help me understand our next steps for the month ahead.

My three top tips for those setting up a marketing strategy for their private practice are as follows:

i. Set aside time each week to write blogs for your website and social media outlets to gather an online following and inform them about you and your services. This service will cost you time and expertise.
ii. Choosing a good website platform (e.g., Wix) means you have all you need to integrate your website with all leading social media outlets, and you can track your progress by tracking who visits your website and following their guidance to grow your online audience.
iii. Choose whether you want to spend your money on professional service providers (e.g., SEO, PPC advertising, blog writing) and focus on delivering sport psychology services or whether you wish to take on the whole process yourself. This decision is critical because you will need to invest in your passion and that might just be doing sport psychology rather than being a marketing consultant.

Note

1 You can learn more about the company and their offerings at www.sportingbounce.com

8
GOING ONLINE

How to Enhance Consultancy Practice Using Digital Technology

Stewart T. Cotterill and Olivia A. Hurley

Going Online: How to Enhance Consultancy Practice Using Digital Technology

Increasingly in the 21st century, Sport and Exercise Psychologists are seeing the benefits in engaging with digital technology and the online world to both enhance their consultancy service provision and to enhance their profiles. The global Covid-19 pandemic that hit the world in late 2019 and early 2020 further accelerated this change in perceptions, with significant numbers of Sport and Exercise Psychologists and their clients forced to engage in services delivered through digital and social media channels (Hurley, 2021). However, to be effective in promoting and delivering services online there are key skills that are required, much of which is currently not taught through traditional Sport and Exercise Psychologist training programmes. This chapter will consider crucial aspects of engaging online, exploring the use of digital technology in developing the consultancy brand (e.g., website development), using social media platforms to develop a digital professional presence and networks, and online platforms to conduct consultancy with clients. This chapter will also explore some of the ethical challenges associated with such engagement online and provide guidance on how to safely navigate the challenges associated with these digital spaces.

Social Media Use

The term social media is used to refer to 'tools, platforms and applications that enable consumers to connect, communicate and collaborate with others' (Williams & Chinn, 2010, p. 422). These communication technologies are rapidly evolving (Schivinski et al., 2020) and when used positively within sport settings, they can provide athletes, coaches, Sport and Exercise Psychologists and various sport

DOI: 10.4324/9781003196280-10

organisations with beneficial ways to interact with each other and their fan base (Cotterill, 2020b; Hurley, 2018). Indeed, thinking about sport psychology service users, athletes are some of the most 'followed' individuals across many social media platforms, as was evident from statistics cited mid-way through 2021 when Portuguese soccer player, Cristiano Ronaldo was reported to be the most followed individual on social media, topping the Facebook and Instagram platform lists, with other athletes such as American former professional wrestler, now movie star and businessman, Dwayne 'The Rock' Johnson, in sixth position and Argentinian soccer player, Lionel Messi, in 11th place (Wallach, 2021). Social media use by such athletes has been studied in some depth for approximately a decade. This research has uncovered that athletes employ popular social media platforms and communities, such as Twitter, Instagram, Facebook, WhatsApp, TikTok and LinkedIn for a number of reasons, such as for (i) personal communicating and socialising, (ii) fan engagement, (iii) professional networking, including brand management, ambassadorial roles and advertising opportunities, (iv) volunteering/charity work and (v) political and/or societal influencing roles (Hambrick et al., 2010; Pegoraro, 2010; Whales et al., 2020).

With such expansive use by athletes, as well as both the positive and negative impacts social media communications can now have on many different population groups, knowing 'best practice' when using social media is important for all Sport and Exercise Psychologists practitioners engaging with other people on these platforms. As such, many sport organisations have increased the social media training of their contracted athletes and support staff in this regard, especially considering the degree of influence various postings on social media can have on perceptions of the organisation, perceptions of the athlete and ultimately on the athletes' potential earnings, for example. Qualities such as authenticity, kindness and honesty are typically valued in a similar way in online communications as they are in the offline world (Francis & Hoefel, 2018). However, research on the online representations individuals make of themselves in their online lives, compared to their real-life, offline lives suggests that many people, in general, opt to display themselves in a more favourable light online (Fullwood, 2015) and perhaps understandably so.

The term social media encompasses not just social networking sites such as Facebook, LinkedIn and WhatsApp, but also video and photo sharing sites such as YouTube, Instagram, Snapchat and Flickr; micro-blogging applications such as Twitter; aggregator sites such as Digg; and even virtual worlds (Cotterill, 2019). There are many different formats, platforms and applications that offer a social media function, although these can broadly be combined under the following headings: blogging, social networks, messaging services, team messaging tools, podcasting, video calling/conferencing and video sharing sites.

A lack of awareness of the opportunities and risks that social media presents to both Sport and Exercise Psychologists practitioners and their clients has resulted in several professional bodies seeking to provide greater practitioner guidance. The International Society for Sport Psychology (ISSP) published guidance relating to online interactions as part of the *ISSP Position Stand on the Use of the Internet in Sport Psychology* (Watson et al., 2001). The authors highlighted a need for guidelines to underpin practices relating to confidentiality, record keeping and electronic communications, transfer and sharing of client information, and boundaries of competence. In a recent book chapter focused on social media and sport psychology consulting, Cotterill (2020b) highlighted that social media (i) offers significant opportunities, but also challenges, related to professional boundaries, (ii) is a great way to both share and access professional information (iii) and is a great way to develop subject or context-specific communities of practice.

Social media also provides practitioners with a vehicle to both publicly and privately (via direct messaging functions) support and communicate with the athletes and other sport personnel they work with (such as coaches and officiating personnel). An important point to note in this regard is that the permission of the relevant individuals needs to be secured in advance of communicating in this way using the online social media space. Sport and Exercise Psychologists practitioners using social media in a professional capacity should seek to complete training in its use in the same way that athletes are advised or required to, in order to know how to appropriately communicate with the individuals they work with and wish to interact with via social media. A good approach to such communication is typically as follows: if public acknowledgement of working with a sport and exercise psychologist first comes from an athlete or team, then reciprocated public support by the Sport and Exercise Psychologist is considered acceptable, appropriate and indeed is often well received. This understanding by all parties concerned should be revisited relatively frequently to ensure the circumstances regarding attitudes toward online social media public or private communications do not change for either party and to avoid any uncomfortable situations from arising. Why? Well, it is always important to be mindful that despite the increasing acceptance of the use of sport psychology principles in many sports, some stigma regarding being seen to work with a sport and exercise psychologist does still exist, especially the type of support or service provision being provided. For example, performance enhancement remains more widely welcomed and accepted in contrast to more clinically related, mental illness-related issues. In such cases, the confidentiality of the client remains paramount and any public social media commentary regarding such matters should not happen without the explicit permission of the individual, and even then it should be communicated in a very considered and positively educational way. Practitioners need to be mindful of their own social media posts. While not explicitly saying they are working with a client, they might post photos in a particular environment that could then highlight they are working with certain client groups or might have certain players or staff in the background. That said, the open and honest commentary of many elite athletes who performed at the Tokyo 2020 Olympic Games on their social media platforms regarding the status of their mental health showed that a sea of change may be happening in this regard also and is a very positive thing to see unfolding across the world of sport (Park, 2021).

Website Development

In recent years, both sport and exercise psychologists and trainees alike have been increasingly encouraged to develop their own websites for their consultancy businesses. While there are many reasons to seek to take this step such as to host your own blog, the predominant two reasons are to (i) advertise your services and (ii) raise your own professional profile. Over the last 10 years, website development has evolved significantly. Historically to create a good website, you would have needed to engage the services of a web designer. However, over the last decade, there has been increasing growth in companies that provide templated website development and hosting platforms. Examples of these include Wix, Godaddy, Squarespace, Shopify and Webflow.[1]

In order to develop your own website the first step you would need to take is to purchase and register an internet domain name (the world wide web/internet address for your webpage). You can either do this using a specific online company who will only register the internet domain name you want for your website (e.g., http://www.crazydomains.co.uk/) or use a company who provides both webpage registration and hosting services (e.g., GoDaddy). You then need to register the internet domain name for a period of time (usually 2–3 years) which will then have an associated price you will need to pay. In addition to that, you then need to renew your registration of the internet domain name at the end of this period of time. The cost of the domain name depends on how desirable that internet address is. For example, a .com address will cost more than a .biz address. There are now lots of different website addresses including .com, .co.uk, .org. .org.uk, .biz, .uk, .London, .Wales, .Scot, .online, .info, .net, .pro (among others). Once you have registered your internet domain name, you then have to register with a domain hosting service (who stores all the data relating to your website on permanently accessible servers). Examples of domain hosting services include Hostinger, hostwinds, bluehost and hostgator.[2] You can also use full-service providers such as Wix or GoDaddy who will register your domain, host your website and allow you to build/edit your website. These integrated services are more expensive than separate registration and hosting services, but they do offer the convenience of a 'one-stop shop' and can make the process less time-consuming for you.

Once you have registered your domain and sorted out your web hosting service you then need to design the website itself. Usually, websites consist of several web pages linked together through a menu system. Many of the templated website platforms such as Wix make it very easy to add in professional-looking pages as part of an overall professional-looking website template. There are also options to add in additional features to your website such as a blog post, online booking systems and even online payment services, although these enhanced services usually come with a premium price attached to them. The amount of money you spend and the features you choose to embed really link back to what your rationale is for developing the website. Is it for self-promotion or is it to provide a foundation for your business?

If hosting your own blog is the primary function of your desire to develop a website, you could look at blog hosting providers such as WordPress, IONOS, Weebly or Jimdo,[3] that allow you to build a website around your blog. Another useful feature of setting up a website is that many providers will also provide email addresses that match your website address. So, if your website address is www.sportpsychology.com you could have an email address that is alex@sportpsychology.com. This option can help develop the professional appearance of subsequent email communications.

Once your website is set up you then need to think about Search Engine Optimisation (SEO). In essence, SEO relates to how easy it is for web search engines (e.g., Bing, Google or Yahoo) to find your webpage and how high up the list of search engine results your webpage appears. This factor is particularly important when it comes to business development as potential clients will generally only look at the search engine results from the first two pages of the search. Web hosting services build in some SEO features that you can modify, such as the description of pages, the search engine titles for webpages and the language you use within pages. There is a lot more that you can do to increase the 'findability' of your website, and website holders are continually getting emails from SEO companies saying they can further enhance the findability of the website. It is important to understand what you need and how far you want to go. A good way to increase the findability of your website is to promote your website address through the other communication and media channels that you use such as social media accounts (e.g., Twitter, LinkedIn, Instagram), email signatures and business cards. The other feature to consider when setting up your website is the communication options you want to make available to your webpage visitors. You can just include your static contact details (such as your email address and phone number), or you can use webpage options to add features such as an enquiry or feedback form (where visitors fill in their details which are then emailed to you so that you can reply) or you can even add in 'instant chat' options where short messages are communicated to you (usually using an app on your smartphone) so that you can respond in real-time (where possible). There are a lot of free training and development resources, events and courses you can access to support you in developing your website as well as many paid support services.

Consulting Online

Consulting online, prior to 2020, for many sport and exercise psychologists was arguably a tool that was used infrequently, if at all. However, the Covid-19 pandemic provided practitioners globally with an opportunity to develop their technology-focused skill-set and online consulting skills. With lockdown restrictions imposed by governments around the world requiring individuals to work from home to reduce the spread of the virus, practitioners began to employ various technologies to provide online consulting to their clients, when in-person meetings were not feasible or permitted.

Popular video conference platforms used for online consulting include Microsoft Teams, Zoom, Skype and Google Hangouts (Boyarsky, 2020). These online platforms offer various advantages, disadvantages and degrees of security which users should explore before deciding upon which platforms to use in their work. For example, some platforms offer more hosting and participant number options (an important consideration when consulting with teams, for example, rather than just individuals), as well as interactive chat, recording, screen sharing and invitation functions. These video conferencing platforms all have specific internet access requirements as well as various software and tools to be available on the devices used (i.e., desktop computers, laptop computers, smartphones) to deliver the online consulting option, such as a working camera, in addition to audio and typing features. These knowledge requirements of the various technological possibilities, especially for consultants less comfortable using technology in general, can lead to increased stress and unease when considering online consulting methods (Cotterill, 2020b). Honest dialogue, where both practitioner and client freely voice any concerns regarding the online consulting experience should be a particular focus of initial online meetings. A good understanding between both parties regarding the advantages and disadvantages of online service provision can help to avoid any misconceptions happening, while also managing expectations of the consultancy experience.

There are many advantages to embracing the use of online consulting. These include the following:

i. it removes the necessity for individuals to travel to the same physical location in order to meet and discuss relevant issues
ii. it offers an ability to record the online meetings using some of the types of technologies cited above, if deemed appropriate (however, this should only be used with the prior consent of all parties in attendance)
iii. online sessions can be advantageous for clients who feel more at ease in their own home spaces (it can help them to relax and speak more openly during the session, which in return can help to establish trust between the consultant and client)
iv. large sections of the population are increasingly more comfortable with video calls and communicating via a screen.

There are also, of course, some disadvantages to using the online consulting option. These include the following:

i. a good internet connection is required by all participating parties
ii. you need to have access to the appropriate technology hardware and software (practitioners should be mindful that digital poverty still exists for many individuals globally that prevents them from accessing such online consulting services; Seah, 2020)
iii. the quality of communication is compromised compared to face-to-face (F2F) consulting; there are fewer available body language cues for both parties, due

to the limits of camera positioning and size (that F2F communications provide; in reality, anything other than F2F conversations has been described as a compromise as a result; Cotterill, 2014)

iv. not all individuals are comfortable being 'on camera' as is typically required for online consulting (keeping cameras turned off during online consulting is an available option for such individuals; however, the communication then becomes more like a telephone conversation)

v. the frequent difficulty of a 'time lag' that can occur in many online communications (The Irish Times, 2020) which can lead to individuals 'talking over' each other (this tends to happen less frequently in F2F physical conversations because better conversational turn-taking 'norms' can be observed during such exchanges)

vi. wearing earphones may be necessary to cancel out various background noises during online meetings – these can be uncomfortable for many individuals to wear, especially over lengthy periods of time and are more problematic if online consulting is the full-time position of the individual and sessions are held 'back-to-back' over several hours in a typical working day (Cotterill, 2020a).

Knowledge, Skills and Expertise to Excel Online

It is important to recognise that like any other domain of performance and/or operation, excelling using online platforms, social media and websites takes a specific set of knowledge, expertise and skills. All of which you can develop with sufficient investment in training and developmental activities. Indeed, it has been suggested that every Sport and Exercsie Psychologists should view themselves as entrepreneurs and should seek to develop the appropriate business and communication skills (Hutter et al., 2017). In terms of developing the required knowledge, it is crucial to understand that knowledge can be broken down into two linked but different components: content and skills. Content relates to what you need to do, and relates to facts, principles, processes and procedures. The skills part is then the ability to put the content aspect of knowledge into action. Therefore, it is important to understand what you need to do, then crucially to be able to apply that knowledge. There is a range of skills that are useful in looking to excel online. These include website design and management; marketing and promotion skills; communication skills; social media account management; and understanding the ethical and moral challenges.

Web Design and Management

There are a lot of technical aspects to running a website that vary in terms of complexity. You can outsource and hire freelancers to do some of the work, however, it is a good idea to understand the fundamentals of how things work, in case you encounter any major issues, and to have a handle on the work any web developer is doing on your behalf. Technical skills are particularly important when it comes to running e-commerce aspects of your website including online booking and payment systems. If you are developing your own website, taking time to understand at a basic level how it all works is useful, particularly when it comes to SEO.

Marketing and Promotion

The ability to create interesting content (referred to as content creation) is an important aspect of running your own website and managing your own social media channels. The ability to create high-quality, interesting, value-added and search engine-optimised content is key to running a successful online business in today's increasingly online and digital environment. The fundamental factor that always needs to be remembered is that content drives traffic, builds trust in your brand/identity, and can attract new leads and new visitors to your content and ultimately, hopefully, to your business. The importance of content creation to your online presence is so important that while writing articles and blog posts is a time-consuming process, it can massively benefit your business. Audio podcasts and videos are also quite effective but can be even more intensive in terms of the time, money and effort required. With this in mind, do not underestimate the value of content, as it is likely to be the primary driver of traffic to your website and social media channels. In order to be most effective, you should create and manage an editorial calendar, stick to a publishing schedule and create valuable content that answers the key questions or knowledge requirements of your target audience.

Social Media Account Management

As with the general marketing and promotion point above, content creation and management is crucial. The first decision to make relating to social media use is what is the function of the relevant account (e.g., Twitter), is it for business use only or is it for business and social use? How do you want your social media followers to perceive you and your services? The answer to this question will determine the tone of your messaging. Do you want to be seen as a 'thought leader' a research expert or an expert practitioner? Do you want to be viewed as an expert in certain sports/domains or more broadly? You can choose to share information of things you do or share links to knowledge and information (such as new journal articles). You can also learn to use social media management platforms such as Twitterdeck, eclincher, Falcon.io and sprout social. These platforms allow you to pre-prepare content to be delivered in a time-released manner as well as provide a range of analytics tools.

Understanding Ethical and Moral Challenges

It is also important to understand what happens with the information and data that you share online, often referred to as your digital footprint. It is also important to understand the ethical and moral challenges that you might face when seeking to engage with clients and other professionals online. There are increasing opportunities to engage in continued professional development (CPD) around this topic, whether it is in reading the increased literature relating to psychology and, more recently, sport and exercise psychology (e.g., Cotterill, 2020b; Watson II & Etzel, 2022) or more broadly around the challenges of both consulting and engaging online, there are online courses available.

Professional and Ethical Challenges with Online Engagement

Endeavouring to maintain all reasonable personal and professional online data privacy should be a priority for everyone using the online world and the technologies referred to earlier in this chapter. It is important for sport and exercise psychologists to ensure that the data relating to their clients (including video footage) is safe and secure. It is also important to be aware of your digital footprint (information available online about individuals due to their online activities, including their actions, interactions and contributions). This is important as this information can be damaging in later life situations for many people (i.e., with regard to career opportunities and in an age where anyone can be 'Googled'). This point also relates to what you use social media for. While you might be clear which social media accounts are personal and which professional search engines are not, a potential client searching online via an internet search engine could well bring up all of this information. Therefore, it is important to be aware of the privacy options and data sharing conditions relating to social media account use.

Linked to this topic of data are the requirements to keep client data safe and secure. Due to the sensitive nature of some client-focused online communications, it is vital to have appropriate security and identification features on the computer/smart devices and software used to deliver online services. Also knowing the appropriate steps to take if any unexpected data or security breach occurs is important. Practitioners need to know their own region or country's reporting procedures with regard to specific General Data Protection Regulation (GDPR) breach issues. Indeed, it is beneficial to undertake training in this regard in advance of using relevant online platforms and delivering appropriate virtual services.

It is also important to recognise that employing online service provision does not reduce the responsibility of sport and exercise psychologists to maintain their professional and ethical standards as exercised in F2F consulting situations. For sport and exercise psychologists engaging in online consulting, it is important to be friendly, warm and professional without being overly familiar. The objective is to create a safe, clear and well-understood relationship with online clients (Grant, 2021). This mode of operation should include a clear client agreement, with terms and conditions stated, as well as roles, rights and responsibilities of all parties explained. The use of online booking systems is becoming more prevalent as is the use of various available technologies to take online payments. It is important that only secure options are used for such activity. It is also important to know who to refer clients to if issues arise in online sessions that are outside of the practitioner's areas of expertise. There might be psychological challenges that emerge from client-focused consulting that are outside of the competence and experience of the consultant and having a relevant referral route is important. To help with this some organisations such as the British Psychological Society (BPS) and the Psychological Society of Ireland (PSI) have endeavoured in recent years to provide advice to their members regarding online data security and standards of practice in order to help ensure consultants are 'fit to practice' using online modes of communication (BPS, 2020; PSI, 2020).

As mentioned in the previous section (Understanding Ethical and Moral Challenges), it is important with online consulting to manage expectations and to set clear goals, roles and responsibilities relating to the process. This includes client expectations and consultants' availability – which need to be established in the consulting relationship. Stating clear availability times and days, within usual working hours should be made in advance of commencing online consulting, as well as maintaining appropriate session lengths. If not, the danger of sessions 'running over' and burnout or health-damaging on-screen fatigue occurring is a possibility (Cotterill, 2020b). Screen fatigue and 'technostress' (Brivio et al., 2018) is a real danger for any individual using online technology to consult. Headaches and eye strain can occur, as well as orthopaedic issues (i.e., back pain resulting from long periods spent seated in one position in front of a computer screen). Ways to combat these issues could involve exploring the use of standing/adjustable desks and screen glare protection tools, as well as taking appropriate screen-breaks that could involve some blue and green exercise, which is beneficial for both mental and physical health). If any technological disruptions occur during sessions, given that unstable connections and cut-outs do happen, pre-agreed courses of action should be followed (e.g., a set number of attempts to re-engage made/time taken to re-establish the internet connection and direct text/email messaging using appropriate private and personally secure account options followed to conclude the session if necessary, with later communications agreed where necessary and followed through on – such as sending additional resources and information in a timely fashion – 2/3 days).

As with any mode of service delivery, online sport and exercise psychology consulting has benefits, as cited earlier in the chapter, while also presenting a number of challenges that sport and exercise psychologists should be aware of. Prioritising security and client privacy as well as health and well-being while using the online space should be the main considerations of all engaged parties (Cotterill, 2020a; McCormack et al., 2015).

In discussions with our own trainee Sport and Exercise Psychologists, they have highlighted the particular challenge of booking too many online sessions during a day, which can result in sitting and being quite inactive for long periods of time. It is, therefore, important to also schedule breaks into your day to ensure you can get up more and also to give your eyes a break from staring at a screen. Wearing 'blue light' glasses has been suggested as an effective solution to help reduce eye fatigue when spending a lot of time engaging with screens.

Summary

The online environment offers significant opportunities for sport and exercise psychologists to both enhance their profile and to further develop their consultancy services. However, it is crucial to understand that these new digital environments and platforms require a differentiated skill set and conceptual understanding in order to best understand the opportunities and challenges that consulting online can bring. Taking the time to engage in appropriate training and development activities is crucial to ensure that sport and exercise psychology practitioners and trainees are sufficiently equipped to cope with the challenges while also taking advantage of the opportunities presented.

Key points to consider when using digital technology to enhance consultancy practice:

- Clearly outline the rationale for engaging in social media use relating to your sport and exercise psychology practice. For each platform you engage with consider the purpose of engagement (why) and how it fits with your personal 'brand' as a sport and exercise psychologist.
- In developing a website have a clear plan for why you are developing a site, the target audience and how you want this audience to engage with the content you create.
- Set boundaries in terms of your work engagement online via social media platforms, including when and how it is acceptable for clients to contact you and what the expectations are in terms of response time.
- When seeking to engage in online consulting think about how the sessions will be structured and how you can effectively build rapport through a screen.

Notes

1 Wix (www.wix.com), Godaddy (www.GoDaddy.com), Squarespace (www.squarespace.com), Shopify (www.shopify.com) and Webflow (www.webflow.com).
2 Hostinger (www.hostinger.com), hostwinds (www.hostwinds.com), bluehost (www.bluehost.com) and hostgator (www.hostgator.com).
3 WordPress (www.wordpress.com), IONOS (www.ionas.co.uk), Weebly (www.weebly.com) or Jimdo (www.jimdo.com).

References

Boyarsky, K. (2020, March 2). *The 10 best free video consulting tools to choose from.* Owl Labs. https://resources.owllabs.com/blog/video-conferencing-tools

British Psychological Society (BPS). (2020). *Guidance for psychological professionals during Covid-19 pandemic.* https://www.bps.org.uk/sites/www.bps.org.uk/files/Policy/Policy%20-%20Files/Guidance%20for%20psychological%20professionals%20during%20Covid-19.pdf

Brivio, E., Gaudioso, F., Vergine, I., Mirizzi, C. R., Reina, C., Stellari, A., & Galimberti, C. (2018). Preventing technostress through positive technology. *Frontiers in Psychology, 9*, 2569. https://doi.org/10.3389/fpsyg.2018.02569.

Cotterill, S. T. (2014, August 15). *Applied sport psychology and social media*. Dr. Stewart Cotterill. https://drstewc.wordpress.com/2014/08/15/applied-sport-psychology-and-social-media/

Cotterill, S. T. (2019, April 30). *The impact of social media use on athlete performance*. Dr. Stewart Cotterill. https://www.thinkperformance.org/post/the-impact-of-social-media-use-on-athlete-performance

Cotterill, S. T. (2020a, May 6). *The impact of Covid-19 lockdown on sport and performance psychology consultants*. Think Performance. https://www.thinkperformance.org/post/the-impact-of-covid-19-lockdown-on-sport-and-performance-psychology-consultants

Cotterill, S. T. (2020b). Social media and sport psychology practice. In M. Bertollo, E. Filho, & P. C. Terry (Eds.) *Innovations in Mental Skills Training* (pp. 109–122). Routledge.

Francis, T., & Hoefel, F. (2018, November 12). *'True Gen': Generation Z and its implications for companies*. McKinsey & Company. https://www.mckinsey.com/industries/consumer-packaged-goods/our-insights/true-gen-generation-z-and-its-implications-for-companies#

Fullwood, C. (2015). The role of personality in online self-presentations. In A. Atrill (Ed.) *Cyberpsychology* (pp. 9–28). Oxford University Press.

Grant, A. (2021). The holistic practitioner. *Journal of the Australian Traditional-Medicine Society*, 26(2), 94–96.

Hambrick, M. E., Simmons, J. M., Greenhalgh, G. P., & Greenwell, C. T. (2010). Understanding professional athletes' use of Twitter: a content analysis of athletes' tweets. *Journal of Sports Communication*, 3, 454–471.

Hurley, O. (2018). *Sport Cyberpsychology*. Routledge.

Hurley, O. (2021). Sport cyberpsychology in action during the COVID-19 pandemic (opportunities, challenges and future possibilities): a narrative review. *Frontiers in Psychology*, 12, 621283. https://doi.org/10.3389/fpsyg.2021.621283.

Hutter, R. I., Oldenhof-Veldman, T., Pijpers, J. R., & Oudejans, R. R. D. (2017). Professional development in sport psychology: relating learning experiences to learning outcomes. *Journal of Applied Sport Psychology*, 29(1), 1–16. https://doi.org/10.1080/10413200.2016.1183152.

The Irish Times. (2020, April 3). *'Lagging wifi, internet freezes, distractions'. Students on the reality of online classes*. The Irish Times. https://www.irishtimes.com/news/education/lagging-wifi-internet-freezes-distractions-students-on-the-reality-of-online-classes-1.4220198

McCormack, H. M., MacIntyre, T. E., O'Shea, D., Campbell, M. J., & Igou, E. R. (2015). Practicing what we preach: investigating the role of social support in sport psychologists' well-being. *Frontiers in Psychology*, 6, 1854. https://doi.org/10.3389/fpsyg.2015.01854.

Park, A. (2021). *How the Tokyo Olympics changes the conversation about athletes' mental health*. Time. https://time.com/6088078/mental-health-olympics-simone-biles/

Pegoraro, A. (2010). Look who's talking: athletes on Twitter: a case study. *International Journal of Sport Communication*, 3, 501–514.

Psychological Society of Ireland (PSI). (2020). *Guidelines on the use of online or telephone therapy and assessments*. https://www.psychologicalsociety.ie/source/PSI%20Guidelines%20on%20use%20of%20Online%20or%20Telephone%20Therapy%20%26%20Assessment.pdf

Schivinski, B., Brzozowska-Woś, M., Stansbury, E., Satel, J., Montag, C., & Pontes, H. M. (2020). Exploring the role of social media use motives, psychological well-being, self-esteem, and affect in problematic social media use. *Frontiers in Psychology*, 11, 617140. https://doi.org/10.3389/fpsyg.2020.617140.

Seah, T. K. M. (2020). COVID-19: exposing digital poverty in a pandemic. *International Journal of Surgery, 79*, 127–128. https://doi.org/10.1016/j.ijsu.2020.05.057.

Wallach, O. (2021, May 14). *The world's top 50 influencers across social media platforms*. Visual Capitalist. https://www.visualcapitalist.com/worlds-top-50-influencers-across-social-media-platforms/

Watson, J. C., Tenenbaum, G., Lidor, R., & Alfermann, D. (2001). ISSP position stand on the use of the internet in sport psychology. *International Journal of Sport Psychology, 32*, 207–220.

Watson II, J. C., & Etzel, E. F. (2022). *Considering ethics: using the internet in sport psychology*. https://appliedsportpsych.org/resources/professional-resources-for-mental-performance-consultants/considering-ethics-using-the-internet-in-sport-psychology/

Whales, L., Frawley, S., Cohen, A., & Nikolova, N. (2020). Everyday things change: Australian athlete communication during the coronavirus lockdown. *International Journal of Sport Communication, 13*, 541–550.

Williams, J., & Chinn, S. J. (2010). Meeting relationship-marketing goals through social media: a conceptual model for sport marketers. *International Journal of Sport Communication, 3*, 422–437.

9
ADMINISTRATIVE AND QUALITY ASSURANCE PROCESSES

Andrea M. Firth and Ricardo G. Lugo

Administrative and Quality Assurance Processes

Building trust is an important foundation stone with all clients. Trust is established and emphasised during the initial stages by the implementation of ethical practice. The basics of ethical practice involve beneficence, doing good and non-maleficence, and avoiding harm. Harm to the client is further avoided during the initial stages of client interaction via a thorough and robust intake protocol. The contract or service agreement allows the client to feel reassured and safe by outlining the process of their psychological sessions. It also helps them understand what they should expect from the interaction and through the relationship between the Sport and Exercise Psychologist and themselves. Such an agreement arises when both parties willingly enter into a written or verbal agreement and is regulated by contract law (Section 5, BPS Practice Guidelines, 2017). We asked ten SEP Psychologists (six British; four international) to elaborate on their administrative and quality assurance practices. Their responses will help elucidate the focus of this chapter.

Standards of Proficiency

The Standards of Proficiency (SOP) included within this text, contain detailed information on the requirements for being a Sport and Exercise Psychologist that include, but are not limited to, competence, ethical issues, privacy and confidentiality, and professional behaviour. However, for more information about these aspects, please refer to the appropriate documents.

Although there are numerous national bodies throughout the world, the following provides an overview of four bodies; two of which are the largest national psychological associations that are also renowned internationally (American Psychological Association, APA; British Psychological Society, BPS), and the

DOI: 10.4324/9781003196280-11

two largest international Sport and Exercise psychological associations that are not specific to any one nation (Association for Applied Sport Psychology, AASP; International Society of Sport Psychology, ISSP). Whilst the APA and BPS have designated divisions that are specific to sport and exercise psychology (SEP), in other regions and countries, such as Scandinavia, there is no such distinction. For more specific national qualifications and codes of conduct, please consult national or local chapters of psychological associations.

APA[1]

The APA is the largest professional body for psychology in the United States, with sports and exercise psychology falling under their Division 47. Division 47 was approved for proficiency in 2003 and falls under the APA's 'Ethical Principles of Psychologists and Code of Conduct'. The APA has identified five principles that should guide one's profession: beneficence and non-maleficence, fidelity and responsibility, integrity, justice, respect for other people's rights and dignity. Sections 7–10 of the APA Approved Standards and Guidelines describes the promotion of good practice, including supervision of trainees (Section 7). Section 6 of the APA 'record keeping and fees' details both the legal and professional responsibilities of the Psychologist, including the necessity of establishing client agreements and record keeping. This includes establishing initial agreements detailing the legal aspects of the Psychologist's role and practices, including fees, and the limitations of the therapeutic relationship. The service agreement should also state how client records are registered to ensure the maintenance of confidentiality and privacy for the client.

BPS/BASES/HCPC[2]

Becoming a Sport and Exercise Psychologist in the United Kingdom is achieved independently via either of two professional bodies, the BPS and the British Association of Sports and Exercise Sciences (BASES) or through a professional doctorate in SEP (readers are guided to Chapters 1–3 of the book for further details). Those who have studied on a relevant but non-BPS accredited course will need to complete a conversion course ahead of engagement with the BPS Stage-2 process. These routes then give qualifications leading to registration with the Health Care Professionals Council (HCPC), the regulator of healthcare professions in the United Kingdom.

Since 2009, the HCPC has maintained statutory responsibility for the registration of professional applied psychologists. SEP is included under the 'Practitioner Psychologist' title with set SOP. The HCPC has clear guidelines ensuring ethical practices including the necessity of appropriate documentation in service delivery (see Sections 2, 4, 7, 10) and evaluation of such service (Section 12). The HCPC has also identified specific areas of expertise and limitations pertinent to SEP practitioners (See Sections 13–15) that are relevant for good practice.

AASP[3]

AASP is an international organisation that certifies SEP practitioners, though not at national levels. The AASP's Ethical Principles and Standards consists of a Preamble, six General Principles, and 26 Standards. The Preamble and the General Principles are however not enforceable rules, meaning these act as guidelines with no consequences for practitioners who do not follow or break the principles. Conversely, the 26 Ethical Standards are enforceable. Their standards for documentation of client services is limited (Standard 14) compared to the APA or HCPC but do specify the need for early disclosure of services and compensation (Standard 15).

ISSP[4]

ISSP is an international organisation that promotes research, practice, and development in the discipline of sport psychology. The ISSP has defined ethical codes for the practice of sport psychology using six Principles and 16 Standards. The six Ethical Principles act as guidelines, whereas the 16 Ethical Standards are expectations of conduct in the form of practical recommendations that can have professional and potential legal ramifications when violated. The ISSP's ethical code does specify that practitioners need to provide service terms, maintain documentation (Code 8) and record keeping and supervision in professional practice (Code 13).

Setting Up Service Agreements

The two national associations (APA; HCPC) and the two international associations (AASP; ISSP) have clear requirements for codes of conduct and requirements for documentation and record keeping, albeit at different specificity levels. Only the APA and AASP are specific in setting up service agreements. The APA (2015) has developed 'Professional Practice Guidelines' for quality assurance that promotes evidence-based practice, professional behaviour in different contexts (i.e., health care, child protection), and gender- and cultural sensitivity. Service Agreements should:

- be specific in communicating fees, ethical codes, and limitations of services provided, and
- be presented to clients as early as possible in their interactions, and
- should highlight record-keeping procedures, confidentiality, informed consent, and legal aspects in case of disputes between the practitioner and the client.

As well as setting up robust service agreements, participants we contacted stressed the value of ensuring they could build rapport with the client during the intake assessment and analysis of needs. Engaging in broad and open conversations with the client during the initial stages of contact helped achieve rapport. Such critical dialogue is mutually beneficial; it assists clients to grasp the psychologist's experience and background and enables the psychologist to understand the client's needs better. The process is, however, flexible. More experienced practitioners stated there was no specific process in setting up a service agreement. Agreements were developed 'after rudimentary needs analysis and factors such as organisational specificity, sport specificity, team, individual and financial considerations, and before both the client and sport psychologist have agreed the client proposal between the sport psychologist and the client'. Some of our participants used a selection of several agreements based on the requirements of the client. In order to accommodate the specific needs and circumstances of each client, all psychologists accentuated the need for diversity and flexibility to be employed during the initial stages of consultation.

Irrespective of the various ways the initial stages were implemented, all participants stated they outlined to the client both the limits of confidentiality and the ethical implications within the therapeutic alliance, whilst only a few of the participants mentioned giving clients a client agreement, contract or consent form. Whilst this process may be agreed upon orally, it is preferable, for legal reasons, to document this arrangement officially in writing. In addition, it helps to clarify the rules of engagement within the therapeutic alliance and manage client expectations by providing a clear and concise document, designed to reassure the client that the alliance is safe and professional. As a minimum, the written client agreement should contain the Psychologist's relevant memberships, accreditation details, and the name of their public liability insurer. The agreement is bi-directional as it highlights the psychologist's expectations of client behaviour and of the therapeutic alliance, as well as specifying the consequences of short-notice cancellations and late arrivals of the client. The agreement should also include the fee structure, the client's complaints procedure, and options available to them should they become unhappy with the psychological service they are receiving.

Note Taking and Keeping Records

As you begin working with the client, you will consider how and if you will use note-taking. Any notes should accurately document client interaction and it is part of the process, which ensures the monitoring of quality and the implementation of adequate support for the client (Rosenbloom, 2010). Client notes can protect both the client and practitioner by providing evidence of what occurred within the session (Mitchels, 2017). In addition to monitoring client attendance, the counsellor would keep client notes as a record, a way of managing risk and ensuring correct adherence to procedure. Though many practitioners keep client records as an aide-memoire, it is recommended to write them up as soon as possible after the session to ensure accuracy. This is especially true when dealing with numerous clients in a day as taking notes after you have completed several sessions can make it easy to mix up the facts between sessions.

A useful way of protecting your client's identity with your practice records is to use the split notes method. In this method, the psychologist keeps two sets of files.

One set includes the demographics and contact details of the client (e.g., gender, age, ethnicity, coach details, disability, agreed number of sessions, and a brief description of the issues with which the client came to the session). This file is issued with an identity number which is then the only reference used on the client's case notes. Case notes contain session details and once again should contain only factual information. In the authors' practices, it is not uncommon for clients and coaches to see elements of the case notes, which form a basis for treatment plans. In such instances, the notes act as goal-setting prompts and evidence of what happened in the therapy session.

Client case notes also help Psychologists to reflect accurately with their supervisor, with case notes feeding into the process notes where the psychologist can reflect, and evidence progress during sessions. Such information contributes to Continuing Professional Development (CPD) and growth as a practitioner. The BPS Code of Practice (2017) emphasises the requirement that supervision records, whether case notes or process notes contain no identifiable features of the client.

Although both the client and official agencies may request access to client records, it is important to note that any document which identifies the client may be considered part of a client record and thus may be regarded, in law, as part of the official record for that client. Hence, if the process notes or journal reflections do not identify the client in any way, these may be excluded from court orders or insurance company requests.

Although process notes can be used for both CPD purposes and supervision meetings, the practitioner should:

- Keep self-reflections strictly professional, as clients have the right to see written records (Freedom of Information Act, 2000). The Freedom of information act is specific to the United Kingdom, international readers should refer to the data protection laws governing the region in which they practice.
- Provide assistance to the client in explaining these records to them if necessary.
- Ensure records are stored in a manner that protects client confidentiality and is in line with General Data Protection Regulations (GDPR) requirements, or the relevant data protection act governing the country or region in which the sport and exercise practice takes place.
- Avoid including anything you might not want the client or others to read, such as negative or judgemental comments. Notes should not include anything inaccurate or anything too intrusive.

Reflection

Reflection forms part of the administrative and quality assurance processes. It helps the Sport Psychologist understand the nature of their interaction with their client and consequently the dynamics of the therapeutic relationship. Our interviews with the ten SEPs highlighted the diverse ways in which the practitioners, involved in sport, provided information on their reflective and supervision experiences.

The analysis highlighted the diverse ways in which reflection and supervision are undertaken within sport psychology. The varied responses by participants underscored the ambiguous use of the term reflection (Zeichner & Liston, 1996), further highlighting the requirement for clarity of the term. This helps ensure critical analysis and effectiveness in how Psychologists work with regard to understanding themselves and others and how such understanding leads to change (Jay & Johnson, 2002).

Despite a lack of clarity in the definition of reflection, the distinct overall goal is to be self-aware of one's state and its influence on delivery. Such self-awareness is vital in psychological practice to enable connection with the client. Reflection requires complex decision-making and at various moments in time incorporates, considering the past, thinking in the moment and thinking about the future, reflecting-on-action, in-action, and for-action (Schön, 1983). As reflection informs future practice, it requires a multidimensional method, which is intrinsic and fundamental to effective practice (Cropley et al., 2010).

Reflection entwines the three parts of what Jay and Johnson (2002) called their reflective typology. Descriptive reflection often begins the process and is the point where a definition of the problem occurs. Problems may be covert, overt, cognitively based, or emotionally based, resulting in certain behaviours. Once the problem is appropriately defined, the next stage involves comparative reflection. This entails gaining different perspectives of the issue and an understanding of whether the problem is easily fixed or more complex in nature. In order to attain multiple and alternative perspectives on the issue, the practitioner must be willing to be open-minded and uninhibited by their biases and usual prevailing thought processes. Instead, they should seek to explore and gain understanding of the viewpoint and perspectives of others. The third dimension is that of critical reflection which involves consistently reviewing the issue and seeking to gain understanding of how the problem-solving actions influences the issue at hand.

Adopting a multidimensional method helps the Sport Psychologist explore the effectiveness of applied practice, the usefulness of the interventions implemented and the efficacy of psychology sessions in attaining the desired goals. It also considers the practitioner's ability to be competent and to evidence what constitutes success in their practice (Cropley et al., 2010). Evaluating the effectiveness of practice is one way for the practitioner to demonstrate advancement and practical development within their sport psychology delivery. A response from Participant 1 emphasises this point by stating,

> ...there are several ways I evaluate my practice. The first being through performance statistics. This evaluation is used mainly for clients who are specifically working on performance and is helpful if there is a specific skill they wish to improve. We will have clarified what their goals and aims are in an early session, having tangible goals clarified to work towards.

Here, the link between theory and practice must be transparent to comply with knowledge-in-action (Schön, 1983).

Reflection should also encompass feelings, emotions, and understanding how personal values influence, and are influenced by, how one practices as a sport and exercise psychologist. It is about analysing information and understanding what it means within a specific context. Participant 2, who at the time of writing is the Sport Psychologist for an English Premiership-winning football team, emphasises the importance of continual critical reflection, by stating,

> reflective practice for me is genuinely and generally an everyday process that occurs as a natural consequence of having to deliver perceived value in elite settings. Over the last 10 years there is always a continuous reflective nature to delivery, in the applied setting, in order to survive as a practitioner.

The participant examines specific aspects of their practice,

> What worked? What didn't? What does the client need, really? Who is the client now? How can I improve? What do I need to explore? What has occurred to me in my recent practice that is important for my development? These are all questions that are considered on a weekly basis.

Furthermore, in order to cope with the complex and highly pressurised environment of elite professional sport, the Sports Psychologist compartmentalises their practice to make in-depth examination easier, stating 'I have recently tended to see my professional practice as a cluster of projects. For example; Head of Department Reflective Practice Project; Player development Project; Player Performance & Well Being Support etc....'

Reflection is a career-long exploratory journey, including many aspects of the self, emanating from different sources. Participant 5, with 28 years' experience within the field of elite sport psychology (at the time of writing), has engaged in reflective practice throughout their career and acknowledges it has shaped their personal philosophy, helped to clarify values and beliefs and informed their theoretical approach, along with the chosen interventions. This Psychologist divulges how reflection is of central importance to the professional relationship they have with clients. All ten participants agreed that reflection is important in building an effective therapeutic relationship with their clients, with each participant actively engaging in reflection using varied approaches.

None of the participants acknowledged the necessity to comprehensively reflect on client relationships by understanding the implicit (hidden) and explicit (obvious to others) ways of relating. This distinction is not always clear. Explicit ways of relating are often, although not always, obvious to both the psychologist and to others and may include the gender identity of either party, ethnicity, unintentional statements about the psychologist resulting from the clothes worn, décor within the consulting room, etc. Conversely, implicit ways of relating are unconscious, with one or all parties being aware of them without in-depth reflection. Clients react to both implicit and explicit patterns of relating (Thwaites & Bennett-Levy, 2007). Understanding the self involves recognising one's personal traits, thoughts, beliefs, and characteristics, how this influences behaviour and, in turn, the therapeutic alliance and effectiveness of the relationship with the client (Hanley, 2009). The gift of seeing ourselves as others see us enables us to be self-aware enough to understand how others perceive us both implicitly and explicitly.

Appropriate reflection requires us, as Psychologists, to examine the context within which we work; to explore our own assumptions and views of the world along with our goals and values fundamental to the work involved (Jay & Johnson, 2002). It is doubtful whether we can really ever be properly reflective without reflecting on what we believe; what we understand our clients believe about themselves and about us; and what we believe about ourselves and our clients. Reflection, therefore, needs to be critical. Critical reflection allows the practitioner to analyse the political and social stances and the power dynamics within the sporting environment within which they operate. It examines ways to equalise power imbalances, whilst maximising a democratic relationship between the sport psychologist and the client. During critical reflection, the questions that should be addressed are 'How can we change our own behaviour?', 'Who has the power?', 'What is the power and what are the power dynamics?', and 'How do we engage in transformational change?'. Critical reflection is a good start, but ultimately psychologists should adopt a reflexive approach. The reflexive approach, like critical reflection, examines the power within the relationship, i.e., what and where the power is, but adds to critical reflection by considering our understanding of other experiences. It is also a personal process, which considers automatic responses, such as why the individual responded to a situation in a specific way, and what experiences influenced the individual psychologist's behaviour. Reflexivity helps the Sports Psychologist to understand how we interconnect with our clients and how various aspects of their lives interconnect. Such analysis helps to make sense of these interconnected types of relationships.

One such interconnection concerns the role of self-efficacy within the therapeutic relationship. Efficacy in sport psychology relies on a collaboration between the athlete and the sport psychologist, a collective efficacy. Collective efficacy directly affects the therapeutic relationship, therefore consistent and continuous reflection, involving all types of efficacies in the therapeutic relationship, is important. When reflecting on the self, the sport psychologist must consider not only their own effectiveness as a practitioner but also their perception of the athlete's ability. This informs the practitioner's belief in their own ability to work collaboratively with their athletes, in addition to considering what the athlete believes the practitioner can do. It also reflects on the link in how others, such as the athlete, coach, or supervisor, perceive the psychologist's own self-efficacy. Efficacy in the relationship needs to look through the eyes of the other (Smilde, 2015).

Other efficacy is important as it affects the desire to maintain a relationship (e.g., the willingness of the client to persist in the therapeutic relationship). Other efficacy is reflected in the athlete's view of their Sport Psychologist's belief in them as an athlete or person, resulting in a close connection between other efficacy and collective efficacy. If the athlete believes in the Sport Psychologist, and reciprocally perceives the Sport Psychologist to believe in them (other efficacy), they will be more likely to want to maintain a collaboration with the Sport Psychologist (collective efficacy). Such understanding directly links to Relational Efficacy, also known as Relation-Inferred Self-Efficacy (RISE) (Saville & Bray, 2016).

RISE is useful in examining links or interconnections in relationships. Morrison and Lent (2018) argue that it is important to examine the practitioner's efficacy beliefs and how these beliefs develop and function within actual practice, including within the supervisory relationship. In practice, this forms part of understanding the self. These authors found that RISE and level of experience predicted practitioner self-efficacy, which is in turn moderated by other self-efficacy. Verbal and non-verbal behaviours in intrapersonal relationships influence the formulation of RISE and in turn the pervading self-efficacy beliefs (Saville & Bray, 2016). Realistically challenging the athlete, supporting the athlete, and allowing the athlete to showcase skill, all contribute to strengthening RISE (Saville et al., 2014).

RISE amongst athletes stems from verbal and nonverbal interactions. High self-efficacy perceptions are highly correlated (0.78) to RISE, with RISE being a mediating factor in the relationship with the athlete (Saville & Bray, 2016). Although this study relates to coach/athlete relationships, lessons can be learned from relating these findings to the similarities between the athlete and Sport Psychologist. Of the respondents for this book chapter, Participant 1 highlighted the importance of being aware of their own personal expected outcomes of a client and of the client's personal expected outcomes of the service. In order to measure RISE, they reflected on their own outcomes by examining case formulations after each session and then assessing whether the relationship was progressing, specifically examining their own comfort levels and that of their athlete.

RISE in cross-racial dyads is especially important. Failure to achieve it may result in ruptures in the therapeutic relationship (Williams et al., 2022). Only two participants, both trainees, mentioned the importance of race in the therapeutic alliance. Participant 1 emphasised the importance of addressing issues of race with clients with whom they felt they had a strong relationship. This allowed those athletes to speak about race-related issues in an open way. The issue of overt racism experienced by athletes was prominent in the media at that time. Consequently, practitioners may have been more aware of the issue than usual. Most participants emphasised the importance of ensuring awareness of the experience of diverse groups such as LGBTQI+, with a clear attempt within practice to engage in gender-neutral language in order to create a 'safe space'. The underrepresentation of LGBTQI+ athletes in elite sport has meant that one of the Psychologists (Participant 2) felt that they would need to seek advice on how to progress in providing sport psychology to LGBTQI+ athletes. Other Psychologists, depending on the organisational environment, regularly liaised with other staff within the organisation responsible for player welfare and care.

The ability to 'look through the eyes of the other' (Smilde, 2015) requires emotional connection and the ability to examine emotional intelligence. It requires the Sport Psychologist to embrace the reflection of others. The challenge for Sports Psychologists is to avoid the automatic assumption of being inclusive and multicultural, based on the belief of not being racist, and having engaged extensively with diverse individuals and groups. The viewpoint of Participant 2, that they do not 'distinguish individuals in terms of any newly identified or socially constructed ethnic profile', potentially shows a lack of understanding through the eyes of the other and requires further reflection. Reflection is necessary to ensure adequate compliance with the Health & Care Professions Council (2008) requirement that professionals avoid allowing personal views, beliefs, or ideologies to negatively impact the professional advice given. Good intentions undoubtedly drive the viewpoint that it is a good idea to treat everyone equally; however, whilst psychologists holding such views may well be self-aware enough to avoid discriminatory behaviour, they still may only have a superficial understanding of the athlete's racial experiences.

A great deal more reflection and understanding is required when working with diverse groups to facilitate the Psychologist's ability to understand sufficiently the lived experience of their client. Failure to do so means there is a danger that the Sport Psychologist might lack sufficient emotional intelligence within their practice. Emotional intelligence (Goleman, 2020; O'Neil, 1996) is important when considering an obvious ethical issue whereby, based on the importance of ensuring RISE, practitioners should ethically question their ability to honestly and congruently look through the 'eyes of the other' in order to holistically assist the athlete. The Sport Psychologist may need to be honest and via reflection admit that RISE may never fully occur between them and the athlete, as their life experiences are too different. Nonetheless, understanding this may help the relationship between the client and the sport psychologist to remain effective.

Supervision

Like reflection, supervision, which means to 'oversee', is a two-way process and investigates the role of the self within psychological work. It also helps clarify the type of Psychologist one wants to be and the theoretical framework that works best for the sport psychologist and their clients. Supervision is a working alliance enabling bidirectional feedback, mentoring, guidance, and evaluation of work and support. It is essential for trainees and professional practitioners alike, in order that they might reach optimum competence. Supervision should be more than simply providing corrective feedback for trainees. It goes beyond the aim of acquiring knowledge and expertise in order to 'independently and competently practice sport psychology' (BPS QSEP Stage 2 Candidate Handbook, 2018, p. 11). Supervision is an essential element of ethical practice. It aims to keep the psychologist ethically on track through transparent sharing of information and honest reflection (Mehr et al., 2010), whilst ensuring appropriate client education, support and welfare (Milne & Watkins, 2014).

There are numerous ways to implement and engage in supervision, with differing approaches depending on the personalities involved, the style of the supervisor and the needs of the supervisee. Engagement with supervision varied amongst the participants recruited for this book chapter, ranging from monthly individual sport psychology supervision, to peer group supervision every few months, and regular individual peer supervision. Some of the Psychologists engaged in a combination of supervision, for example, monthly professional supervision and quarterly peer-to-peer supervision. Not all participants had supervision and instead elected for regular mentoring, coupled with personal reflective processes and engagement with contemporary research. Participants who were trainee Sport Psychologists engaged in regular CPD ranging from one CPD event per month to ad hoc CPD events. Communication with other Sport Psychologists and Sport Scientists is crucial but may require time and effort to ensure such relationships are developed. However, being part of a peer group could mitigate these challenges, whilst being useful in providing novel areas of research and independent learning.

The underlying models and theoretical underpinnings will frame what good practice looks like. The type of supervision offered and the underlying model used are dependent upon the specific theoretical underpinnings preferred by the supervisor. Irrespective of the theoretical underpinning used, appropriate supervisory models are necessary to fortify the process. Whilst there will be preferences for specific theoretical perspectives, supervision should encourage both the understanding of different approaches and flexibility in implementing a variety of interventions and frameworks. Widening such understanding is important as it avoids practitioners becoming stale or overly reliant on one method or perspective when an alternative would be more beneficial. It broadens the mind of the practitioner, better enabling them to work with specific client needs in an integrative way. It is important for Sport Psychologists to keep in mind what type of practitioner they want to be, what exactly they are doing within their practice, how they as Psychologists are affecting their clients and their practice overall, and how in turn they are being affected by their clients and their practice. These factors form the core context of supervision.

Trainee Sport and Exercise Psychologists should discuss practice implications regarding their current caseload. For trainee Sport and Exercise Psychologists, the issue is often a lack of clients rather than a problem of too many. Supervision should include regular discussions of the direction of learning and intended career professional development. Such discussions are required, as the supervisor will guide the trainee to ensure appropriate, effective, and ethical practice takes place. They will share the responsibility for ensuring adherence to a good standard of practice by the trainee. An understanding of the requisite supervisory methods and interventions is also a necessity, along with a thorough understanding of ethical and legal considerations.

Rapport within the relationship is reliant upon:

- a comprehension of interpersonal issues (e.g., the processes involved in the supervisory relationship, including feedback on assessment and evaluation)
- an understanding of cultural diversity, individual differences, and the implication for inclusion.

All of this forms part of self-reflection within supervision (Watkins Jr, 2013). This type of relationship, especially between neophyte Psychologists and their supervisors, can indicate a power imbalance. Therefore, it is important that the supervision process focuses on neutralising the power dynamic within the relationship through both parties working collaboratively (Hawkins & Shohet, 2006) and offering continual support, learning and career development. As an essential part of the reflective process, supervision should aim to enhance self-understanding (Feltham & Dryden, 1994). By allowing the Sport Psychologist to collaborate with a trained professional a core aim is to identify psychological and behavioural changes in the Psychologist.

Supervision encompasses self-efficacy, going beyond simply knowing what to do by understanding how to engage with the client and the pervading environment surrounding the client. The aim of supervision within this context is to enhance the level of self-efficacy necessary to function well (Wheeler & Richards, 2007). Regular and good-quality supervision increases self-efficacy in the ability to deliver desired therapeutic outcomes effectively (Cashwell & Dooley, 2001). However, such supervision requires a thorough acceptance of, and compliance to, reflective practice in order to avoid the erosion of self-efficacy experienced in some forms of supervision (Wilson et al., 2015). Intrinsically, supervision must allow the supervisee the time and space to feel comfortable by allowing them to be vulnerable in exploring, then revealing, their inner thoughts and feelings. For trainee or newly qualified Sport and Exercise Psychologists, it is important to address the power imbalance within the relationship openly and honestly, as it can affect the nature of the relationship and the willingness of the supervisee to bring up anything negative. It can affect their freedom to share their feelings, thoughts, and emotions about their own practice or client issues. When conducting group sessions, supervisors should be cognizant that the presence of peer groups may elicit this reluctance to share negative emotions or thoughts relating to their practice. Conversely, group sessions can work well by allowing the supervisee to feel they are not alone in the types of concerns they are experiencing. In such well-run groups, the supervisee is likely to give open and honest feedback to the supervisor and their peers on how they are doing. Whatever the format of supervision, feedback should always be bidirectional to ensure the supervisor and the supervisee both benefit from the process.

Contracting in any form of therapeutic relationship is important. As with client relationships, supervision contracts enable clarity of the supervisory process. It helps manage mutual expectations and divulges vital information to the supervisee ahead of their commitment to the process. The contracting of the supervisory process is vital and is a requirement of the initial enrolment of BPS QSEP Stage-2.

The BPS provides a template of a supervisory contract for trainees. Lack of role clarity is commonplace within supervision when trainees are part of an organisation in which a line manager, or superior, conducts supervision. In such situations, there is often ambiguity regarding the legal implications of the supervisory process (Callicott & Leadbetter, 2013). There is no reason to avoid conducting supervision under such circumstances, so long as it is under a clear, concise, and informative written agreement.

To ensure the on-going effectiveness and efficiency of the service Sport Psychologists provide to their clients, deliberate efforts to engage in reflective practice and supervision are essential. Lifelong learning and knowledge acquisition is equally crucial (readers are referred to Chapter 13 for further information on Continued Professional Development). All practitioners we consulted consistently engaged with reading of peer-reviewed and non-peer reviewed publications, feeling that it helped them to keep up-to-date with current topics within the field. Those Psychologists who also lecture within higher education and/or supervise trainee sport and exercise psychologists find their teaching contributes to keeping them abreast of relevant and contemporary ideas and research. Regular review and monitoring of the progress made on agreed goals is also another way psychologists engage in quality control. This includes awareness of both the client's expected outcomes and the Psychologist's expected outcomes. Although none of the participants responded with how they would differentiate between these expectations, reflection and discussion within supervision should address such differentiation to enable the Psychologist to contemplate and formulate a suitable plan of action with their client.

Conclusion

This chapter has endeavoured to briefly outline the most important aspects of the administrative and quality assurance processes within SEP consultancy. The chapter seeks to encourage trainee and fully qualified Sport Psychologist to consider how they build trust and use the various types of efficacy needed to support their clients (see Figure 9.1). This also includes practitioners gaining knowledge of national guidelines and requirements for Psychologists. Practitioners should also take into account the necessary and desired continued professional development and establish mentorship and supervision networks for personal development. For all Sport and Exercise Psychologists, on-going good reflection is essential. Whilst currently not a BPS requirement for SEP, the authors argue that even when fully qualified, practitioner engagement in regular supervision, in some form, is essential. This view is mirrored by the HCPC, who also recommends practitioners to engage in regular reflection[5]. Following reading this chapter, readers are encouraged to consider and reflect upon the following questions:

- What is your responsibility as a practitioner to ensure RISE (relationship-inferred self-efficacy) in the practitioner–client dyad?

FIGURE 9.1 Quality assurance for practitioners.

- How can you as a practitioner diminish unbalanced client relationships (e.g., culturally and/or gender-diverse dyads)?
- Supervision of own practice
    a. How often should you as a practitioner engage in personal supervision?
    b. What could prevent you from disclosing personal experiences when being supervised?

Notes

1 See https://www.apa.org/about/policy/approved-guidelines
2 See https://www.hcpc-uk.org/standards/standards-of-proficiency/practitioner-psychologists/
3 See https://appliedsportpsych.org/about-the-association-for-applied-sport-psychology/ethics/
4 See https://issponline.org/index.php/issp-r-ethics-code
5 For further details, visit https://www.hcpc-uk.org/standards/meeting-our-standards/reflective-practice/

References

Callicott, K., & Leadbetter, J. (2013). An investigation of factors involved when educational psychologists supervise other professionals. *Educational Psychology in Practice*, 29(4), 383–403.

Cashwell, T. H., & K. Dooley (2001). The impact of supervision on counsellor self-efficacy. *Clinical Supervisor Special Issue*, 20(1), 39–47.

Cropley, B., Hanton, S., Miles, A., & Niven, A. (2010). Exploring the relationship between effective and reflective practice in applied sport psychology. *The Sport Psychologist*, 24(4), 521–541.

Feltham, C., & Dryden, W. (1994). *Developing counsellor supervision*. London: Sage.

Goleman, D. (2020). *Emotional intelligence*. New York: Bloomsbury Publishing.

Hanley, T. (2009). The working alliance in online therapy with young people: Preliminary findings. *British Journal of Guidance & Counselling*, 37(3), 257–269.

Hawkins, P., & Shohet, R. (2006). *Supervision in the helping professions*. Glasgow: Bell and Bain Ltd.

Jay, J. K., & Johnson, K. L. (2002). Capturing complexity: A typology of reflective practice for teacher education. *Teaching and teacher education*, 18(1), 73–85.

Mehr, K. E., Ladany, N., & Caskie, G. I. (2010). Trainee nondisclosure in supervision: What are they not telling you? *Counselling and Psychotherapy Research*, 10, 103–113.

Milne, D., & Watkins Jr, C. E. (2014). Defining and understanding clinical supervision: A functional approach. In C.E. Watkins, Jr. & D.L. Milne (Eds.), *The Wiley international handbook of clinical supervision* (pp. 3–19). Chichester: Wiley-Blackwell. https://doi.org/10.1002/9781118846360.ch1

Mitchels, B. (2017). Confidentiality, note taking and record keeping. In C. Feltham, T. Hanley & L. A. Winter (Eds.), *The Sage handbook of counselling and psychotherapy* (pp. 132–136). London: Sage.

Morrison, M. A., & Lent, R. W. (2018). The working alliance, beliefs about the supervisor, and counselling self-efficacy: Applying the relational efficacy model to counsellor supervision. *Journal of Counseling Psychology, 65*(4), 512.

O'Neil, J. (1996). On emotional intelligence: A conversation with Daniel Goleman. *Educational Leadership, 54*(1), 6–11.

Rosenbloom, S. T. (2010). Generating clinical notes for electronic health record systems. *Applied Clinical Informatics, 1*, 232–243.

Saville, P. D., & Bray, S. R. (2016) Athletes' perceptions of coaching behavior, relation-inferred self-efficacy (RISE), and self-efficacy in youth sport. *Journal of Applied Sport Psychology, 28*(1), 1–13. DOI: 10.1080/10413200.2015.1052890.

Saville, P. D., Bray, S. B., Martin Ginis, K. A., Cairney, J., Marinoff-Shupe, D., & Pettit, A. (2014). Sources of self-efficacy and coach/instructor behaviors underlying relation-inferred self-efficacy (RISE) in recreational youth sport. *Journal of Sport & Exercise Psychology, 36*, 146–156. DOI: 10.1123/jsep.2013-0144.

Schön, D. A. (1983). *The reflective practitioner: How professionals think in action*. New York: Basic Books. (Reprinted in 1995).

Smilde, R., (2015). Leadership and empathy: Looking through the eyes of another. In Vecomming an Artist and Supporting a Lifelong Career. London UK, However suggest this reference instead. Retrieved from https://rcconference.wordpress.com/rineke-smilde/

Thwaites, R., & Bennett-Levy, J. (2007). Conceptualizing empathy in cognitive behaviour therapy: Making the implicit explicit. *Behavioural and Cognitive Psychotherapy, 35*(5), 591–612.

Watkins Jr, C. E. (2013). On psychotherapy supervision competencies in an international perspective: A short report. *International Journal of Psychotherapy, 17*(1), 78–83.

Wheeler, S., & Richards, K. (2007). The impact of clinical supervision on counsellors and therapists, their practice and their clients. A systematic review of the literature. *Counselling and Psychotherapy Research, 7*(1), 54–65.

Williams, J., Lugo, R. G., & Firth, A. M. (2022). Exploring the therapeutic alliance and race from sports psychologists' and athletes' lived experiences: A pilot study. *Heliyon, 8*(1), e08736.

Wilson, H. M. N., Weatherhead, S., & Davies, J. S. (2015). Clinical psychologists' experiences of accessing personal therapy during training: A narrative analysis. *International Journal of Practice-based Learning in Health and Social Care, 3*(2), 32–47.

Zeichner, K. M., & Liston, D. P. (1996). *Reflective teaching: An introduction*. Hillsdale, NJ: Lawrence Erlbaum Associates.

PART III
Personal and Professional Development

Vaithehy Shanmuganathan-Felton

Until recently, applied sport psychology literature has heavily focused on understanding the processes involved in consultancy, the philosophy underpinning practitioners' service delivery and interventions that practitioners use to enhance performance (Tod et al. 2017). The role of the applied sport psychology practitioner was also considered to be mainly focused on enhancing athletic performance client welfare and wellbeing has not been at the forefront of psychological support and interventions (McCormack et al., 2015). Over the past decade, there has been an increase in the visibility of literature focusing on the factors that influence and are in turn influenced by clients' wellbeing and mental health (e.g., Uphill et al., 2016). Yet, little attention has been paid to understanding the practitioner, the stressors that they face and the personal and professional factors that influence their development (Tod et al., 2017).

Do as I Say, Not as I Do!

Applied practitioners are dedicated to facilitating their clients to thrive and flourish and play a critical role in the success and effectiveness of their service delivery (Poczwardowski, 2019). However, the impact of working in a helping profession on the mental health and psychological wellbeing of sport psychology consultants has only recently started to receive attention. For example, McCormack et al. (2015) found cases of emotional exhaustion and burnout. Practitioners in their study also reported finding it difficult to detach from their work; taking their work home to complete, staying late in the office and attending sporting events outside of office hours. This lack of detachment was more prevalent when working during competitions or on site at camps. It is important to pause here to recognise that while the *nature* of an applied sport psychology practitioner's work is like those operating in psychology, counselling and psychotherapy domains, the *context* of the applied sport psychology practitioner's work differs greatly from these professions, fuelling additional stressors (Quartiroli et al., 2019). These include but are not limited to providing psychological support in non-traditional settings, limited career opportunities, volatile and precarious working conditions and environment, limited professional support and networks and often ambiguous/multiple professional roles (see Gilmore et al., 2018; Quartiroli et al., 2019). These unique stressors subsequently add further burden on the practitioner's wellbeing.

Engagement in self-care strategies and practices is a must for practitioners for effective ethical practice but also to enhance personal and professional wellbeing (Quartiroli et al., 2021b). However, there is little literature on the widespread use of self-care strategies by sport psychology practitioners, although the benefits of taking care of the self have been documented in other helping professions (e.g., Rupert & Dorociak, 2019). Nonetheless, for a thriving career as well as career longevity, you must take care of your personal self by developing and integrating sustainable strategies and practices to manage your work-related stressors, maintain clear personal and professional boundaries, balance your personal and professional time effectively and make effective use of your social support networks (McCormack et al., 2015; Quartiroli et al., 2019; Quartiroli et al., 2021b).

Developing and Practicing with Cultural Competence

If I ask you to think back to 2020, it may be a fair assumption to make that the two key events you recalled were the COVID-19 pandemic and the murder of George Floyd. While this was not the first case of its kind[1], the unlawful murder of George Floyd by a law enforcement officer in the USA particularly struck a chord with many of us. You may also remember witnessing friends, families, acquaintances and organisations broaching the conversation about race, in some cases, for the first time. The sport psychology profession was no different, with increased attention, dialogue and commitment to promoting and addressing Equity, Diversity and Inclusion. With greater numbers of clients and more diverse groups of clients seeking psychological support from applied sport psychology practitioners, especially as we are now in an era where the use of cyberpsychology for consultancy has grown (Hurley, 2021), operating with cultural competence is paramount for effective and ethical practice; practitioners must be able to work with clients from cultural backgrounds different than their own (Quartiroli et al., 2020). Engagement in courses, workshops and training that promote cultural awareness, knowledge and skills are included in several professional bodies' requirements for certification and accreditation (e.g., AASP, FEPSAC, ISSP, BASES). However, you must also independently and purposefully make concerted efforts to develop, integrate and maintain cultural competence in your commitment to professional growth but also to enrich your practice (Quartiroli et al., 2020).

Commit to Learning for Effective Personal and Professional Development

Engagement in Continued Professional Development (CPD) is a requirement of all applied sport psychology training routes and engagement in continued education is a requirement to maintain accreditation or registration as a practitioner with professional bodies. However, your learning journey does not cease once you have qualified, rather to mature into experienced professionals and maintain effectiveness and excellence, you need to commit to renewing your knowledge and skills (Quartiroli et al., 2020; Wylleman et al., 2009). Otherwise, you may risk losing the competencies that you have spent time developing. In addition to benefits for professional development, continued engagement in learning has also been linked to reduced levels of burnout (Goodman & Schorling, 2012). That said, there are barriers to engaging with learning, including time and financial costs, which can be further exacerbated if you are working solely in applied practice, or trying to balance family and work to name a few. Interestingly, one of the advantages of the COVID-19 pandemic reported by sport psychology practitioners was the increased availability of workshops, seminars, events and activities online, with practitioners reporting greater involvement and engagement due to the times and costs associated with not needing to travel (Byrne & Shanmuganathan-Felton, 2020). However, it is important to note that beyond these formal events and activities, informal learning through critical reflection, self-directed reading, supervision and peer consultation, also contribute to professional development and underline commitment to learning (Quartiroli et al., 2021a). The key to be able to commit to learning, is the shifting of your mindset from perceiving engagement in such activities as mandatory for professional credentials, to genuine interest and passion for learning (Neimeyer et al., 2009).

Over to You...

You may be at the beginning of your journey in applied practice, contemplating your options, a trainee or a seasoned practitioner reading this text. Despite which stage you are at, the take-home message is that you are at the heart of effective practice. The closing section of the book brings together a selection of personal and professional themes that are central to your development and effectiveness as a practitioner and I hope that they act as a helpful aid in your journey in applied sport psychology.

Note

1 https://www.amnesty.org/en/what-we-do/police-brutality/

References

Byrne, L., & Shanmuganathan-Felton, V. (2020). The impact of COVID-19 lockdown and social isolation on the provision of psychological support by sport and exercise psychologists. Presented at the Virtual *British Psychological Society Division of Sport & Exercise Psychology (DSEP) Conference* 2020, 16–17th December.

Gilmore, S., Wagstaff, C., & Smith, J. (2018). Sports psychology in the English Premier League: 'It feels precarious and is precarious'. *Work, Employment and Society*, 32(2), 426–435. doi: 10.1177/0950017017713933.

Goodman, M.J., & Schorling, J.B. (2012). A mindfulness course decreases burnout and improves well-being among healthcare providers. *International Journal of Psychiatry in Medicine*, 43, 119–128. doi: 10.2190/PM.43.2.b.

Hurley, O. A. (2021). Sport cyberpsychology in action during the COVID-19 pandemic (opportunities, challenges, and future possibilities): A narrative review. *Frontiers in Psychology*. doi: 10.3389/fpsyg.2021.621283.

McCormack, H. M., MacIntyre, T. E., O'Shea, D., Campbell, M. J., & Igou, E. R. (2015). Practicing what we preach: Investigating the role of social support in sport psychologists' well-being. *Frontiers in Psychology*, 6, 1854. doi: 10.3389/fpsyg.2015.01854.

Neimeyer, G. J., Taylor, J. M., & Wear, D. M. (2009). Continuing education in psychology: Outcomes, evaluations, and mandates. *Professional Psychology: Research and Practice*, 40, 617–624. doi: 10.1037/a0016655.

Poczwardowski, A. (2019). Deconstructing sport and performance psychology consultant: Expert, person, performer, and self-regulator. *International Journal of Sport and Exercise Psychology*, 17(5), 427–444. https://doi.org/10.1080/1612197X.2017.1390484.

Quartiroli, A., Knight, S. M., Etzel, E. F., & Zakrajsek, R. A. (2019). Fostering and sustaining sport psychology professional quality of life: The perspectives of senior-level, experienced sport psychology practitioners. *The Sport Psychologist*, 33(2), 148–158. doi: 10.1123/tsp.2017-0140.

Quartiroli, A., Vosloo, J., Fisher, L., & Schinke, R. (2020). Culturally competent sport psychology: A survey of sport psychology professionals' perception of cultural competence. *The Sport Psychologist*, 34(3), 242–253.

Quartiroli, A., Wagstaff, C. R. D., Herms, M., & Kemmel, C. (2021a). The future of continuing education and lifelong learning in sport psychology professionals: A Delphi study. *Professional Psychology: Research and Practice*, 52(2), 173–185. doi: 10.1037/pro0000362.

Quartiroli, A., Wagstaff, C. R. D., Zakrajsek, R. A., Knight, S.M., & Etzel, E. F. (2021b). The role of self-care and professional quality of life in sustaining a long-lasting career in sport psychology: A qualitative exploration. *Journal of Applied Sport Psychology*. doi: 10.1080/10413200.2021.1907483.

Rupert, P. A., & Dorociak, K. E. (2019). Self-care, stress, and well-being among practicing psychologists. *Professional Psychology: Research and Practice*, 50(5), 343–350. doi: 10.1037/pro0000251.

Tod, D., Hutter, R. I. V., & Eubank, M. (2017). Professional development for sport psychology practice. *Current Opinions in Psychology*, 16, 134–137. doi: 10.1016/j.copsyc.2017.05.007.

Uphill, M., Sly, D., & Swain, J. (2016). From mental health to mental wealth in athletes: Looking back and moving forward. *Frontiers in psychology*, 7, 935. doi: 10.3389/fpsyg.2016.00935.

Wylleman, P., Harwood, C. G., Elbe, A.-M., & de Caluwé, D. (2009). A perspective on education and professional development in applied sport psychology. *Psychology of Sport and Exercise*, 10, 435–446. doi: 10.1016/j.psychsport.2009.03.008.

10
THE MENTAL HEALTH OF SPORT PSYCHOLOGY CONSULTANTS

Margaret McCarthy, Tadhg E. MacIntyre, Laura McMahon and Hannah McCormack

The Mental Health of Sport Psychology Consultants

Sport psychology could be described as having a long past but a short scientific history. This field of psychology arguably dates back to Norman Triplett's early observations in the late 1800s (Kremer & Moran, 2008). From there, a drive for performance enhancement shaped the field with an emphasis on peak performance and flow states, psychological skills training, and belatedly, mental toughness. This discourse dominated the zeitgeist until recent years when the mental health and wellbeing of the key stakeholders in sport were understood to be critical for the wellbeing and performance of all concerned (MacIntyre et al., 2017).

Consultants' mental health, psychological wellbeing, and consequential performance capacity have, to date, received limited consideration in the literature (McCormack et al., 2015). In this chapter, we address this gap by exploring the mental health of consultants, tracing the historical antecedents, the ethical considerations, and the consequences, notably in terms of burnout. Finally, implications for practice and recommendations for future research will be provided to ensure that lessons learned from our long history might inform our future and help to shape a shared mandate for mental health in sport.

A Shared Mandate

Moran and Toner (2017) defined 'sport psychology', simply, as seeking to understand the performance, mental processes and wellbeing of people engaged in sport. This definition reflects a recent shift in the field towards the promotion of mental health and wellbeing, which is now viewed as complementary to, and not competing with, a focus on performance enhancement (Henriksen et al., 2019). This pivot in focus has not been without debate among researchers and practitioners.

DOI: 10.4324/9781003196280-13

For example, some have suggested that the primary role of Sport Psychologists is performance enhancement, based on the foci of professional training with limited exposure to mental health interventions (Martindale et al., 2014). Others advocated that supporting mental health be viewed as central to sport psychology practice (MacIntyre et al., 2014). Some consensus has emerged regarding a shared mandate among consultants and practitioners in sport to address the prevention of mental illness and the promotion of mental health and wellbeing (MacIntyre et al., 2017). Sport psychology consultants play a critical role as advocates for this shared agenda, and ensure it is embedded within practices, particularly across multi-disciplinary teams (Alfano & Collins, 2021). The mental health of consulting Sport Psychologists is central to this approach, not only because the healthy practitioner self is central to effective consulting practice (Tod et al., 2017), but because practitioners serve as role models for the promotion of mental health best practice in the behaviours and attitudes of others.

The Ethical Imperative

Consultants' mental health when challenged can lead to a diminished capacity for service delivery with possible long-term implications for the practitioner, client-users, and ultimately the performance environment. Consulting at Olympic Games over 16 days of competition has been associated with potentially detrimental effects at many levels with one study noting that consultants in this setting frequently experienced burnout despite high levels of work engagement (McCormack et al., 2015).

Not surprisingly, the preservation and promotion of practitioner mental health and wellbeing have been highlighted as an ethical imperative. The APA ethics code (APA, 2017), states, in part, 'psychologists strive to be aware of the possible effect of their own physical and mental health on their ability to help those with whom they work' (p. 1062). Similarly, the British Psychological Society (2018) code of ethics and conduct states that 'psychologists should monitor their own personal and professional lifestyle in order to remain alert to signs of impairment' (p. 15). While professional accreditation within sport psychology requires a 'deep knowledge of professional ethics' (Schinke et al., 2018) and good practice delivery is predicated on a deep understanding of self and others (Alfano & Collins, 2021), the aforementioned ethics frameworks in sport psychology, may not provide sufficient guidance for practitioners on preserving their own mental health. Clearly, there is a widely accepted ethical obligation to maintain an awareness of and promote practitioner mental health and wellbeing, given the knock-on effects for client-users and across the sport setting. If we are to prioritise mental health in sport, we need to recognise the risks of diminished practitioner mental health and wellbeing on a personal, client, and stakeholder level.

Multi-Dimensional Model of Mental Health

The consideration of the mental health of a Sport Psychologist is best viewed in light of the constructs and mechanisms of mental health and psychological wellbeing. The World Health Organisation (WHO) viewpoint brings these two constructs together in its definition of mental health as a state of well-being in which the individual realises his or her own abilities, copes with the normal stresses of life, works productively and fruitfully, and makes a contribution to his or her community (WHO, 2004) thus "challenging the idea that mental health is simply the opposite of mental ill-health" (Barry, 2009, p. 6). It is now widely accepted that the conceptualisation of mental health has evolved beyond the absence of mental disorders.

For the purposes of this chapter, the 'complete state model of mental health' is applied (Keyes & Martin, 2017), which defines mental health as a complete state, consisting of the presence and absence of symptoms of mental health and mental illness, respectively. The presence of high levels of positive mental health is referred to as *flourishing*, reflected in symptoms of emotional, psychological, and social wellbeing (Keyes, 2005), and the absence of positive mental health is referred to as *languishing*. Vitality and engagement are deemed to be present in flourishing and absent in languishing (Keyes & Martin, 2017).

Vitality reflects emotional wellbeing (e.g., the presence of positive feelings towards life). Emotional vitality is understood as 'the energy that is available to the self—the energy that is exhilarating and empowering, and that actions that lead to need satisfaction can enhance energy available for self-regulation' (Deci & Ryan, 2008). Engagement in this model reflects psychological and social wellbeing – positive functioning in life and the extent to which individuals can thrive in their private, personal lives and public, social lives, respectively (Keyes & Martin, 2017). Seligman (2011) describes *engagement* as a psychological state in which individuals feel absorbed by what they are doing, and at its high end, engagement has been referred to as 'flow' (Csikszentmihalyi, 1997).

In summary, the multi-dimensional model asserts that mental health is underpinned by vitality and engagement which reflect emotional energy and optimal psychological and social functioning. This supports the expanded view articulated earlier in this chapter, that the optimisation of both positive functioning and personal and professional performance outcomes, can be widely understood to be entwined with mental health and wellbeing – not just for the athlete, but for the Sport Psychologist too. When this emotional energy and engagement are compromised, so too is mental health.

Professional Challenges

McCormack et al. (2018) assert that the work engaged in by sport psychology consultants is very similar to the person-focused work of medical professions, arguably with issues around professional boundaries (e.g., consulting in different settings) with some idiosyncratic challenges (e.g., Olympic/Paralympic events). In 2001, Andersen et al. (2001) predicted that future training and practice of sport psychology would more closely resemble counselling psychology than performance enhancement training. Over a decade later, researchers identified four areas of training required to practice performance psychology competently: performance excellence, mental health counselling, consulting psychology, and performance speciality domain (Aoyagi et al., 2012).

Despite a paucity of research specific to the mental health and wellbeing of sport psychology consultants as a sub-discipline (McCormack et al., 2018), the importance of robust mental health among practicing Psychologists is widely recognised in the literature, as are the detrimental effects of its compromise, which can lead to both personal distress and impaired professional functioning, with the potential to cause harm to clients (Smith & Moss, 2009). Sport psychology practitioners are at risk of experiencing various mental health challenges. Many of these risks are common across the 'caring professions', and many more are specific to the wider body of practising applied Psychologists, but some of the risks to mental health are contextually unique to the applied Sport Psychologist. To begin with, it is widely understood that many practicing Psychologists enter the profession in part to more deeply understand and perhaps resolve, their own problems, and some may have a predisposition to mental illness or mental ill health (Bearse et al., 2013). Due to the caring nature of the work, most practicing Psychologists demonstrate a predisposition to put the needs of their clients ahead of their own (Bearse et al., 2013). Even when Psychologists do become aware of concerns in their own lives, they often neglect their own needs, engaging in few leisure activities and inadequate self-care, and may be less likely to seek help when experiencing mental health challenges (Smith & Moss, 2009).

Work stressors of mental health professionals, both in independent and institutional roles, across applied practice and academia, can include heavy emotional demands, transference, negative client behaviours, lack of therapeutic progress, over-involvement with clients; lack of support, lack of development opportunity, excessive workload, mismanaged workload, hours of work, salary, negative team environments, life stresses, work–life balance, management within academia and insufficient time to balance research, teaching, supervision, and applied practice (Hammond et al., 2018; Maslach et al., 2001). In addition to the above stressors, factors unique to the Sport Psychologist role include disparate training and qualification pathways; practice environments and contexts; multiple (rather than single or even dual) role relationships, role ambiguity, role conflict and role overload; multiple clients within multi-disciplinary teams; potential client goal conflict; client issues specific to the sporting sub-culture (e.g., 'making weight'); limitations on time, space and location of support provision; blurred reporting lines, confidentiality concerns, payment issues, out-of-hours practice and immersive engagements with 'always-on' performance requirements; restrained emotional expression; post-competitive loss, travel and feelings of isolation (Aoyagi & Portenga, 2010; McCann, 2008).

Training pathways in sport psychology were traditionally rooted in physical education, kinesiology, and the sport sciences preparing practitioners to impart support relevant to performance enhancement and psychological skills training (Andersen et al., 2001). This approach may not have adequately prepared the practitioner for the array of challenges experienced in the provision of mental health and wellbeing support within the sporting context. While this focus on performance enhancement was undoubtedly useful in terms of the acceptability of the interventions, in reality, it may have overlooked the more generalisable aspects of these psychological skills to support mental health and wellbeing. However, mental skills training alone is unlikely to be sufficient to address the expanding needs of those operating in contemporary elite sport.

Clinical psychological training, for example, requires the qualifying practitioner to personally engage in psychotherapy and supervised practice, and promotes the maintenance of career-long peer support. However, the disparate pathways for qualification to sport psychology are not always aligned in this area and as a result, many neophyte sport psychology consultants enter professional practice less equipped to deal with the mental health challenges posed by the work (McCormack et al., 2018; Smith & Moss, 2009). While supervised practice is an integral part of professional training pathways, peer support for accredited practitioners is typically not mandated (Rhodius & Sugarman, 2014) and it is often up to individual practitioners to maintain these professional networks (McCormack et al., 2018). Thus, some of the safeguards for sport psychology consultants may not be integrated into practice scenarios, yet the setting is potentially laden with risks. For example, traditional practice boundaries in applied psychology relating to time, space and place rarely apply in sport psychology settings, where consultants often deliver support in non-traditional settings (e.g., locker rooms) usually in much less than the standardised session duration of one hour (Andersen et al., 2001; McCann 2008).

Applied practitioners meet with and support athletes, coaches and multi-disciplinary team members, individually and collectively. The flexibility in service delivery potentially blurs the boundaries that are ubiquitous in other applied psychological therapeutic settings. When one reflects upon the impact of the workload upon the Sport Psychologist, not only should practitioners be concerned with the mental health of athletes, but they should also be focused on the maintenance of their own mental wellbeing, both of which are arguably complimentary to performance. Ethical issues and conflicts of interests can arise in service provision within the immersion practitioner framework (i.e., practitioner is embedded within the team or organisation) and the 'just-visiting' consultative role (e.g., working with individuals sometimes within a team sport). Both service delivery scenarios pose challenges in terms of prevention of mental health issues and personal growth. When embedded within a large team organisation it can be difficult to distinguish who the real client is – the individual who receives support or the individual or body who pays for support, thus blurring lines of reporting and accountability and raising ethical concerns, the burden of which sits with the practitioner, but for which the applied Sport Psychologist has received little training (Andersen et al., 2001; McCormack et al., 2015).

Furthermore, travelling with a client or team, to training camps or competitions, can cause the Sport Psychologist to experience isolation while away from home for long periods, during which practicing 'out-of-hours' and being 'always-on' are commonplace (McCann, 2008). Within a team hierarchy, practitioners may be part of a multi-disciplinary team but without access to peer support or supervisors or mentors, it may be difficult for them to recognise whom they can seek support from. Ironically, while immersed in a sporting group, the Sport Psychologist may still feel like an 'outsider' (Aoyagi & Portenga, 2010). The solo consultant may be at further risk, without a multi-disciplinary team for social support and with challenges in the continuity of care as they may have to overcome barriers to gain access to their athlete(s) given competing organisational demands. This consultant may also feel disempowered in their role being one step removed from the sport ecosystem, which may limit their capacity to influence the team culture. However, they benefit from the limited face time with athletes in the team context as applied Sport Psychologists are also expected to refrain from emotional outbursts or stress-related displays of emotions to avoid emotional contagion to the performers. Consulting in all its guises, as we shall see arguably provides a myriad of challenges to mental health for the sport psychologist.

Five-Ring Focus: Consulting at the Olympic Games

Working at an Olympic Games offers a window into these context-specific challenges experienced by the applied Sport Psychologist. In this case, it is possible that the practitioner is away from home for up to three weeks, working up to 22-hour days (MacIntyre et al., 2014), in typically unscheduled, non-traditional time segments and locations (Andersen et al., 2001), delivering up to nine interventions per day (Birrer et al., 2012), but where every action can be viewed as an intervention in the 'always-on' environment. The demands of supporting athletes, coaches, and members of multi-disciplinary teams on a rollercoaster of perceived success and failure all while self-regulating to stay cool under pressure can be overwhelming (Gould & Maynard, 2009). More recently, Arnold and Sarkar (2015) identified that practitioners were cognisant of the fact that athletes felt that they were inadequately prepared for the aftermath of an Olympic Games, and the same may be true for the applied Sport Psychologist. More recently, the impact and aftermath of COVID-19 on the structure of service provision for the applied Sport Psychologist within and beyond the Olympic context brought an added layer of complexity. Virtual consulting, postponed and cancelled sporting milestones and adaptation to public health protocols were a further layer of stressors for the practitioner to cope with (Lundqvist et al., 2021). In summary, 'in performance environments, especially when traveling, the work is fast-paced, demanding, and many times exhausting' (Aoyagi & Portenga, 2010, p. 255).

Consequences: From Work-Related Stress to Burnout

Despite the perceived ethical and professional obligations to maintain and advance practitioner Psychologists' mental health and wellbeing, the extant literature in this area presents significant evidence of mental illness and impaired mental health among practitioner Psychologists. Findings include depression, anxiety, emotional exhaustion, burnout, compassion fatigue, secondary traumatisation, vicarious traumatisation, countertransference, and a history of personal trauma (Bearse et al., 2013; Figley, 2002; McCormack et al., 2018). Among mental health professionals, approximately 75% have received mental health support in comparison to one-quarter of the general adult population (Bearse et al., 2013).

Burnout – Engagement Continuum

The psychological relationship an individual experiences with their job has been conceptualised as a continuum between the negative experience of burnout and the, opposite, positive experience of engagement. Burnout is one of the most cited and most concerning mental health impairments among Psychologists and is found to be commonly experienced by Sport Psychologists despite positive engagement with their work (Fletcher et al., 2011; McCormack et al., 2018). Maslach et al. (2001) observed that the significance of burnout lies in its link to important outcomes, through impaired functioning.

Burnout refers to the emotional depletion and loss of motivation that result from prolonged exposure to chronic emotional and interpersonal stressors on the job (Leiter et al., 2015) and is characterised by three key dimensions: emotional exhaustion (feeling overextended and depleted in one's emotional and psychological resources), cynicism, or depersonalisation (feelings of detachment or negativity towards people or aspects on the job) and inefficacy (feelings of incompetence and reduced productivity) (Maslach et al., 2001). On the other hand, engagement is characterised by energy, involvement, and efficacy.

The synergy with the Keyes and Martin (2017) account of mental health is striking, which described impaired wellbeing as *languishing* – when vitality and engagement are absent. This chapter situates the Burnout – Engagement continuum along the mental health axiom – with burnout presented in the lower half of the wellbeing axiom aligned to languishing, and engagement in the upper half of the axiom, aligned to flourishing. According to the British Association of Sport and Exercise Scientists Expert Statement on Burnout in Sport, burnout is an extreme and persistent form of sport disillusionment that can affect both athletes and coaches (Madigan et al., 2019). A future expansion of this statement might capture the effect of burnout on the wider multi-disciplinary team including the sport psychology consultant. However, in its current form, parallels must be drawn between the experience of burnout amongst sport coaches and practitioners in sport psychology.

To explore more deeply the factors that may lead to the experience of burnout in applied Sport Psychologists, the Job Demands–Resource Theory JD–R Theory) is instructive. This theory posits that all job characteristics can be classified as either job demands or job resources. Job demands are physical, psychological, social, or organisational aspects of the job that require sustained physical and/or psychological effort and are therefore associated with certain physiological or psychological costs.

Conversely, job resources are those physical, psychological, social, or organisational aspects of the job that help to either achieve work goals, reduce job demands and the associated physiological and psychological costs, or stimulate personal growth, learning, and development. Personal resources, the belief people hold regarding the degree of control they exert over their environment (e.g., self-efficacy and optimism) can play a role similar to job resources (Bakker & Demerouti, 2017).

Job Demands as a Predictor of Burnout

The extant research strongly supports that job demands are predictors of burnout. The antecedents of both burnout and engagement can be classified as situational factors (e.g., work overload, job autonomy) and individual factors (e.g., individual differences or personal characteristics, e.g., neuroticism, self-efficacy) (Bakker & Demerouti 2008, Maslach et al., 2001). Situational antecedents of burnout include job demands such as role ambiguity, role conflict, role stress, stressful events, workload, and work pressure and to a lesser extent a lack of job resources including lack of development opportunity, lack of feedback, and monotony.

In a sport-specific context, situational antecedents to burnout include excessive workload, post-competitive loss, feelings of isolation (Hill et al., 2021), teaching, research, consulting, workload, hours, perceived gap between required and provided resources, lack of social support, negative social interactions, funding and income, presentation issues (media interest), evaluation in the workplace and ethical obligations (Fletcher et al., 2011). Academic Sport Psychologists were reported to experience more organisational stressors than applied practitioners (Fletcher et al., 2011). However, effective organisational culture, transformational leadership, and access to quality social support were identified as key structural protective factors (Hill et al., 2021).

The current literature suggests that stressful aspects of the work environment are more important predictors of burnout than personality. In general, individuals who believe they have control over their (work) environment, deal better with their job demands and are less predisposed to develop burnout. Sport-specific individual antecedents include perfectionistic concerns, extrinsic motivation, and thwarting of basic psychological needs of autonomy, competence, and relatedness (Madigan et al., 2019). More recently, McCormack et al. (2018) found that Sport Psychologists reported bringing work home, working from home, staying on-site late, attending sporting events our-of-hours, and lack of detachment from work especially at training camps and competitions, and that burnout tends to 'creep into this profession despite the high levels of work engagement'. Previously, McCormack et al. (2015) reported that demographics such as age and gender predict burnout, with age negatively associated with burnout. Tod et al. (2017) noted that with experience, comes a deeper appreciation of the influence of a practitioner's own relationships, needs, histories, and issues on their professional practice. Women are found to be more predisposed to experience emotional exhaustion than men, whereas men experience more depersonalisation than women (Purvanova & Muros, 2010). However, women were found to engage more significantly in career-sustaining behaviours (especially relational or educational) than men (Stevanovic & Rupert, 2004).

Job Resources as a Predictor of Engagement

Research supports the contention that job resources predict engagement. Situational job resources found to predict work engagement include task variety, task significance, autonomy, feedback, social support from colleagues, high-quality relationships with the supervisors, transformational leadership, innovativeness, organisational climate, autonomy, and social support. Individual factors include emotional stability, extraversion, conscientiousness, proactive personality, self-efficacy, optimism, and self-esteem (Mäkikangas et al., 2013).

Burnout Outcomes

The JD–R theory proposes that job demands, and job resources instigate two very different processes, namely a health-impairment process and a motivational process. More specifically, job demands predict burnout and by extension less favourable job-related outcomes including poor performance, in-role performance due to exhaustion, absence duration (an indication of ill-health), future depression, and higher future job demands through self-undermining behaviour and loss spiralling (Hobfoll, 2001, 2011).

Health-related outcomes of chronic burnout (chronic fatigue and cynicism in particular) include impaired physical and psychological health, as represented by measures of self-perceived health, depression, anxiety, sleep disturbance, memory impairment, neck pain, infections, musculoskeletal problems, cardiovascular issues, and type 2 diabetes (Armon et al., 2010; Kim et al., 2011). The consequences of burnout for sports coaches, which may be extrapolated to sport psychologists, suggest reduced work capacity, negative impact on relationships with athletes, and many ultimately leaving the profession (Madigan et al., 2019).

Engagement Outcomes

Job Resources are predictors of engagement, and by extension, more favourable job-related outcomes including positive performance, extra-role performance through engagement, absence frequency (an indicator of motivation), organisational commitment, and increased future resources through job crafting and gain spiralling (Hobfoll, 2001, 2011). While research suggests some links between engagement and better health, the main focus has been on motivational consequences, such as individuals feeling more inspired, energetic, enthusiastic, and cheerful (Schaufeli et al., 2009), and consistent with the Broaden-and-Build theory (Fredrickson, 2001) and conservation of resources theory (Hobfoll, 2001, 2011), experiencing positive emotions and gains spirals as a result.

Research suggests that job resources can buffer job demands. Specifically, the more resources practitioners have available, the better they will cope with the demands of their work, especially when needed most. Jobs that combine high demands with high resources are so-called active jobs (Karasek, 1979) that challenge employees to learn new things on the job and motivate them to use new behaviours (Bakker & Demerouti, 2017, p. 275).

Applied Implications and Practitioner Recommendations

Research has only recently focused on the mental health and wellbeing of Sport Psychologists, and their experience of burnout. As previously noted, the antecedents of burnout can be situational or individual, yet the recommendations reported in the research are weighted heavily towards individual practitioner self-care (readers are referred to Chapter 11 for integrating self-care strategies into daily practice). Whilst practitioner self-care is undoubtedly critical in the preservation and promotion of practitioner mental health, this emphasis puts the onus on the applied Sport Psychologist to carry the burden, not only of ethical obligation and duty of care to almost all those involved in their sporting sphere, but also to care for the practitioner self, which can be a particular burden for solo practitioners compared to those embedded within multi-disciplinary teams.

Fletcher et al. (2011) note that while Sport Psychologists are encouraged to 'practice what they preach' through self-care, 'Sport Psychologists are typically trained to design and deliver stress management interventions for others. It is a different skill to effectively implement such techniques in one's own life'. Wagstaff (2019) observed that the education and training of Sport Psychologists continue to be dominated by psychological skills, and Smith et al. (2009) noted the persistence of deficiencies in personal and professional impairment education among trainee Psychologists.

Extant research posits that factors related to the work environment are more important predictors of burnout than individual factors such as personality. However, according to Wagstaff (2019, p.18), 'Sport organizations, professional societies and regulatory bodies, and education and training providers are currently failing in their duty of care to individuals in sport'. Therefore, recommendations for the prevention of burnout in the practice of sport psychology should reflect the duty of care sporting bodies hold in relation to the wellbeing of all who work in sport, and the ethical obligations to create environments and organisational culture which promote flourishing (Fletcher & Wagstaff, 2009). Recommendations which consider the situational, structural and systemic aspects of the sporting organisational environment might include the following:

i. As a sub-discipline of psychology, sport psychology could broaden its focus to the mental processes, wellbeing, and performance of *all* people involved in sport, such that stress management interventions and psychological skills would not solely focus on athletes but also incorporate the broader multi-disciplinary teams surrounding the performer, including sport psychology staff (Fletcher et al., 2011). The discipline could shift the emphasis away from short-term, corrective intervention to envision and promote a broader view of cultural excellence within sport, where mental health and wellbeing are a shared mandate by all, for all.

ii. Training pathways could be reviewed to reflect and best prepare the applied Sport Psychologist for modern-day practice demands, with an increased alignment to therapeutic training, counselling and organisational/cultural psychology. This has implications for accreditation pathways and the role of public statutory and regulatory bodies (e.g., HCPC).

iii. Taking a Strength-Based Approach, professional bodies within sport psychology could advance impairment education to create awareness regarding the risk factors and undesirable outcomes of burnout, for the practitioner (rather than just for the athlete), emphasising the role of job and personal resources in the promotion of engagement. This theory-orientated approach could also include the conservation of resources model (Hobfoll, 2001) and test specific hypotheses relating to psychological recovery to ameliorate work-related stress.

iv. Education on career-sustaining behaviours may help Psychologists-in-training to best prepare for challenges later in their careers (Smith & Moss, 2009). This could be reflected through in-curriculum focus on the need for, and the provision of practical training in self-care, ethics, direct supervision and feedback, referral pathway provision, in-curriculum therapeutic support, formal/informal peer support, proactive boundary management; transition support (into and out of sports/engagements/competitions) and ongoing systemic support structures to facilitate optimal engagement and service delivery.

v. Professional bodies could incentivise and reward evidence of protective and sustaining practice and behaviours on a longitudinal basis; consider the merits of a mentoring or buddy-up system for recently accredited professionals and develop forums to enable and facilitate shared best practice, complex case reviews and group peer support.

vi. As with all employer–employee relationships, sporting bodies and academic institutions have a responsibility to uphold their duty of care to the Sport Psychologist, through fostering an attractive motivational climate, provision of regular feedback and social support. Working in teams in the provision of psychological support is encouraged where possible, as is the provision of peer support where needed.

vii. Promotion of autonomy-supportive working environments, improving role clarity, balancing workload, and hours, and reducing dissonance between perceived job demands and resources could protect against burnout. In practice, recent initiatives by professional bodies may support a more holistic approach to reducing work-related stress. In 2020, the BPS, in response to the COVID-19 global pandemic, developed guidelines for the use of outdoor therapy, a consulting setting with benefits for the client, co-benefits for the mental health of the practitioner, and additional benefits in terms of sustainability. This offers a useful pathway for future research on work-related stress and wellbeing in the field.

viii. A key challenge in this field is the recognition and reward of applied practice to enrich course content and delivery, ensuring an appropriate balance is achieved between teaching, research, supervision and applied practice, funding, and student-contact hours. For example, given the REF (Research Excellence Framework, UK) model which is focused on research impact, applied psychology practice has a potential role in advancing this narrative within Higher Education Institutions.

In consideration of the widely perceived ethical and professional obligations to maintain and advance practitioner psychologist mental health and wellbeing, these recommendations reach beyond individual differences and self-care. They present an opportunity for a proactive review of the systemic work environments and cultural excellence within high-performance sport and sport psychology service provision. Such a review could focus on appropriate, aligned training pathways to best prepare the modern practitioner; to practice within the contemporary high-performance sport environment; and post qualification support structures and professional environments, bodies, and forums which facilitate and enable a community of shared practice rather than promoting competing practitioners.

Conclusion

Sport Psychology is concerned with the mental processes, wellbeing, and performance of people involved in sport. This frames the link between the Sport Psychologist's mental health and wellbeing and their own performance, and the potential implications on client-users, key stakeholders and the broader performance environment. The present-day practitioner aims to promote an athlete's ability to perform and ability to thrive which conveys how the role has expanded beyond the traditional framework of performance enhancement and psychological skills training, to complement counselling and clinical psychology roles. The many risks to psychology practitioner mental health and wellbeing are documented here and, in the extant literature. In addition, this chapter has explored the context-specific challenges experienced uniquely by the applied Sport Psychologist, which may result in a diminished capacity for preparation for client work and limited preventative buffers from mental health risks.

Practitioner mental health and wellbeing are understood here through the Keyes and Martin (2017) model in which mental health and wellbeing are underpinned by vitality and engagement (reflecting emotional, psychological, and social wellbeing). On the other hand, burnout is one of the most common manifestations of impaired mental health amongst practitioner Psychologists characterised by emotional exhaustion, depersonalisation, and reduced efficacy. The burnout–engagement continuum is situated here along the vertical axiom of the complete state model of mental health, running from languishing – flourishing. The situational and individual antecedents and consequences of burnout and engagement amongst Sport Psychologists are understood here in the context of the Job Demands–Resources Model. By extrapolation, the recommendations presented here go beyond the clear need for individual self-care by the practitioner Sport Psychologist, to explore the situational, organisational, and systemic supports that might be considered to protect and promote the mental health and wellbeing of the consultant.

References

Alfano, H., & Collins, D. (2021). Good practice in sport science and medicine support: practitioners' perspectives on quality, pressure and support. *Managing Sport and Leisure*. DOI: 10.1080/23750472.2021.1918019.

American Psychological Association. (2017). Ethical principles of psychologists and code of conduct. American Psychological Association. https://www.apa.org/ethics/code

Andersen, M. B., Van Raalte, J. L., & Brewer, B. W. (2001). Sport psychology service delivery: staying ethical while keeping loose. *Professional Psychology: Research and Practice*, 32(1), 12. DOI: 10.1037/0735-7028.32.1.12.

Aoyagi, M. W., & Portenga, S. T. (2010). The role of positive ethics and virtues in the context of sport and performance psychology service delivery. *Professional Psychology: Research and Practice*, 41(3), 253.

Aoyagi, M. W., Portenga, S. T., Poczwardowski, A., Cohen, A. B., & Statler, T. (2012). Reflections and directions: The profession of sport psychology past, present, and future. *Professional Psychology: Research and Practice*, 43(1), 32.

Armon, G., Melamed, S., Shirom, A., & Shapira, I. (2010). Elevated burnout predicts the onset of musculoskeletal pain among apparently healthy employees. *Journal of Occupational Health Psychology*, 15(4), 399–408. DOI:10.1037/a0020726. PMID: 21058854.

Arnold, R., & M. Sarkar. 2015. Preparing athletes and teams for the Olympic Games: experiences and lessons learned from the world's best sport psychologists. *International Journal of Sport & Exercise Psychology*, 13(1): 4–20. DOI: 10.1080/1612197X.2014.932827.

Bakker, A. B., & Demerouti, E. (2008). Towards a model of work engagement. *Career Development International*, 13, 209–223.

Bakker, A. B., & Demerouti, E. (2017). Job demands–resources theory: taking stock and looking forward. *Journal of Occupational Health Psychology*, 22(3), 273.

Barry, M. M. (2009). Addressing the determinants of positive mental health: concepts, evidence and practice. *International Journal of Mental Health Promotion*, 11(3), 4–17.

Bearse, J. L., McMinn, M. R., Seegobin, W., & Free, K. (2013). Barriers to psychologists seeking mental health care. *Professional Psychology: Research and Practice*, 44(3), 150.

Birrer, D., Röthlin, P., & Morgan, G. (2012). Mindfulness to enhance athletic performance: theoretical considerations and possible impact mechanisms. *Mindfulness*, 3(3), 235–246.

British Psychological Society (2018). Code of ethics and conduct. Retrieved 7 March 2022, from https://www.bps.org.uk/news-and-policy/bps-code-ethics-and-conduct

Csikszentmihalyi, M. (1997). *Flow and the psychology of discovery and invention*. New York: Harper Perennial.

Deci, E. L., & Ryan, R. M. (2008). Self-determination theory: a macrotheory of human motivation, development, and health. *Canadian Psychology/Psychologie canadienne*, 49(3), 182.

Dreison, K.C., Luther, L., Bonfils, K.A., Sliter, M.T., McGrew, J.H., & Salyers, M.P. (2018). Job burnout in mental health providers: A meta-analysis of 35 years of intervention research. *Journal of Occupational Health Psychology*, 23(1), 18–30. DOI:10.1037/ocp0000047. Epub 2016 Sep 19. PMID: 27643608.

Figley, C. R. (2002). Compassion fatigue: psychotherapists' chronic lack of self care. *Journal of Clinical Psychology*, 58(11), 1433–1441.

Fletcher, D., Rumbold, J.L., Tester, R., & Coombes, M.S. (2011). Sport psychologists' experiences of organizational stressors. *The Sport Psychologist, 25*(3), 363–381.

Fletcher, D., & Wagstaff, C. R. (2009). Organizational psychology in elite sport: its emergence, application and future. *Psychology of Sport and Exercise, 10*(4), 427–434.

Fredrickson, B.L. (2001). The role of positive emotions in positive psychology. The broaden-and-build theory of positive emotions. *The American Psychologist, 56*(3), 218–226.

Gould, D., & Maynard, I. (2009). Psychological preparation for the Olympic Games. *Journal of Sports Sciences, 27*(13), 1393–1408.

Hammond, T. E., Crowther, A., & Drummond, S. (2018). A thematic inquiry into the burnout experience of Australian solo-practicing clinical psychologists. *Frontiers in Psychology, 8*, 1996.

Henriksen, K., Schinke, R., Moesch, K., McCann, S., Parham, W., Larsen, C., & Terry, P. (2019). Consensus statement on improving the mental health of high performance athletes. *International Journal of Sport and Exercise Psychology, 18*(5), 553–560.

Hill, D. M., Brown, G., Lambert, T. L., Mackintosh, K., Knight, C., & Gorczynski, P. (2021). Factors perceived to affect the wellbeing and mental health of coaches and practitioners working within elite sport. *Sport, Exercise, and Performance Psychology, 10*(4), 504–518. DOI: 10.1037/spy0000263.

Hobfoll, S. E. (2001). The influence of culture, community, and the nested-self in the stress process: Advancing conservation of resources theory. *Applied Psychology: International Review, 50*(3), 337–370.

Hobfoll, S. E. (2011). Conservation of resources theory: Its implication for stress, health, and resilience. In S Folkman (Ed.), *The Oxford Handbook of Stress, Health, and Coping* (pp. 127–147). New York: Oxford Univ. Press.

Karasek, R. A. (1979). Job demands, job decision latitude, and mental strain Implications for job redesign. *Administrative Science Quarterly, 24*, 285–308.

Keyes, C. L. M. (2005). Mental illness and/or mental health? Investigating axioms of the complete state model of health. *Journal of Consulting and Clinical Psychology, 73*(3), 539–548. DOI: 10.1037/0022-006x.73.3.539.

Keyes, C. L. M., & Martin, C. C. (2017). The complete state model of mental health. In M. Slade, L. Oades, & A. Jarden (Eds.), *Wellbeing, recovery and mental health* (pp. 86–97). Cambridge University Press. DOI: 10.1017/9781316339275.009.

Kim, H., Ji, J., &Kao, D. (2011). Burnout and physical health among social workers: A three-year longitudinal study. *Social Work, 56*(3), 258–268. DOI: 10.1093/sw/56.3.258. PMID: 21848090.

Kremer, J., & Moran, A. (2008). Swifter, higher, stronger: the history of sport psychology. *The Psychologist, 2*(8), 740–742.

Leiter, M. P., Day, A., & Price, L. (2015). Attachment styles at work: measurement, collegial relationships, and burnout. *Burnout Research, 2*(1), 25–35.

Lundqvist, C., Macdougall, H., Noguchi, Y., Malherbe, A., & Abejean, F. (2021) When COVID-19 struck the world and elite sports: psychological challenges and support provision in five countries during the first phase of the pandemic. *Journal of Sport Psychology in Action*. DOI: 10.1080/21520704.2021.1931594.

MacIntyre, T., Jones, M., Brewer, B., Van Raalte, J., O'Shea, D., & McCarthy, P. (2017). Editorial: mental health challenges in elite sport: balancing risk with reward. *Frontiers in Psychology, 8*. DOI: 10.3389/fpsyg.2017.01892.

MacIntyre, T. E., Barr, J., & Butler, C. (2014). The good, the bad and the ugly of elite sport: a reply to Martindale, A., Collins, D. & Richards, H. (2014). It's good to talk…Is elite sport good for you? *Sport and Exercise Psychology Review, 10*(3), 68–76.

Madigan, D., Gustafsson, H., Smith, A., Raedeke, T., & Hill, A. (2019). *The BASES expert statement on burnout in sport* [Ebook] (https://www.bases.org.uk/spage-resources-bases_expert_statements.html). Online: The Sport and Exercise Scientist Issue 61. Retrieved from https://www.bases.org.uk/imgs/tses___issue_61_autumn_19_expert_statement_online__pages_579.pdf

Mäkikangas, A., Feldt, T., Kinnunen, U., & Mauno, S. (2013). Does personality matter? A review of individual differences in occupational well-being. In *Advances in positive organizational psychology* (pp. 107–143). Emerald Group Publishing. DOI: 10.1108/S2046-410X(2013)0000001008.

Martindale, A., Collins, D., & Richards, H. (2014). It's good to talk… Is elite sport good for you? *Sport and Exercise Psychology Review*, 10(3), 68–76.

Maslach, C., Schaufeli, W. B., & Leiter, M. P. (2001). Job burnout. *Annual Review of Psychology*, 52(1), 397–422.

McCann, S. (2008). At the Olympics, everything is a performance issue. *International Journal of Sport and Exercise Psychology*, 6(3), 267–276.

McCormack, H. M., MacIntyre, T. E., O'Shea, D., Campbell, M. J., & Igou, E. R. (2015). Practicing what we preach: investigating the role of social support in sport psychologists' well-being. *Frontiers in Psychology*, 6, 1854. DOI: 10.3389/fpsyg.2015.01854.

McCormack, H. M., MacIntyre, T., O'Shea, D., Herring, M., & Campbell, M. (2018). The prevalence and cause(s) of burnout among applied psychologists: a systematic review. *Frontiers in Psychology*, 9, 2018. Frontiers, https://www.frontiersin.org/article/10.3389/fpsyg.2018.01897

Moran, A., & Toner, J. (2017). *A critical introduction to sport psychology* (3rd ed.). New York: Taylor and Francis.

Purvanova, R., &Muros, J. (2010). Gender differences in burnout: A meta-analysis. *Journal of Vocational Behavior*, 77, 168–185. DOI:10.1016/j.jvb.2010.04.006.

Rhodius, A., & Sugarman, K. (2014). Peer consultations with colleagues: the significance of gaining support and avoiding the "lone ranger trap". In J.G. Cremades & L. S. Tashman (Eds.), *Becoming a sport, exercise, and performance psychology professional* (pp. 359–366). Psychology Press.

Schaufeli, W.B., Arnold, B. Bakker, & Willem Van Rhenen. (2009). How changes in job demands and resources predict burnout, work engagement, and sickness absenteeism. *Journal of Organizational Behavior*, 30, 893–917. DOI: 10.1002/job.595.

Schinke, R. J., Si, G., Zhang, L., Elbe, A. M., Watson, J., Harwood, C., & Terry, P. C. (2018). Joint position stand of the ISSP, FEPSAC, ASPASP, and AASP on professional accreditation. *Psychology of Sport and Exercise*, 38, 107–115.

Seligman, M. E. P. (2011). *Flourish: a visionary new understanding of happiness and well-being*. New York: Free Press.

Smith, P. L., & Moss, S. B. (2009). Psychologist impairment: what is it, how can it be prevented, and what can be done to address it? *Clinical Psychology: Science and Practice*, 16(1), 1.

Stevanovic, P., & Rupert, P. A. (2004). Career-sustaining behaviors, satisfactions, and stresses of professional psychologists. *Psychotherapy: Theory, Research, Practice, Training*, 41(3), 301.

Tod, D., Hutter, R. V., & Eubank, M. (2017). Professional development for sport psychology practice. *Current Opinion in Psychology*, 16, 134–137. DOI: 10.1016/j.copsyc.2017.05.007.

Wagstaff, C. R. (2019). A commentary and reflections on the field of organizational sport psychology. *Journal of Applied Sport Psychology*, 31(1), 134–146.

WHO (2004). *Promoting mental health: concepts, emerging evidence, practice: summary report*. Geneva: WHO.

11

PRACTISING WHAT WE PREACH

Self-Care as an Avenue for Effective Practice

Alessandro Quartiroli, Heather Hunter and Daniel R. F. Martin

Practising What We Preach: Self-Care as an Avenue for Effective Practice

As sport psychology practitioners (SPPs), we dedicate our working hours to facilitating our clients' thriving in the pursuit of performance (Poczwardowski, 2019). To continue providing effective and ethical psychological support, practitioners may consider learning to tend to their wellbeing, with an intention toward thriving and subsequent professional performance (McCormack et al., 2018). This chapter will make a case for the importance of self-care for SPPs, including the embedding of self-care into the foundation of ethical professional practice. As will be explored later, it is impossible to be prescriptive in the types of self-care activities practitioners should engage in. Instead, in this chapter, we will explore the nuanced challenges of the SPP environment, how these nuances affect self-care needs, and the barriers to practising self-care that practitioners may experience. The nascent research in this area has begun to explore the mechanisms that underpin effective self-care practices, so we will delve into how these findings may be applied when developing a self-care plan. For the most part, the work we present in the chapter is grounded in scholarly efforts aimed to be globally and culturally inclusive; however, we recognise that the existing knowledge is heavily grounded in Westernised worldviews. For this reason, we believe it is paramount to highlight how cultural SPPs' context and background and their cultural intersectionality play an important role in the individual conceptualization of self-care as well as in the implementation of their self-care practices (readers are referred to Chapter 12 for further guidance on broaching culture and diversity in sport, exercise and performance psychology practice). Above all, in this chapter, we aim to make it clear to neophytes and experienced practitioners alike that the payoff associated with effective self-care is worth the conscious and purposeful endeavour.

DOI: 10.4324/9781003196280-14

Sport Psychology's Unique Challenges

The work of psychology practitioners is associated with both personal (e.g., emotional exhaustion) and professional (e.g., impairment) challenges (Stevanovic & Rupert, 2004). These challenges may negatively impact an individual's personal and professional wellbeing if they are unable to manage or prepare for them effectively. Consequently, this may negatively influence SPPs' professional effectiveness (Cropley et al., 2010, 2016).

Evidence suggests that due to a complex interplay of workplace conditions and stressors (Acker, 2012), mental health practitioners experience a variety of career-related challenges (Malinowski, 2014), ranging from relationship difficulties to psychological isolation and loneliness (Norcross & VandenBos, 2018), as well as emotional exhaustion (Baker, 2003; Rupert & Dorociak, 2019). While SPPs experience some of the same career-related stressors as 'traditional' mental health practitioners, they also face additional unique professional challenges. These challenges include SPPs' roles (e.g., dual relationships, scientist-practitioner), non-traditional working environments (e.g., hotel lobbies, during air travel) and conditions (e.g., quick meetings during breaks or within fast-paced competition), and ambiguous ethical and professional boundaries (e.g., room sharing on extended trips). These demands differentiate the professional experience of SPPs from those experienced by mental health professionals working in more traditional environments (Andersen et al., 2001; Quartiroli, Knight, et al., 2019b; Stapleton et al., 2010; Waumsley et al., 2010).

Self-Care Is Our Responsibility

Similar to other psychology practitioners, SPPs are mandated by the ethical guidelines of their profession to maintain the highest ethical standards (Barnett et al., 2007) while reaching their fullest potential (Knapp et al., 2017). Given that the neglect of pursuing professional mandates would be unethical, it is incumbent on practitioners to engage in self-care practices that promote personal and professional wellbeing (Quartiroli, Wagstaff, & Thelwell, 2021a). Practitioners who fail to care for their wellbeing could experience higher levels of burnout and secondary traumatic stress (Butler et al., 2017; Santana & Fouad, 2017), while also potentially engaging in practices that are harmful to their clients (e.g., abandonment), themselves (e.g., addictive behaviours), and possibly the profession (e.g., loss of competence; Barnett et al., 2007).

For this reason, practitioners must assume the personal and professional responsibility to develop and maintain their own wellness (e.g., Venart et al., 2007) and to engage in self-care as an ethical imperative (e.g., Norcross & VandenBos, 2018; Wise et al., 2012). Additionally, engaging in self-care may protect practitioners from negative outcomes whilst fostering personal flourishing and promoting good practice outcomes (Wise et al., 2012; Skovholt & Trotter-Mathison, 2016). For practitioners who do engage in self-care, evidence suggests that they are more likely to experience greater wellbeing (Colman et al., 2016). This may be a result of lower levels of stress and negative affect; combined with higher levels of positive affect, flourishing, self-rated academic and clinical performance (Zahniser et al., 2017), compassion satisfaction (Butler et al., 2017), quality of life (Goncher et al., 2013), and professional wellbeing and practice outcomes (Rupert & Dorociak, 2019).

Although the construct of self-care has received considerable attention within general psychology literature (e.g., Baker, 2003; Dorociak et al., 2017), the body of research detailing how SPPs experience self-care is still relatively young (Quartiroli, Etzel, et al., 2019a). An initial exploration of the self-care construct in globally situated SPPs recently provided novel insights into how SPPs understand and experience self-care (Quartiroli, Etzel, et al., 2019a). According to these initial findings, self-care can be described as grounded in one's values and characterised by the engagement in activities aimed to support physical, emotional, cognitive, spiritual, and social health. While these results offer an initial understanding of self-care in the context of the sport psychology profession, they do fall short of providing a coherent and shared definition of the construct.

Understanding Self-Care for Sport Psychologists

While there is emerging evidence that SPPs generally perceive self-care to be important in their professional and personal lives, the lack of a clear conceptualisation of self-care has limited the ability of researchers to advance our understanding of self-care in SPP populations (Dorociak et al., 2017; Quartiroli, Etzel, et al., 2019a). To contribute to the development of a clear and coherent conceptualization of self-care within the sport psychology context, (Quartiroli, Wagstaff, & Thelwell, 2021a) shared a definition of Sport Psychology Self-Care (SPSC) consensually co-constructed and agreed upon by a panel of globally situated SPPs across the career-span development.

This new definition provides a solution to the lack of consensus that existed within the general and sport psychology literature on self-care. This definition does not aim to standardise self-care but instead highlights the rooted individual nature of its practices (and challenges) while providing a shared language to describe self-care. The possibility of a shared language is especially valuable for professional organizations, credentialing bodies, and training programs to contribute to highlighting the value of SPSC for SPPs. At an individual level, clarity on self-care for SPPs will encourage current and future SPPs to focus on proactively engaging in practices that foster their health and wellbeing as foundations of ethical and effective practice.

Core to the newly developed definition of SPSC is the idea that SPSC is grounded in one's values. In addition to highlighting the individual nature of SPSC, the salience of one's values also indicates the importance for SPPs to reflect upon and explore their values. That self-care should be grounded in one's values impedes the possibility for researchers to prescribe unified and standardised practices and strategies that support SPSC. However, it encourages SPPs to engage in reflective and explorative efforts aimed to develop one's awareness of their own values. The development of such awareness may then represent the foundation for SPPs to explore, develop, and implement practices aimed to support their SPSC, and consequently their wellbeing, health, and potentially professional practice.

Moreover, this sport-psychology-specific definition highlights how self-care occurs through deliberate engagement in activities aimed at prioritizing, developing, preserving, protecting, monitoring, and restoring one's health, wellbeing, and life satisfaction. While somewhat wordy, these diverse sets of foci of self-care are important given the numerous ways self-care relates to positive life outcomes. These foci are not necessarily goals or aims that must be reached concurrently or in a specific order. Instead, they represent the possible reasons to engage in SPSC practices.

Considerations at the Outset

To best foster effective self-care, SPPs need to consider the intention behind incorporating self-care into their lives. The way they choose to approach this bears significance due to what is referred to in the literature as the 'plurality of purpose' of self-care (Quartiroli Wagstaff, Thelwell, 2021a). Indeed, the purpose of self-care may be to promote good outcomes such as restoring health and wellbeing and improving satisfaction, or it could be to protect against adverse outcomes such as burnout and professional impairment. While the decisions to engage in self-care proactively or reactively are not mutually exclusive, it appears that depending on their stages of professional development, SPPs lean more toward one or the other. Early career SPPs seem more likely to engage in self-care practices only as a response in the face of adversity and challenge when they already feel tired or are experiencing some form of physical or emotional deficit. Conversely, in the later stages of their professional journey, SPPs report being proactively invested in self-care, developing and maintaining self-care practices and strategies aimed to support their personal and, consequentially, professional journey (Martin et al., 2021; Quartiroli, Etzel, et al., 2019a). Moreover, in addition to their stage of professional development, it appears that the tendency for SPPs to feel a greater affinity for and to have more experience with the restorative and reactionary role of self-care can be linked to the uncertain and unpredictable nature of professional challenges unique to the early stages of a psychology professional's journey (Quartiroli, Knight, et al., 2019b). Engaging in reactive self-care practices can have an important impact in helping SPPs to adjust to their work-life balances (Quartiroli, Wagstaff, et al., 2021b; Waumsley et al., 2010). However, scholars are developing a body of evidence that stresses and highlights the importance of a more proactive exploration, development, and implementation of self-care practices and strategies that serve to foster self-care throughout the entire professional developmental continuum (Martin et al., 2021; Quartiroli, Etzel, et al., 2019a).

The deliberate decision to engage in self-care is fundamental to the development of effective practice. The intention of the activity must be aimed towards observing, preserving, safeguarding, prioritising, developing, and restoring one's own health, wellbeing, and life satisfaction. For example, neophyte practitioners have described how they prioritised and deliberately engaged in self-care actions that met their daily functioning needs because they attributed those actions as being important to their overall health and wellbeing (Martin et al., 2021). These types of behaviours could include but are not limited to good sleep hygiene, attention to nutrition, regular physical activity, and making time to be in nature. Like the work practitioners perform with the clients they serve, examining one's motivations and what leads them to the decision to practice (or not practice) certain skills may lead down a myriad of avenues weighing up benefits and challenges. Practitioners understand that here is where some of the most valuable work potentially lies, as this is where there is the space to address mechanisms that no longer work for their clients and create the potential for change. Applying this in a reflective manner may allow practitioners to do the same for themselves.

Engaging in Self-Care

While it is recognised that SPPs must engage in self-care, both through scholarship (e.g., Quartiroli, Etzel, et al., 2019a) and anecdotally, the main questions posed by SPPs are precisely *what is* self-care, *how to* engage in self-care, and *how often* engage in self-care. While early on in their professional development, SPPs seem to seek out easy-to-follow instructions related to self-care practices, however, self-care does not and cannot work in a prescriptive manner (Quartiroli, Etzel, et al., 2019a; Quartiroli, Wagstaff, & Thelwell, 2021a).

Engaging in self-care is a deeply individual endeavour and self-care practices are not universal and cannot be reduced to a finite list, one-size-fits-all, set of prescriptive recommendations. Instead, SPPs are encouraged to look inwards to their own personal values and needs to understand, develop, and implement practices that fit such values and needs. This personal exploration also enables SPPs to engage in practices that will be sustained across their career span and contribute to long-term successful engagement in self-care. Through self-discovery, awareness, and reflection, SPPs can develop a clear understanding of what their values are and consequently develop self-care strategies and practices that align with them. It is only by engaging in this process that SPPs can start conceptualising and developing their self-care plan, and it is only by extending this process throughout one's career span that this plan can be adapted, modified, adjusted, and maintained.

How Does Self-Care Work?

Regardless of the self-care practices and strategies developed and implemented by SPPs, recent research data suggest that effective SPPs' self-care practices are underpinned by a set of foundational mechanisms (Martin et al., 2022; Quartiroli, Etzel, et al., 2019a). Comprised of self-awareness, self-reflection, psychological flexibility, and interconnection of one's self-care practices, these mechanisms serve to build the foundations of self-care practices that are underpinned by an understanding of oneself, an understanding of one's needs in relation to self-care as well as an appreciation for the holistic nature of self-care.

Self-Awareness

Self-awareness is the most salient of these mechanisms as it enables a practitioner to understand their own personal needs and to develop and implement subsequent self-care skills and techniques that serve to meet these needs. Moreover, for the practitioner with established self-care, greater levels of self-awareness may improve their ability to evaluate, and sense-check how aligned their existing self-care practices and personal needs are. Since self-care practices evolve alongside career maturation and the new challenges and demands that may come with that, it is important that not only neophyte practitioners explore their self-awareness to best generate self-care practices that meet their needs, but that SPPs across the career span maintain levels of self-awareness that afford them an insight into in how existing self-care practices meet their evolving needs.

Self-Reflection

Self-reflection is the key to integrating all these considerations into a coherent and effective self-care practice. Reflections on one's own personal story, on the purpose of self-care, on core personal values, and our awareness of the self are key to deliberate engagement in effective self-care. Self-reflective exercises allow practitioners to review, plan, and refine their self-care practices and goals. They have been reported by practitioners to hugely influence their understanding and awareness of their self-care needs (Martin et al., 2021), and some scholars have even discussed the perception of self-reflection as a form of self-care (Quartiroli, Wagstaff, Zakrajsek, et al., 2021b). It is of paramount importance that practitioners across the career span develop self-reflection and meta self-reflection skills so that they may explore, become aware of, and monitor their own personal values, professional beliefs, and subsequent effective and intentional self-care practice. The first of these steps may be for the practitioners to engage in a deliberate exploration of self and their own journey. While there are a variety of approaches to this practice, we recommend SPPs to engage in a modified version of the McAdams' Life Story (McAdams, 2001). The Life Story Interview promotes self-exploration of authenticity, fundamental beliefs and values, and visions for the future. See Table 11.1.

Grounded in this process of self-exploration, SPPs may choose to engage in reflective exercises focused on developing some clarity about their own individual values. Deliberately engaging in this process of self-reflection may lead SPPs to develop an in-depth understanding of the main values leading their life as well as a greater awareness of their adherence to these values in their day-by-day. Finally, as presented in the definition offered in Box 11.1, a clear understanding of one's value represents a principal bedrock for the development, implementation, and maintenance of self-care. In Box 11.2, we offer a few suggestions in terms of reflective

TABLE 11.1 McAdams' Life Story Interview Outline – Modified

Interview Component	Description
Life Chapters	When I bring to mind the story of my life, the distinct chapters that would make up the book telling my story are… (Provide a title and a brief summary of the plot.) The end of one chapter and the beginning of the next is marked by…

Key Scenes
  High Point
  Low Point
  Turning Point
  Positive Childhood Scene
  Negative Childhood Scene
  Vivid Adolescent Scene
  Vivid Adult Scene
  One Other Important Scene
	In an especially significant scene in my life… (What happened, how did you feel, what were you thinking about, and who else was there?) This scene stands out in my life story because… (Why did you choose it? What might it say about who you were or are now?)

Life Challenge	The most significant challenge I have faced in my life is… It came to be because… I have addressed/understood/coped with this by…
Future Script	When thinking about the next chapter in my life, I see… I am heading towards… My goals are… I plan to achieve them by…

Ideological Setting
  Religious
  Political
  Most Important Value
	When thinking about my beliefs about life and the world, my most important personal, spiritual, or ethical values are… I came to these values by… My most important values around politics and/or social relationships are… I developed these through… Looking broadly, I think the most important value in life is … because…

Life Theme	Thinking back over this exercise, do you see a theme or motif that runs through the story of your life? What might it be?

Adapted from McAdams & Guo, 2014.
According to the Study of Lives Research Group at Northwestern University website, the Life Story II protocol is free to use and does not require explicit permission. Researchers should feel free to adapt that instrument, or any of the other interview protocols, to the specific needs of their own projects.

questions that may facilitate SPPs to engage in this reflective experience. Finally, grounded in their newly developed in-depth understanding and awareness of themselves, their journey, and their own values, we encourage SPPs to engage in further reflective exercises focused on their own current approach to self-care. These reflective experiences may also guide the SPP to develop a greater awareness of their engagement in self-care practices and of the challenges and barriers they

> **BOX 11.1 DEFINITION OF SELF-CARE**
>
> SPSC is the purposeful engagement in activities grounded in one's values. It involves prioritizing, developing, preserving, protecting, monitoring and restoring holistic (i.e., physical, psychological, social, spiritual, and emotional) health, wellbeing and satisfaction with work and life.
>
> (Quartiroli, Wagstaff, & Thelwell, 2021a)

> **BOX 11.2 REFLECTIVE QUESTIONS ON VALUES**
>
> What is most important to me?
> Am I living in line with my values?
> How have my values changed over time?
> How are my values integrated into the way I care for myself?
> Does my self-care address my holistic health and wellbeing?

> **BOX 11.3 REFLECTIVE QUESTIONING ON SELF-CARE**
>
> What does self-care mean to me?
> What makes self-care important in my journey?
> How does self-care fit my life?
> How do I embrace self-care?
> What is my self-care practice like?
> How did it come to be this way?
> What aspects would I like to improve?
> What nourishes and/or constrains what I do?
>
> Adapted from Anderson et al. (2004)

perceived as hindering their self-care and limiting their engagement in self-care practices (see Box 11.3).

Psychological Flexibility

Psychological flexibility represents another foundational mechanism underpinning effective self-care across a practitioner's career span. Here, we refer to elements of flexibility present in both the practitioner and the self-care plans that they develop. Given the uniqueness of their working lives in comparison to other psychology professionals (Andersen et al., 2001; Stapleton et al., 2010), it is important that SPPs develop and maintain an element of flexibility in experiencing and implementing their self-care practices. For example, SPPs often travel with teams abroad, to training camps or competitions, facing the expectation for them to be always available (Williams & Andersen, 2012). In these situations, it is important for SPPs to anticipate that the same self-care practices that are employed on a weekly basis cannot be continued whilst working away and that instead, alternative or modified practices may need to be implemented (Quartiroli, Etzel, et al., 2019a). In such a case, SPPs must then exercise a degree of flexibility in both their thinking toward the likelihood of engaging in their regular self-care and in the formulation of their self-care plan whilst away. A self-care plan that has room to be modified and is adaptable, as well as an SPP who understands the need for such flexibility, is far more likely to experience more positive outcomes for their personal and professional wellbeing than self-care plans that are rigid or immovable.

Interconnection of One's Self-Care Practices

The final underpinning mechanism of self-care is the interconnection of various self-care skills and techniques. Self-care cannot be effective as one technique or approach in isolation. Rather, several interconnected skills, techniques, or approaches will better serve an SPP in developing a self-care practice that is holistic in nature (Martin et al., 2021). This is not to say that self-care practices must require a multitude of elements, but it is important that self-care practices are varied and tend to the individual's emotional, physical, social, and psychological needs. Simply relying on one single self-care practice may not be sufficient to prepare a practitioner with the requisite resources to conduct their role in an ethical and competent manner (Martin et al., 2021; Quartiroli, Wagstaff, & Thelwell, 2021a). Given the many possibilities and combinations of self-care activities, it is important for SPPs to explore how they select the self-care practice activities that are most relevant to their personal and professional needs and how these practices are implemented in a coherent, holistic, and effective manner.

Barriers to Implementing a Self-Care Plan

While the body of evidence relating to the benefits of developing a self-care practice is compelling, SPPs have reported that there are challenges that hinder the implementation of self-care practices as well as the development of effective self-care plans (Quartiroli, Etzel, et al., 2019a; Quartiroli, Wagstaff, & Thelwell, 2021a). Primarily, extrinsic factors associated with the uniqueness of the sport psychology profession may pose a significant challenge to self-care. Having to seek and remain aware of professional opportunities, coping with unsupportive professional environments, and continually striving to meet clients' expectations and needs make it paramount that SPPs devote time and energy to their self-care (Quartiroli, Etzel, et al., 2019a; Quartiroli, Wagstaff, & Thelwell, 2021a).

In addition to the specific professional factors, SPPs may also experience a series of barriers to their self-care that limit their ability to live a healthy lifestyle. Among these hindering factors, SPPs list a lack of personal and professional social support, a lack of time, a lack of self-compassion, and awareness of their own self-care needs. Finally, SPPs also perceive their conscious or unconscious tendency to professionally over-commit, combined with their inability to set reasonable personal and professional boundaries, as hindering their self-care by sacrificing themselves and their own lives for their professional journey. Similarly, to self-care practices, this list of challenges potentially faced by SPPs is not meant to be a finite list. SPPs reported encountering most of these challenges at one stage or another. As such, SPPs who are considering exploring their self-care for the first time may use these reports as a way to prepare for possible bumps in the road ahead (Quartiroli, Wagstaff, & Thelwell, 2021a). However, SPPs must engage and sustain the abovementioned self-explorative journey so that, in addition to identifying their own most beneficial self-care practices, they can also identify potential unique challenges present in their lives and consequentially adopt these practices.

The Payoff

With multiple challenges and barriers to overcome, as well as the deliberate, conscious engagement required for effective self-care, aspiring and neophyte SPPs might wonder if it is worth giving all the necessary effort. The simple conclusion from the research is yes. Investigations from both general psychology and sport psychology have shown the positive effects of engaging with self-care (Quartiroli, Etzel, et al., 2019a; Rupert & Dorociak, 2019). SPPs who engage in self-care report greater wellbeing and positive affect in their personal life, as well as improved quality and effectiveness in their professional practice, leading to an improved professional experience. More broadly, engaging in self-care practices is associated with increases in wellbeing, compassion satisfaction, and quality of life and decreases in stress and negative affect (Dorociak et al., 2017; Quartiroli, Wagstaff, Zakrajsek, et al., 2021b; Rupert & Dorociak, 2019).

Despite the many challenges and work-related stressors, most practitioners can manage such pressures well enough to function competently and to ensure for themselves a long-lived and positive career (Quartiroli & Etzel, 2012; Quartiroli, Etzel, et al., 2019a; Quartiroli, Knight, et al., 2019b). Scholars have argued that those psychology practitioners able to sustain a long-lasting and effective career have learned to attend to the personal self, as well as the professional one, allowing them to experience their professional journey positively (Rønnestad & Skovholt, 2013; Tod, 2007). Exploring this parallelism between personal and professional life in SPPs, Quartiroli and colleagues highlighted the inextricably interrelated relationship existing between SPSC and SPPs' professional quality of life (Quartiroli, Wagstaff, Zakrajsek, et al., 2021b). Practitioners along the career development spectrum have described how taking care of themselves is paramount for the enjoyment of their professional experiences, and in not doing so, there is a negative impact on SPPs' ability to embrace their work meaningfully and positively and to provide effective services to their clients (Martin et al., 2021; Quartiroli, Wagstaff, Zakrajsek, et al., 2021b).

The Self-Care Plan

The processes of developing awareness about oneself and their values, about what self-care is in one's life, about what makes engaging in self-care relevant in one's journey, about identifying the self-care practices that, as grounded in their personal

---

BOX 11.4 BRINGING IT ALL TOGETHER – THE BEGINNING OF A SELF-CARE PLAN

1. Reflections on one's journey – see Table 11.1
2. Reflections on one's values – see Box 11.2
3. Reflections on one's self-care – see Box 11.3

Finally, to develop a self-care plan grounded in one's values and to be able to bring together a series of practices that can be assimilated within each other and in the individual's life, it is important for SPPs to also consider how the outcomes of these reflections may be integrated. Some examples of possible higher-level reflective questions are:

Keeping in mind my life story, my values, and worldviews…

1. How does my understanding of self-care fit my past, present, and future journey?
2. What am I am currently doing to support my wellbeing?
3. What self-care practices can I implement to prioritise my wellbeing?
4. How can I develop self-care practice that aligns with who I am and my values?

Considering what is presented in this chapter…

1. What can I do to realign my life to my values?
2. How can I engage in self-care practices that align with who I am and my values?
3. How can re-assess my current journey to integrate these reflections?
4. What areas of my own journey need to be the primary focus of my personal work?
5. …..

---

values, would fit the individual SPP's journey, and about the factors limiting their implementation could be brought together in the act of developing a self-care plan.

While it is possible for practitioners to identify different models to develop a self-care plan, as described throughout this chapter, we believe that self-care is a *purposeful engagement in activities grounded in one's values* and therefore an intimately personal journey. For this reason, we believe that offering a prescriptive approach to the development of a self-care plan is neither useful nor necessary, and instead, it may become potentially detrimental to the process of self-exploration needed by SPPs to develop the foundational awareness of themselves, their journey, their values, and their worldview on self-care. For this reason, in Box 11.4, we tried to bring together in a more succinct manner what we presented throughout the chapter in the hope that this will help the readers to begin the self-exploratory journey needed to develop their own self-care.

Conclusion

Based on the results of our scholarly efforts, we can conclude that SPPs should consider engaging in self-care as it is beneficial in a multitude of ways (e.g., greater wellbeing, higher levels of positive affect, flourishing, compassion satisfaction, quality of life, professional wellbeing, and practice outcomes). Failing to engage in self-care may lead to SPPs experiencing negative outcomes, which may result in engaging in practices that are harmful to clients, themselves, their reputations, or the profession. For this reason, practitioners must take on the personal and professional responsibility to develop and maintain their own wellness by actively – and not just retroactively – engaging in self-care.

Being grounded in personal values, self-care should be intrinsically driven and individual in nature and must become a foundational aspect of SPPs' personal and professional journey. For this reason, as already indicated, instead of directing SPPs to a prescriptive list of *ready-to-go* practices that they must engage in, we strongly encourage them to engage in a variety of self-explorative activities that may enable them to develop the required self-awareness of their core personal values, critical to the development of effective and individualised self-care practices. By engaging in this process, SPPs may be able to identify and decide for themselves which specific activities are beneficial for them. By engaging in this process, SPPs will also become more aware of the potential unique set of challenges and barriers they may face or are already facing which hinder their own self-care, considering them as part of the development of their individualised self-care practices. This process can be applied across the career span, from neophyte practitioners developing a self-care plan for the very first time through to experienced and expert SPPs seeking to revisit, re-evaluate, and sense-check their established practices.

We acknowledge that the scholarly work we referred to throughout the chapter and in which we ground our work and the suggestions for reflective exercises as well as for developing a self-care plan offered in this chapter aimed to keep in consideration cultural differences. However, it is important to highlight that many of the constructs and activities we present here may be heavily influenced by Westernised approaches to practice and life and may not be directly transferable to other cultural contexts and backgrounds. We recognise the importance of humbly engaging in an exploration of self that also keeps in consideration the cultural self. While we understand self-care as intimately personal and therefore unique for each individual, we also recognise that the cultural context and background of the single SPPs as well as their cultural intersectionality play an important role in their personal development as well as in the conceptualization of self-care and in the implementation of their self-care practices.

Take-Home Message

From what the research to date allows us to conclude, the bottom line is that self-care must be grounded in one's personal values. To identify one's values and to identify how to best meet one's self-care needs, practitioners are encouraged to purposefully engage in the process of reflection and actively seek to develop their self-awareness so that they may be better equipped to prioritise, develop, preserve, monitor, and restore their holistic health, wellbeing, and satisfaction within their professional and personal lives. Armed with this information, it is likely that practitioners will be able to better identify the types of self-care that will be the most meaningful and impactful for them. To illustrate this with an example of how core values may be translated into meaningful self-care practices, SPPs who perceive love and compassion to be personal values may look to tailor their self-care to include activities, behaviours and intentions that are driven by that value, such as dedicating time to spend with loved ones and engaging in self-compassionate practices. It is important that these practices are congruent with one's values and fit one's personal and professional journey. While self-care is somewhat *aspirational*, as any individual may strive toward it, SPPs must keep in mind that self-care practices must be realistic and practical as they need to fit a professional life that is already characterised by intrinsic and unique challenges.

An individual's self-care, similar to a mosaic or tapestry, is a unique and complex expression of one's personal values, self-care needs, and a myriad of behaviours, intentions, and activities that are guided by and serve to align with such values and needs. To gain clarity upon the arrangement, frequency, and intensity of their self-care practices, SPPs are encouraged to purposefully dedicate time and attention to self-exploration through reflection to maximise self-care's potential positive and protective effects.

References

Acker, G. M. (2012). Burnout among mental health care providers. *Journal of Social Work*, *12*(5), 475–490. https://doi.org/dgc9k6.

Anderson, A. G., Knowles, Z., & Gilbourne, D. (2004). Reflective practice: A review of concepts, models, and practical implications for enhancing the practice of applied sport psychologists. *The Sport Psychologist*, *18*(2), 188–203. https://doi.org/dm3q.

Andersen, M. B., Van Raalte, J. L., & Brewer, B. W. (2001). Sport psychology service delivery: Staying ethical while keeping loose. *Professional Psychology: Research and Practice, 32*, 12–18. https://doi.org/cn3gvs.

Baker, E. K. (2003). *Caring for ourselves: A therapist's guide to personal and professional wellbeing.* American Psychological Association Press.

Barnett, J. E., Baker, E. K., Elman, N. S., & Schoener, G. R. (2007). In pursuit of wellness: The self-care imperative. *Professional Psychology: Research and Practice, 38*, 603–612. https://doi.org/dwpd3j.

Butler, L. D., Carello, J., & Maguin, E. (2017). Trauma, stress, and self-care in clinical training: Predictors of burnout, decline in health status, secondary traumatic stress symptoms, and compassion satisfaction. *Psychological Trauma: Theory, Research, Practice, and Policy, 9*(4), 416–424. https://doi.org/gbn6fq.

Colman, D. E., Echon, R., Lemay, M. S., McDonald, J., Smith, K. R., Spencer, J., & Swift, J. K. (2016). The efficacy of self-care for graduate students in professional psychology: A meta-analysis. *Training and Education in Professional Psychology, 10*(4), 188–197. https://doi.org/f9bhjx.

Cropley, B., Baldock, L., Mellalieu, S. D., Neil, R., Wagstaff, C. R. D., & Wadey, R. (2016). Coping with the demands of professional practice: Sport psychology consultants' perspectives. *The Sport Psychologist, 30*(3), 290–302. https://doi.org/dt8x.

Cropley, B., Hanton, S., Miles, A., & Niven, A. (2010). Exploring the relationship between effective and reflective practice in applied sport psychology. *The Sport Psychologist, 24*(4), 521–541. https://doi.org/dm5c.

Dorociak, K. E., Rupert, P. A., & Zahniser, E. (2017). Work life, wellbeing, and self-care across the professional lifespan of psychologists. *Professional Psychology: Research and Practice, 48*(6), 429–437. https://doi.org/gcv77c.

Goncher, I. D., Sherman, M. F., Barnett, J. E., & Haskins, D. (2013). Programmatic perceptions of self-care emphasis and quality of life among graduate trainees in clinical psychology: The mediational role of self-care utilization. *Training and Education in Professional Psychology, 7*(1), 53–60. https://doi.org/f4r6qf.

Knapp, S. J., VandeCreek, L. D., & Fingerhut, R. (2017). *Practical ethics for psychologists: A positive approach* (3rd ed.). American Psychological Association. https://doi.org/f6hv.

Malinowski, A. J. (2014). *Self-care for the mental health practitioner: The theory, research, and practice of preventing and addressing the occupational hazards of the profession.* Jessica Kingsley Publishers.

Martin, D. R. F., Quartiroli, A., & Wagstaff, C. R. D. (2021). An exploration of sport psychology professional quality of life in neophyte practitioners. *The Sport Psychologist.* Advanced Online Publication. https://doi.org/g52w.

Martin, D. R. F., Quartiroli, A., & Wagstaff, C. R. D. (2022). A qualitative exploration of neophyte sport psychologist practitioners self-care experiences and perceptions. *Journal of Applied Sport Psychology.* Advanced Online Publication: https://doi.org/hp2q.

McAdams, D. P. (2001). The psychology of life stories. *Review of General Psychology, 5*(2), 100–122. https://doi.org/fnhdfz.

McAdams, D. P., & Guo, J. (2014). How shall I live? Constructing a life story in the college years. *New Directions for Higher Education, 2014*(166), 15–23. https://doi.org/gn8h96.

McCormack, H. M., MacIntyre, T. E., O'Shea, D., Herring, M. P., & Campbell, M. J. (2018). The prevalence and cause (s) of burnout among applied psychologists: A systematic review. *Frontiers in Psychology, 9*, 1897. https://doi.org/gfg3tw.

Norcross, J. C., & VandenBos, G. R. (2018). *Leaving it at the office: A guide to psychotherapist self-care* (2nd ed.). Guilford Press.

Poczwardowski, A. (2019). Deconstructing sport and performance psychology consultant: Expert, person, performer, and self-regulator. *International Journal of Sport and Exercise Psychology, 17*(5), 427–444. https://doi.org/dzgk.

Quartiroli, A., & Etzel, E. (2012, August 2–5). Ethics and self-care of sport and exercise psychology professionals. Paper presented at the APA 2012 Convention, Orlando, FL, United States.

Quartiroli, A., Etzel, E. F., Knight, S. M., & Zakrajsek, R. A. (2019a). Self-care as key to others' care: The perspectives of globally situated experienced senior-level sport psychology practitioners. *Journal of Applied Sport Psychology, 31*, 147–167. http://doi.org/dzgm.

Quartiroli, A., Knight, S. M., Etzel, E. F., & Zakrajsek, R. A. (2019b). Fostering and sustaining sport psychology professional quality of life: The perspectives of senior-level, experienced sport psychology practitioners. *The Sport Psychologist, 33*(2), 148–158. https://doi.org/dtxs.

Quartiroli, A., Wagstaff, C. R. D., & Thelwell, R. (2021a). The what and the how of self-care for sport psychology practitioners: A Delphi study. *Journal of Applied Sport Psychology*. Advanced Online Publication. https://doi.org/gthc.

Quartiroli, A., Wagstaff, C. R. D., Zakrajsek, R. A., Knight, S. M., & Etzel, E. F. (2021b). The role of self-care and professional quality of life in sustaining a long-lasting career in sport psychology: A qualitative exploration. *Journal of Applied Sport Psychology*. Advanced Online Publication. https://doi.org/f7bw.

Rønnestad, M. H. & Skovholt, T. M. (2013). *The developing practitioner. Growth and stagnation of therapists and counselors.* Routledge.

Rupert, P. A., & Dorociak, K. E. (2019). Self-care, stress, and wellbeing among practicing psychologists. *Professional Psychology: Research and Practice, 50*(5), 343–350. https://doi.org/gg9n8r.

Santana, M. C., & Fouad, N. A. (2017). Development and validation of a self-care behavior inventory. *Training and Education in Professional Psychology, 11*(3), 140–145. https://doi.org/gbsdmh.

Skovholt, T. M., & Trotter-Mathison, M. (2016). *Counseling and psychotherapy: Investigating practice from scientific, historical, and cultural perspectives. The resilient practitioner: Burnout prevention and self-care strategies for counselors, therapists, teachers, and health professionals* (3rd ed.). Routledge.

Stapleton, A. B., Hankes, D. M., Hays, K. F., & Parham, W. D. (2010). Ethical dilemmas in sport psychology: A dialogue on the unique aspects impacting practice. *Professional Psychology: Research and Practice, 41*(2), 143–152. https://doi.org/bgpzv3.

Stevanovic, P., & Rupert, P. A. (2004). Career-Sustaining Behaviors, Satisfactions, and Stresses of Professional Psychologists. *Psychotherapy: Theory, Research, Practice, Training, 41*(3), 301–309. https://doi.org/fsbrbz.

Tod, D. (2007). The long and winding road: Professional development in sport psychology. *The Sport Psychologist, 21*, 94–108. https://doi.org/dt86.

Venart, E., Vassos, S., & Pitcher-Heft, H. (2007). What individual counselors can do to sustain wellness. *The Journal of Humanistic Counseling, Education and Development, 46*(1), 50–65. https://doi.org/fzg85k.

Waumsley, J. A., Hemmings, B., & Payne, S. M. (2010). Work-life balance, role conflict and the UK sport psychology consultant. *The Sport Psychologist, 24*, 245–262. http://doi.org/dt88.

Williams, D. E., & Andersen, M. B. (2012). Identity, wearing many hats, and boundary blurring: The mindful psychologist on the way to the Olympic and Paralympic Games. *Journal of Sport Psychology in Action, 3*(2), 139–152.

Wise, E. H., Hersh, M. A., & Gibson, C. L. (2012). Ethics, self-care and well-being for psychologists: Re-envisioning the stress-distress continuum. *Professional Psychology, Research and Practice, 43*(5), 487–494. http://dx.doi.org/10.1037/a0029446.

Zahniser, E., Rupert, P. A., & Dorociak, K. E. (2017). Self-care in clinical psychology graduate training. *Training and Education in Professional Psychology, 11*(4), 283–289. https://doi.org/gckdk4.

12

'DOING THE WORK'

Broaching Culture and Diversity in Sport, Exercise, and Performance Psychology Consultancy Practice – An Intersectional Consideration for Working with Stakeholders of Marginalised Racial and Ethnic Identities

Shameema Yousuf and Rob Owens

Broaching Culture and Diversity in Sport, Exercise, and Performance Psychology Consultancy Practice

In this chapter, the authors explore how "doing the work" in sport, exercise, and performance psychology (SEPP) consultancy is contingent on how well consultants can broach issues of culture and diversity with stakeholders (athletes, coaches, athletic staff), especially when their lived experience may include multiple, intersecting marginalised identities. The authors consider it important to advocate for practices that are inclusive of multicultural perspectives. One way is to draw from a social justice framework and study the personal, social, and organisational issues that affect consultants in their interactions with peers and clients; and offer guidance and practical advice on how consultants-in-training and those more experienced, hereby referred to as practitioners, can co-create relationships with clients that are meaningful, intentional, and authentic. These issues are considered from a racial and ethnic intersectional lens of marginalised identities, although the authors recognise that when speaking to the need for inclusive practice and diversity, it implies much more than consideration of race and ethnicity.

Broaching conversations related to culture, diversity, and inclusion may indeed present some difficulty and discomfort. Developing expertise in multicultural psychology and cultural perspectives in SEPP requires practitioners to commit to developing competency in the field. Recognising this need, practitioners developing cultural competence should acknowledge that it has no finite destination and is rather more of a lifelong journey on which one is continually exploring their worldview, by self-reflecting, and engaging in cultural reflexivity to inform practices (Quartiroli et al., 2020). As will be explained later in this chapter, broaching race, ethnicity, and culture (the when, where, how, and why to do it) is contextual, fluid, and dynamic. It necessitates an understanding of the self, appreciating the

DOI: 10.4324/9781003196280-15

client's worldview, and a willingness to engage in uncomfortable, yet crucial conversations. It also provides for rich opportunities where applied SEPP practitioners can co-create spaces with clients that are authentic, growth fostering, and transformative for the client and the practitioner. Developing cultural competence is an ethical responsibility (Fisher & Anders, 2010) with some associations' ethics codes outlining principles of social justice and responsibility, and standards that guide multicultural and diversity awareness in professional practice.[1] Additionally, when planning and selecting interventions, the authors posit that by developing cultural competence, one aligns with "avoiding harm".

In this chapter, the term practitioner will be used to refer to those who coach, counsel, and consult with elite performers and organisations, and readers are encouraged to seek an understanding of the differences. The reader will gain understanding of (1) the meaning of multicultural psychology; (2) consider some of the theoretical considerations when working with diverse ethnic individuals of intersectional backgrounds; (3) learn about the work that practitioners need to commit to in their own growth, and (4) gain practical solutions to anti-discrimination practice.

Multiculturalism and the Need to Work from an Intersectional Lens

Multicultural psychology is the study of human behaviour and includes topics related to identity development, acculturation and assimilation, prejudice and stereotyping, and developing multicultural competence. Understanding multicultural aspects of human identity is important as SEPP practitioners may find themselves working with individuals of different cultural backgrounds and identities (Cunningham, 2019). These include race, ethnicity, gender, sexual orientation, socio-economic status (SES), age, spirituality, geographical location, nationality, and language (Comas-Diaz, 2011; Oglesby, 2010), and the intersections amongst these social constructs. Dimensions of identity and their intersections, render different cultural perspectives, and influence the behaviours of sport and physical activity participants (Ryba, 2017), and culturally informed intervention strategies employed by practitioners, can impact engagement, performance and wellbeing outcomes, and the therapeutic relationship (Comas-Diaz, 2011; Fisher & Anders, 2010; Ryba, 2017). Hence, an understanding of multicultural psychology and cultural sport psychology is a necessary antecedent in the provision of psychological services in SEPP. Practitioners who lack multicultural competence may ignore differences in cultural identity and are likely to misinterpret cultural norms and overgeneralise or stereotype (McGannon & Schinke, 2013; Parham 2005). They could rely on monocultural and Eurocentric approaches driven by values of the Western White middle class that do not align with stakeholder values (Parham 2005). This can also result in decreased sport participation and distress among athletes of more collective cultures (Blodgett et al., 2011; Parham, 2005; Ryba & Schinke, 2009).

Contextualising the Work: Interrogating Sport through an Intersectional Lens

The intersectional experiences of marginalised racial and ethnic stakeholders in sport, and how oppression negatively impacts the health, wellbeing and performance of these stakeholders, is the focus of this chapter. Since no single variable can describe the nuanced experiences of athletes or other stakeholders in sport (Parham 2005), interrelated constructs of race, ethnicity, SES, international–transnational status, and spirituality are examined through theoretical frameworks of cultural humility (Hook et al., 2013) and intersectionality (Crenshaw, 1989). The purpose is to provide practitioners with a deeper understanding of the experiences of marginalised individuals in sport.

Examining the intersectional experiences of marginalised individuals within sport, the practitioner may have several roles that include being a supporter, carer, facilitator (Friesen & Orlick, 2011), and even advocate. The authors posit that cultural competence can provide impetus for practitioners to lead policy work in sport organisations and associations, work with senior leaders and staff teams within sport environments to implement inclusive structures and practices that dismantle discriminatory barriers, educate and mentor other practitioners, and work with marginalised athletes to empower them (McGannon & Johnson, 2009).

Intersectionality describes the social and political power relations of intertwined individual identity characteristics producing distinct systems of privilege and discrimination. Consequently, practitioners are encouraged to go beyond the development of cultural competence by considering intersectional cultural humility (Ortega & Faller, 2011; Tervalon & Murray-Garcia, 1998). Cultural humility and cultural competence differ, in so much as humility surrenders to never fully knowing how an individual's culture may differ from one's own, whereas competence assumes defined attributes (Krane & Waldron, 2021; Quartiroli et al., 2020). Hence, in practice, this leads to the continuous need to explore with curiosity. Considering the complexity of cultural practice, it is essential that practitioners also consider some of the stigmas and stereotypes associated with different group belonging. This includes examining the interrelational and intersectional experiences that are considered within the constructs of race, ethnicity, SES, and international/transnational/diaspora status, with the latter referring to aspects of migration. An extensive overview of intersectionality is beyond the scope of this chapter; however, the authors encourage practitioners to expand their knowledge of this topic by engaging in continuing professional development, education, and training offered through sport psychology associations and social justice organisations.

Race, Racism, and Eurocentrism

Race, a social construct, categorises individuals based on ancestral lineage, and is historically constructed based on phenotypic characteristics by groups and cultures who considered them significant. The socio-historical processes that categorise perceived physical differences, such as skin colour and hair texture, are what render it a social construct (Hylton, 2013). The interrelation between race and racism through other social characteristics (e.g., gender, class, ethnicity, sexuality, geography, spirituality) must also be considered as they correspond to significant disparities in and among social groups' experiences.

Scholars posit that practitioners often engage with a race-blind approach that treats all athletes the same (Butryn, 2002; Schinke & Hanrahan, 2009), where the dominance of Eurocentric practices in SEPP assumes equality across society. An explanation used to condemn this dominance in applied sport psychology is Critical Race Theory (CRT). It highlights racism exists and persists because it is embedded in institutions to protect and preserve the privileges of those who are White identifying (Bell, 1976; Hylton, 2013). Considering CRT, the construct "white privilege" first structured by Peggy Mcintosh (1989) examined the privileges afforded to white people, describing the "knapsack" of tools, maps, and cultural codes that white individuals, in particular, white men, have in navigating society, that were unavailable to Black women. This entitlement for white men is an unearned privilege. In the field of sport psychology, as far as one can tell visually, many of the positions held by psychologists on teams in the UK, for instance, as well as the positions of coaches and managers are held by white individuals (Farenet, 2014).[2] If practitioners and coaches are ill-informed in cultural practice, the question remains what harm may be inflicted on those whose experiences may differ from the hegemonic view and Eurocentric monocultural approaches, and who are maintaining the privileges and superiority of the white race?

In essence, Eurocentrism in sport psychology is preserved because it is underpinned by racism, where research, teaching, and practices until the past decade have remained systematically and consistently unchallenged and uncorrected, with the multicultural perspective excluded. Many mainstream sport psychology texts, for example, exclude collective ideologies and theories of motivations, self-esteem, and learning, thereby preserving the importance of "self" or individualism aligned with monoculturalism and Eurocentrism, above collectivist practice. Racism and Eurocentrism have also impacted professionals as they develop a career in the field (Gunter, 2019; Yousuf, 2022). A growing momentum in cultural sport psychology provides the impetus to address some of the disparities through several other theories and principles that include feminism, diaspora, transnationalism, neo-racism, and Islam when considering the interrelational and intersecting racialised identities and experiences.

Intersectionality and Women in Sport

Being Black and Female. Historically, feminist theory and practice were critiqued for failing "to respond to experiences of women of colour and non-heterosexual working class and/or disabled women" (Buffington & Lai, 2011, p. 3). The hegemonic western feminist debate centred on the differences of other women of cultural belonging, marginalised ethnic origins and the "third world", being transformed and colonised (Mohanty, 1988, p. 62). For example, Black feminist thought (Collins,

1998, 2005; hooks, 1981) emerged from women of colour who believed that white women in the feminist movement were focusing on gender without considering how race, class, sexuality, and other social identities contributed to the marginalisation of women. Intersectionality, defined as the various ways in which gender and race interact to shape the experiences of Black women (Crenshaw, 1989), became a focal point and a means for explaining how the lived experiences of women of colour were structured on gender, race, and class oppression, and how traditional feminist thought (first wave and second wave feminisms) ignored the privileges afforded to white women based on their race. Third wave feminism sought to remedy the harm created by slavery, imperialism, capitalism, and colonialism, and led to the development of not only intersectionality but also trans-feminism (Califia, 1997; Koyama, 2001) and transnational feminisms (Grewel & Kaplan, 1994). Transnational feminist thought critiqued the notion that white western feminist thoughts and ideas can act to liberate all women. Considering the intersection of gender and race, misogynoir (Bailey & Trudy, 2018) speaks more accurately to the inequities faced by Black women of indigenous African descent (hereby referred to as Black women) in society. While the construct has been applied to all women of colour, the authors contend that the unique experiences of Black women from differing national cultures must also be examined independently, without mass grouping.

In sport, Black women may face being stigmatised as the "angry Black woman" such as in the case of Serena Williams with caricatures that depict them in an unflattering manner. They may be called names such as the case with teenager Alice Dearing, a Great Britain swimmer, and Sienna Devow, a 12-year-old basketball player of Aboriginal descent in Australia. Additionally, practitioners are also urged to consider these unique contexts and experiences through a socio-political national lens, since experiences in one part of the world may differ greatly from another and are often shaped by historical political ideologies in a region. As detailed already, when viewed through a hegemonic lens, it is essential that practitioners consider the multi-layered cultural backdrop of an environment and the client.

Islam and Feminism in Applied Sport Psychology. Analysing the convergence of Islam and feminism (Barlas, 2008; Seedat, 2013), one must be aware of the multiple forms of convergence that allows for an understanding of historical overlaps between the two, while being aware not to preclude other ways of being Muslim and feminist (Seedat, 2013). Several authors argue against the single terminology of Islamic feminism suggesting that by doing so, Islamic traditions are set aside (Seedat, 2013). Indeed, considering the history of feminist sport psychology, there has been little discussion and research to discuss and examine Muslim female experiences through a faith-based approach, though as proposed through this chapter, it is imperative that practitioners improve the focus on women and marginalised groups.

Considering variable experiences and cultural beliefs amongst Muslim women, the authors assert that discussions on Muslim women's experiences, and programming in sport psychology for Muslim women, must be considered without a "one size fits all" approach. For instance, the majority of UK Muslims come from immigrant and diaspora backgrounds such as majority identities from origins in Pakistan,

Bangladesh, Yemen, Syria, and Somalia. Between these countries and societies alone, there may be variations in gender norms. In addition, in the UK, there are also large variations in the gender norms within their adopted home country (Knott, 2017c). Consequently, values, cultures, backgrounds, and languages differ amongst Muslim women and are linked to different upbringings and lifestyles. In view of this, the way in which Islam is interpreted into their lifestyles that include sport, will vary, given differing values and cultural attitudes (Knott, 2017a).

To illustrate these differences, Muslims may share similar barriers to those of other religions and no religion, such as financial and economic stress, confidence concerns, and balancing commitments, though it is important to recognise that social mobility difficulties despite educational successes are more prevalent amongst Muslims (Di Stasio & Heath, 2019; Stevenson et al., 2017). There are also generational differences and attitudes amongst Muslim women with some younger Muslims having stronger Islamic views than the older generations and vice versa. Many younger generations believe that modernity can improve their faith and hold their right to equal participation, respect, and role in society (Janmohamed, 2016). Some adorn the hijab with comfort in their identity that challenges stereotypical assumptions, seeing it as a symbol that represents assertiveness, defiance, or independence (McKenna & Francis, 2019). The principle of modesty is valued in Islamic society, though this may indeed vary amongst girls and women with some choosing not to wear headdresses (British Broadcasting Corporation, 2009). In the UK, family structures are multigenerational in Muslim societies with household sizes generally larger than other religious groups with more women than the general population taking up the role of looking after home and family (The Muslim Council of Britain, 2015).

In Islam, healthy lifestyles are encouraged for men and women with psychological, emotional, and physical health maintained through diet, activity, and spirituality that includes abstinence from alcohol and tobacco (Rassool, 2014). There has been equal attention to the importance of exercise for boys and girls for good health (McGee & Hardman, 2012), but organisations contend that female sport habits are influenced by cost, perceived inclusivity and lack of diversity, single-sex activities, and clothing policies (Muslimah Sports Association, 2019), with lower levels of participation amongst Muslim women,[3] compared to women of no religion or Christian faith in the UK (Sport England, 2019). While healthy lifestyles are encouraged, the barriers and negative experiences and stereotypes faced by Muslim women impact participation (Knott, 2017c; McGee & Hardman, 2012; Mckenna & Francis, 2019), with Muslim women being more susceptible to illnesses such as diabetes, dementia, and depression (The Muslim Council of Britain, 2015). Such stereotypes and negative experiences include constructing Muslims as a monolithic group (Knott, 2017b), faith-based hatred (Mckenna & Francis, 2019), Islamophobia towards those whose faith is more visible like women wearing hijab and niqab, bans that prohibit Muslim women from participating in national and international sport impacting representation, and feeling disengaged in sport programs (McGee & Hardman, 2012). Being aware of the complexities within a group and faith has practical implications in terms of the numerous ways in which barriers may be present affecting participation, performance, mental health, and wellbeing. Practitioners must consider these in the consulting relationship, so they can better support the client in these areas as well as advocate for, and on behalf of the client if necessary. Failure to recognise these nuances and demonstrate cultural sensitivity/humility may lead to a client being marginalised by Eurocentric and monocultural practices that do not speak to their worldview and cultural identity.

Transnational Perspectives. Considering international differences, practitioners are required to examine the different cultural adaptations that athletes and stakeholders are required to make as they cross boundaries. These individuals maintain strong economic, social, and political connections with their countries of origin (Vertovec, 2009). Historically, *Neo-Racism Theory* explained racism in Europe while CRT explained domestic racism in the USA. Examined through the lens of Neo-Racism Theory, subordination and exclusion of ethnic and immigrant individuals are underpinned by cultural and nationalistic superiority perceiving them to be a threat to national existence (Barker, 1981). In addition, what underpins neo-racism is a rationale for marginalising or assimilating certain non-dominant groups in the dominant cultural group. As such, neo-racism is still racism in that it functions to maintain racial hierarchies of oppression (Spears, 1999).

Consequently, international student athletes and transnational stakeholders with intersecting racial identities may be subjected to marginalisation, which cannot be explained through the lens of CRT, since it does not explain the temporary status of international student athletes and employees. International students who migrate are typically on sojourn, a temporary stay, but their identity may be primed and stereotyped even before their entry through processes that categorise them as non-resident "aliens" in the USA, for example, and the numerous paperwork processes required of them before entering their host nation. Neo-racism in the applied settings can show itself in the form of student athletes being rejected admission to US college, un-objective academic appraisal in the classroom, excessive fees for education in the UK, not being able to gain financial aid or losing it if awarded, and even struggling to find sufficient work given the limited hours work rule applied to international students. The theory may also show itself in negative remarks from faculty or fellow students, and barriers to forming interpersonal relationships in the host society.

Rather than assimilate to overcome the challenges presented within the host country, it is suggested that institutions and practitioners must examine the ways in which international student athletes may be marginalised based on their cultural differences through the lens of the theory (Lee & Rice, 2007). While transformation and transitional adaptation by all international stakeholders, may require repositioning, negotiation of cultural practices as one moves into a host nation, and meaning reconstruction (Ryba et al., 2016), one must support stakeholders to maintain authenticity in their cultural way of being. Such *transnational* experiences of stakeholders may be considered through an intersectional lens in which several systems related to cultural identities of ethnicity, disability, diaspora, and gender intertwine, and stakeholders seek to make meaning of their experiences through several approaches including ethnography (Forber-Pratt, 2017, 2021; Yousuf, 2022).

Essential too, that practitioners appreciate the nuanced cultural narrative of those who seek asylum and are displaced from their homelands. They may continue to recount their identity in terms of being displaced (Sayyid, 2000). Indeed, athletes at international athletic events have been seeking *asylum* for decades (Hart, 2021), and, historically, several are displaced from war-torn nations and impoverished societies, and seek refuge from persecution. Resettling and as *diaspora* communities, these individuals will similarly go through a transitional process where acculturation and adaptation, must be mediated by the practitioner acknowledging and understanding the power present in the therapeutic relationship, validating the experiences of those displaced, and meeting the client where they are in the adaptation process. This requires a counselling approach that considers the intersection of their cultural identities, mental health and performance, while seeking to understand the experiences through a cultural lens, by (a) doing a culturally informed intake (Taylor et al., 2018), (b) using active listening skills, (c) understanding if they need any practical support with, for example, food options, language assistance, and housing difficulties, (d) learning about their faith needs, and (e) doing the work described below.

Doing the Work

Effectively broaching conversations on culture with stakeholders/clients from marginalised racial and ethnic identities requires diligence, cultural competence/humility, and self-reflexivity. Applied sport psychology work can do harm when practitioners are unable to engage in conversations about race, gender, and culture, and ignore the nuanced and multifaceted experiences of individual athletes that contribute to minority stress (Lee et al., 2019). This includes the myriad of ways athletes interact with coaches, managers, teammates, and other service providers like sport dietitians, athletic trainers, strength and conditioning coaches, etc. This also applies to other high-performance domains like the military, business, medicine, and the performing arts. Practitioners who are not (multi)culturally competent and humble, can do damage to the performers they serve by not attending to their needs and the systemic barriers the performer might face within the organisation. Prior to designing performance interventions, practitioners should ask essential cultural questions of themselves as outlined in Box 12.1.

BOX 12.1 ESSENTIAL CULTURAL QUESTIONS FOR PRACTITIONERS TO CONSIDER ABOUT THEIR PRACTICE

Are interventions culturally informed?

- What do I know about the athlete's culture?
  - How do they identify?
  - What is their nationality?

- How do they observe their faith if any?
- What are their belief sets and values?
- What intersectional lenses do I need to consider?
  - How might the athlete's multiple identities influence their belief systems?
- What are my worldviews and what preconceived notions do I have?
  - Have I done some self-reflexivity work? (discussed in the chapter)
  - Have I researched historical and political processes of systems that may have affected the client?
- How will all these things affect how I design and implement interventions for this particular athlete or performer?
  - What theories may be necessary to consider when conceptualising your treatment and interventions?
- How do I engage with stakeholders in a way that empowers the client-stakeholder relationship?
  - Is there an inherent power dynamic that may be necessary to acknowledge?
  - Can I submit to not knowing about their experience and am open to listening with cultural humility (later discussed)?
  - How can I acknowledge failure if I have said something that makes the client uncomfortable by demonstrating cultural humility and empowering them to correct me?
  - Am I asking the right questions with an open-ended stance to learn more about them?

Towards Cultural Competency

Fundamental to current applied SEPP practice is the idea of cultural competence. Cultural competence is about gaining the understanding, skills, and knowledge to deliver appropriate culturally informed interventions. It is about being alert to how practitioners' worldviews and those of their clients may shape behaviours, and how personal values, attitudes, and beliefs are influenced by their cultural backgrounds. It is about developing the skills needed to effectively broach conversations on race, ethnicity, and culture. In this chapter, the authors emphasise that cultural competence is developed over time and is a lifelong journey of learning demonstrating cultural humility (Krane & Waldron, 2021) where the practitioner continues to engage with self-awareness and self-reflection with intentionality. Furthermore, with sport and the field of sport psychology becoming more globalised and involving movement across borders, there has been a growing interaction among practitioners and clients in numerous differing cultural contexts (Ryba et al., 2018, Yousuf, 2022). Thus, practitioners may find themselves working within environments and contexts that are unfamiliar to their own cultural background and unlike their previous consulting experiences. These diverse multicultural contextual settings along with increased interactions, necessitates developing cultural competence (Parham, 2005).

Sensitivity, Reflexivity, and Self-Reflection

Through a process of exploring clients' unique identity and individualised experiences, alongside exploring one's own cultural perspective and worldview, one strives towards cultural sensitivity (Schinke et al., 2012). Cultural sensitivity is produced through self-exploration and understanding one's biases, values, social position, and power (Blodgett et al., 2011; McGannon & Johnson, 2009; Schinke et al., 2012). For example, when an athlete of colour demonstrates emotions of anger and the immediate assumption is made that the athlete has behavioural issues, it is necessary to question this assumption. Simply, it is incumbent upon practitioners to self-reflect on systems of oppression, privilege, and inequality and how they have been influenced professionally and personally (Brutus & Yousuf, 2019). Cultural reflexivity enables practitioners to be more open to alternative worldviews (Saukko, 2003), be more responsive to people of other cultures, and enables practitioners to understand the experiences of marginalised individuals (McGannon et al., 2014; Schinke et al., 2012). Some experts go further to encourage practitioners to interrogate and disrupt systemic intersectional disempowering cultures by committing to self-reflexivity (Fisher & Anders, 2010). One might consider this to be the nature of advocacy.

Humility

Cultural humility involves a self-exploration of the limits of the practitioner's cultural knowledge or skills within applied settings and is about gaining the knowledge and skills needed to effect design and deliver interventions for clients based on the client's cultural background. Hook et al. (2013) defined cultural humility as other-oriented "characterised by respect for others and lack of superiority" (p. 2) denoting that when practitioners demonstrate cultural humility, there is a strengthening therapeutic alliance and that clients' perceptions of practitioners' cultural humility, is positively associated with improved therapeutic outcomes. Clients also place importance on humility when their worldview is addressed and Hook et al. (2013), proposed that the role of the practitioner is not to assume they understand the cultural background of the client based on their own knowledge and experience, but rather to be active equal partners (Dorpat, 1996). The practitioner must explore with the client what aspects of their cultural background may be protective factors or alternatively harmful to the client. Humility is not about overstating one's own perspective when positioning with an interpersonal stance, but more about forming an alliance where the client is guided towards self-realisation through their own worldview.

Similarly, it is important for those in training to recognise that humility is about demonstrating curiosity and interest in the client's worldview and perspective with a willingness to ask questions when uncertain about the client's worldview, while continuing to develop knowledge and skills (Hook et al., 2013). This practice and search for knowledge and skill improvement is essential, so as not to fall into the trap of gaslighting (American Psychological Association, n.d.) to coerce clients or stifle the therapeutic conversation when questioning. The trainee is encouraged to adopt the values and stance of openness and respect with a humble approach.

Broaching Conversations: The Four Styles

At this point in the chapter, the reader has been provided with a context, to understand or contemplate how culture affects the consulting process and a brief overview of the theories that have surfaced in cultural sport psychology and feminist sport psychology research. In doing so, the authors hope practitioners gain theoretical tools and insights into how (hegemonic) power, culture, and identity affect the consultant–consultee relationship, and highlight the *power-over* nature of consultant work that is often unintentionally oppressive for clients. The chapter turns now to a discussion of broaching styles and how practitioners can broach conversations on race, ethnicity, and culture with stakeholders/clients whose worldviews or experiences may not align with the practitioner's. The aim is to provide practitioners with practical tools for engaging in dialogues that are diffused with a sense of humility and courage, and self-reflective practice.

As previously mentioned, effectively broaching conversations is a skill that requires self-awareness on the part of the practitioner, an active-oriented approach to understand the stakeholder or client's worldview, and the recognition and attendance to power imbalances that influence the consulting relationship (Ratts et al., 2016). Day-Vines et al. (2007) assert broaching conversations on race and ethnicity is a multicultural competence that falls along a continuum of five styles: avoidant, isolating, continuing/incongruent, integrated, and infusing. They posit that practitioners who *avoid* broaching conversations on race in the consulting process do so because they believe race is not part of the presenting concern, or they minimise the effects of racial discrimination and oppression on the client's mental health. This can include achieving optimal performances. Additionally, they suggest that unlike avoidant practitioners who ignore cultural factors, practitioners who *isolate* tend to broach issues of race and culture in a simplistic fashion. For example, cultural differences between the practitioner and the client might be discussed as part of the initial intake process utilising assessments like the Performance Interview Guide (Aoyagi et al., 2017) or the Sport Interviewing Protocol (SIP; Taylor et al. 2018) but are then never discussed again in future sessions. Day-Vines et al. (2007) highlighted that continuing/incongruent practitioners encouraged clients to explore race and other cultural factors in their dialogues but were doing so in ways that reified cultural stereotypes or disempowered the client. Assuming that a client is (not) experienced with playing a particular sport or is (not) a fan of that sport based on the client's race, is a prime example. They posit that *integrated/congruent* and *infusing* practitioners broach race and ethnicity with clients by attending to the intersectional and dynamic nature of the client's identities. They further highlight that the difference is that infusing practitioners view broaching as a way of life, and more than just a professional obligation as potential change agents. Infusing practitioners are more likely to engage in social justice advocacy on behalf of clients. The authors suggest that this extends to all stakeholders.

Consider an elite athlete like four-time Olympic gold medallist Simone Biles who generated much media controversy after pulling herself out of the team competition during the 2020 Tokyo Olympic Games citing her mental health and a case of the "twisties" as the primary reasons for her decision to withdraw. Practitioners who avoid, isolate, and are incongruent with how they broach race with athletes (or other high-level performers) would not have considered Biles' multiple, marginalised identities as a young Black woman, who was under immense pressure to perform not only for her team and country, but also for other people of colour who consider her a role model. Practitioners who are integrated/congruent or infusing in their broaching styles would understand that Biles was also competing against the racial ideologies and cultural stereotypes that represent the "natural" gymnast body as white and female. These styles would also consider the backdrop of 2020 in which people of colour and especially Black people, were reliving experiences of racial trauma after the murder of George Floyd by law enforcement, while coping with the grief and injustice of a disproportionate number of ethnic people lost in the COVID-19 pandemic. They may have contemplated that Biles was also contending with mainstream media depictions that centred visible aspects of her identity in their narratives, ignoring other aspects of it like her Catholic faith (Zimmerman, 2021), as well as her sexual victimization by former US Gymnastics team doctor, Dr. Larry Nassar.[4] Biles' withdrawal generated several comments on listservs and social media from applied SEPP practitioners, with several citing her case as a reason why elite sport organisations need more applied practitioners. Underlying some of these discussions and assertions was the unspoken premise that if Biles had someone at the Olympics who could have helped her with her mental game, she may not have withdrawn from the team competition. Given the fact the United States Olympic and Paralympic Committee (USOPC) employs mental health clinicians and SEPP practitioners, this inference makes little sense, but it does speak to how SEPP practitioners are not immune to neoliberal masculine values that pride individualism and individual responsibility above all else.

Within sport, Coakley (2011) highlights the value of assuming individual responsibility for risk, especially in high-performance sport, but these neoliberal ideologies are pervasive in sport, and difficult to combat. An example is the Association for Applied Sport Psychology's (AASP, 2021) statement on mental health and its relationship to performance. The statement illustrates the organisation's expressed commitment to social justice, but it does not go far enough to place communal responsibility for risk of the overall health and wellbeing of athletes on all stakeholders, including SEPP practitioners. Thus, broaching conversations on race, gender, ethnicity, and culture within the context of athlete wellbeing, should extend beyond the consultancy space and permeate across the profession.

Practical and Applied Setting Considerations

In this chapter, the authors outlined a few theories from cultural sport psychology and applied feminist sport psychology research, as well as delved into a few theories that are underrepresented in applied SEPP scholarship. The intent has been to help practitioners at all stages in their career engage in cultural praxis and self-reflexivity when broaching conversations on race ethnicity with stakeholders of marginalised cultural backgrounds. Considerations on the types of broaching styles were the primary focus. Notwithstanding, the authors realise that practitioners must consider not only the conversations and the language used, but also the communication channels used. In addition, how the practitioner creates space to allow for stakeholder access, safety, and comfort is also necessitated. Many practitioners are aware of the benefits of creating a physical environment that is conducive to fostering an alliance with stakeholders, with consideration for how virtual environments may not be accessible for stakeholders with physical and/or other limitations.

While the chapter was primarily focused on consulting with stakeholders of diverse cultural backgrounds, practitioners must also become comfortable with broaching conversations related to diversity, equity, and inclusion with stakeholders from non-marginalised backgrounds. Being an ally does not only mean advocating for or supporting individuals who have faced discrimination. It is not only about dismantling systems. It is about holding difficult conversations with those of dominant culture to help them become allies in the agency of change.

There is no cookie-cutter approach when working with clients. Meeting clients where they are, is the responsibility of the practitioner. Utilising intake forms and questionnaires such as in Box 12.1, the SIP (Taylor et al., 2018) and The Saliency of Race in Sport Questionnaire (SORIS-Q; Forster-Scott, 2005) to design interventions that are culturally sensitive and use appropriate language, are hallmarks of cultural competency/humility. For example, practitioners can use forms and questionnaires to understand how an athlete identifies and how important their racial identity is to them. They may seek understanding of experiences of racism and how they hinder mental and physical health, impact performance, while also exploring feelings of isolation or distress (Forster-Scott et al., 2018; Taylor et al., 2018). Terminology is especially important when targeting the specific inequalities to be addressed and reducing individuals to acronyms is considered disrespectful (Sporting Equals, 2021). Acronyms may equally disengage individuals, especially if intending to build a trusting therapeutic relationship. Lastly, practitioners are urged to continuously seek to educate themselves and evolve with respect – an ethical responsibility.

Notes

1 Association for Applied Sport Psychology (AASP); American Psychological Society (APA); British Psychological Society (BPS); International Society of Sport Psychology (ISSP).

2 Of 92 UK professional soccer clubs, 19 out of 552 senior coaching positions were held by coaches from Black and ethnic 'minority backgrounds'. A total of 3.4% of the coaches employed.
3 50.7% doing 150 minutes of moderate activity a week, as compared to 72% for those with no religion, and 63% for Christians.
4 See https://www.judiciary.senate.gov/meetings/dereliction-of-duty-examining-the-inspector-generals-report-on-the-fbis-handling-of-the-larry-nassar-investigation

References

American Psychological Association. (n.d.). Gaslight. In *APA Dictionary of Psychology*. Retrieved October 4, 2021 from https://dictionary.apa.org/gaslight

Aoyagi, M.W., Poczwardowski, A., Statler, T., Shapiro, J.L., & Cohen, A.B. (2017). The performance interview guide: Recommendations for initial consultations in sport and performance psychology. Professional Psychology: *Research and Practice*, 48(5), 352–360.

Association for Applied Sport Psychology. (2021, August 17). Statement on the continuum of mental health & relationship to performance: a response to the conversation supporting Naomi Osaka and Simone Biles. https://appliedsportpsych.org/media/news-releases-and-association-updates/aasp-statement-on-the-continuum-of-mental-health-and-relationship-to-performance-a-response-to-the-conversation-supporting/

Bailey, M. & Trudy (2018). On misogynoir: citation, erasure, and plagiarism. *Feminist Media Studies*, 18(4), 762–768. https://www.tandfonline.com/action/showCitFormats?doi=10.1080%2F14680777.2018.1447395

Barlas, A. (2008). Engaging Islamic feminism: provincializing feminism as a master narrative. In A. Kynsilheto (Ed.), *Islamic Feminism: Current Perspectives*. Tampere Peace Research Institute Occasional Paper No. 96.

Bell, Jr., D. A. (1976). Racial remediation: an historical perspective on current conditions. *Notre Dame Law*, 52(5), 5–29.

Barker, M. (1981). *The New Racism. Conservatives and the Ideology of the Tribe*. Junction Books.

British Broadcasting Corporation. (2009, September 3). Hijab. https://www.bbc.co.uk/religion/religions/islam/beliefs/hijab_1.shtml

Blodgett, A., Schinke, R., Smith, B., Peltier, D., & Pheasant, C. (2011). Exploring vignettes as a narrative strategy for co-producing the research voices of Aboriginal community members. *Qualitative Inquiry*, 17, 522–533.

Brutus, A. & Yousuf, S. (2019). Meeting student-athletes where they are: counseling and psychological services for college student-athletes of diverse racial, ethnic, and socioeconomic backgrounds. In M. J. Loughran (Ed.), *Counseling and Psychological Services for College Student-Athletes* (pp. 221–244). FIT Publishing.

Buffington, M. & Lai, A. (2011). Resistance and tension in feminist teaching. *Visual Arts Research*, 37(73), 1–13.

Butryn, T. M. (2002). Critically examining white racial identity and privilege in sport psychology consulting. *The Sport Psychologist*, 16, 316–336.

Califia, P. (1997). *Sex Changes: The Politics of Transgenderism*. Cleis Press.

Coakley, J. (2011). Ideology doesn't just happen: sports and neoliberalism. *Revista da Asociación Latinoamericana de Estudios Socioculturales del Deporte*, 1(1), 67–84.

Collins, P. H. (1998). *Fighting Words: Black Women and the Search for Justice*. University of Minnesota Press.

Collins, P. H. (2005). *Black Sexual Politics: African-Americans, Gender, and New Racism*. Routledge.

Comas-Diaz, L. (2011). Interventions with culturally diverse populations. In D. H. Barlow (Ed.), *The Oxford Handbook of Clinical Psychology* (pp. 868–887). Oxford University Press.

Crenshaw, K. (1989). Demarginalizing the intersection of race and sex: a Black feminist critique of antidiscrimination doctrine, feminist theory, and antiracist politics. In *The black feminist reader* (pp. 208–238). Blackwell Publishers.

Cunningham, G. B. (2019). *Diversity and Inclusion in Sport Organizations: A Multilevel Perspective*. Routledge.

Day-Vines, N. L., Wood, S. M., Grothaus, T., Craigen, L., Holman, A., Dotson-Blake, K., & Douglass, M. J. (2007). Broaching the subjects of race, ethnicity, and culture during the counseling process. *Journal of Counseling & Development, 85*(4), 401–409.

Di Stasio, V. & Heath, A. (2019, January 18). *Are Employers in Britain Discriminating against Ethnic Minorities?* Centre for Social Investigation Nuffield College. http://csi.nuff.ox.ac.uk/?p=1299

Dorpat, T. L. (1996). *Gaslighting, the Double Whammy, Interrogation, and Other Methods of Covert Control in Psychotherapy and Psychoanalysis*. Jason Aronson.

Farenet (2014). *Ethnic Minorities and Coaching in Elite Level Football in England: A Call to Action*. Sports People's Think Tank and the University of Loughborough. https://www.farenet.org/wp-content/uploads/2014/11/We-speak-with-one-voice.pdf

Fisher, L. A. & Anders, A. D. (2010). Critically engaging with sport psychology ethics through cultural studies: four commitments. In T. V. Ryba, R. J. Schinke, & G. Tenenbaum (Eds.), *The Cultural Turn in Sport Psychology* (pp. 101–126). FIT.

Forber-Pratt, A. J. (2017). "Not everybody can take trips like this": a paralympian's perspective on educating about disability around the world. In S. Hadler & L. Assaf (Eds.), *Inclusion, Disability & Culture: Ethnographic Approach Traversing Abilities and Challenges* (pp. 59–75). Springer.

Forber-Pratt, A. J. (2021). The insider looking out: discovering the real me. *Qualitative Inquiry, 28*(6), 609–617.

Forster-Scott, L. (2005, May 13). The creation of the saliency of race in sport questionnaire: exploring issues of Black racial identity development in sport (Unpublished doctoral dissertation). Temple University. https://www.proquest.com/openview/ef47ea1f44d4c51798d9e154f57ac6d4/1?pq-orisite=gscholar&cbl=18750&diss=y

Forster-Scott, L., Tinsley, T. M., Ng, K., Withycombe, J. L., & Poudevigne, M. (2018). Diversity in sport psychology assessment. In J. Taylor (Ed.), *Assessment in Applied Sport Psychology* (pp. 35–56). Human Kinetics.

Friesen, A. & Orlick, T. (2011). Holistic sport psychology: investigating the roles, operating standards, and intervention goals and strategies of holistic consultants. *Journal of Excellence, 14*(1), 18–42.

Grewel, I. & Kaplan, C. (1994). *Scattered Hegemonies: Postmodernity and Transnational Feminist Practices*. University of Minneapolis Press.

Gunter, K. K. (2019). The unintentional feminist. In L. Carter (Eds.), *Feminist Applied Sport Psychology* (pp. 182–189). Taylor Francis.

Hart, R. (2021, August 4). Belarusian sprinter joins long list of Olympic defectors: here's how athletes have sought asylum at the games. Forbes. https://www.forbes.com/sites/roberthart/2021/08/04/belarusian-sprinter-joins-long-list-of-olympic-defectors---heres-how-athletes-have-sought-asylum-at-the-games/?sh=52614a398489

Hook, J. N., Davis, D. E., Owen, J., Worthington, Jr., E. L., & Utsey, S. O. (2013). Cultural humility: measuring openness to culturally diverse clients. *Journal of Counseling Psychology, 60*(1), 353–366.

hooks, b. (1981). *Ain't I a Woman: Black Women and the Search for Social Justice*. Routledge.

Hylton, K. (2013). *Sport Development Policy, Process and Practice* (3rd ed.). Routledge.

Janmohamed, S. (2016). *Generation M: Young Muslims Changing the World.* Bloomsbury.
Knott, K. (2017a). *British Muslims: A History.* CREST.
Knott, K. (2017b). *British Muslims: Demography and Communities.* CREST.
Knott, K. (2017c). *British Muslims: Gender and Generations.* CREST.
Koyama (2001, July 26). Trans feminist manifesto. https://eminism.org/readings/pdf-rdg/tfmanifesto.pdf
Krane, V. & Waldron, J. J. (2021). A renewed call to queer sport psychology. *Journal of Applied Sport Psychology, 33*(5), 469–490.
Lee, S. M., Lombera, J. M., & Larsen, L. K. (2019). Helping athletes cope with minority stress in sport. *Journal of Sport Psychology in Action, 10*(3), 174–190.
Lee, J. J. & Rice, C. (2007). Welcome to America? International student perceptions of discrimination. *Higher Education, 53*(3), 381–409.
McGee, J. E. & Hardman, K. (2012). Muslim schoolgirls' identity and participation in school-based physical education in England. *SportLogia, 8*(1), 49–71.
McGannon, K. R. & Johnson, C. R. (2009). Strategies for reflective cultural sport psychology research. In R. J. Schinke & S. J. Hanrahan (Eds.), *Cultural Sport Psychology* (pp. 57–75). Human Kinetics.
McGannon, K. R. & Schinke, R. J. (2013). "My first choice is to work out at work; then I don't feel bad about my kids": a discursive psychological analysis of motherhood and physical activity participation. *Psychology of Sport and Exercise, 14*, 179–188.
McGannon, K. R., Schinke, R. J., & Busanich, R. (2014). Cultural sport psychology considerations for enhancing cultural competence of practitioners. In L. S. Tashman & J. G. Cremades (Eds.), *Becoming a Performance Psychology Professional: International Perspectives on Service Delivery and Supervision* (pp. 135–142). Routledge.
McIntosh, P. (1989, July/August). White Privilege: Unpacking the Invisible Knapsack. *Peace and Freedom Magazine*, 10–12.
McKenna, U. & Francis, J. (2019). Growing up female and Muslim in the UK: an empirical enquiry into the distinctive religious and social values of young Muslims. *British Journal of Religious Education, 41*(4), 388–401.
Mohanty, C. (1988). Under Western eyes: feminist scholarship and colonial discourses. *Feminist Review, 30*(1), 61–88.
Muslimah Sports Association (2019). *Insight pack: Muslim women and girls*. https://www.womeninsport.org/wp-content/uploads/2019/12/Muslim-Women-and-Girls-Insight-Pack-FINAL.pdf
Oglesby, C. (2010, October). *Diversity Lecture*. Lecture presented at the Association of Applied Sport Psychology Annual Congress. Providence, RI.
Ortega, R. M. & Faller, K. C. (2011). Training child welfare workers from an intersectional cultural humility perspective: a paradigm shift. *Child Welfare, 90*(5), 27–49.
Parham, W. D. (2005). Raising the bar: developing an understanding of athletes from racially, culturally, and ethnically diverse backgrounds. In M. B. Anderson (Ed.), *Sport psychology in Practice* (pp. 201–215). Human Kinetics.
Quartiroli, A., Vosloo, J., Fisher, L. A., & Schinke, R. J. (2020). Culturally competent sport psychology: a survey of sport psychology professionals' perception of cultural competence. *The Sport Psychologist, 34*(3), 242–253.
Rassool, G. H. (2014). *Cultural Competence in Caring for Muslim Patients*. Palgrave MacMillan.
Ratts, M. J., Singh, A. A., Nassar-McMillan, S., Butler, S. K., & McCullough, J. R. (2016). Multicultural and social justice counseling competencies: guidelines for the counseling profession. *Journal of Multicultural Counseling and Development, 44*(1), 28–48.
Ryba, T. V. (2017). Cultural sport psychology: a critical review of empirical advances. *Current Opinion in Psychology, 16*, 123–127.

Ryba, T. V. & Schinke, R. J. (2009). Methodology as a ritualized eurocentrism: introduction to the special issue. *International Journal of Sport and Exercise Psychology*, 7, 263–274.

Ryba, T. V., Schinke, R. J., Stambulova, N. B., & Elbe, A. M. (2018). ISSP position stand: transnationalism, mobility, and acculturation in and through sport. *International Journal of Sport and Exercise Psychology*, 16(5), 520–534.

Ryba, T. V., Stambulova, N., & Ronkainen, N. J. (2016). The work of cultural transition: an emerging model. *Frontiers in Psychology*, 7, 427.

Saukko, P. (2003). *Doing Research in Cultural Studies*. SAGE Publications Ltd.

Sayyid, S. (2000). Beyond Westphalia: nations and diaspora: the case of the Muslim "Umma". In B. Hesse (Eds.), *Un/settled Multiculturalisms: Diasporas, Entanglements, Transruptions* (pp. 33–51). Zed Books.

Seedat, F. (2013). Islam, feminism, and Islamic feminism: between inadequacy and inevitability. *Journal of Feminist Studies in Religion*, 29(2), 25–45.

Schinke, R. J., & Hanrahan, S. J. (Eds.). (2009). *Cultural sport psychology*. Human Kinetics.

Schinke, R. J., McGannon, K. R., Parham, W. D., & Lane, A. (2012). Toward cultural praxis: strategies for self-reflexive sport psychology practice. *Quest*, 64(1), 34–46.

Spears, A. (1999) Race and ideology: an introduction. In A. Spears (Ed.), *Race and Ideology Language, Symbolism, and Popular Culture* (pp. 11–59). Wayne State University Press.

Sport England. (2019). Active lives November 2017/2018 data. Retrieved from https://www.sportengland.org/adultnov1718tables/

Sporting Equals. (2021, October 13). Terminology resource. http://www.sportingequals.org.uk/news-and-blogs/sporting-equals-terminology-resource.html

Stevenson, J., Demack, S., Stiell, B., Abdi, M., Clarkson, L. Ghaffar, F., & Hassan, S. (2017). *The Social Mobility Challenges Faced by Young Muslims*. Social Mobility Commission.

Taylor, J., Simpson, D., & Brutus, A. L. (2018). Interviewing: asking the right questions. In J. Taylor (Ed.), *Assessment in Applied Sport Psychology* (pp. 101–114). Human Kinetics.

Tervalon, M. & Murray-Garcia, J. (1998). Cultural humility versus cultural competence: a critical distinction in defining physician training outcomes in multicultural education. *Journal of Health Care for the Poor and Underserved*, 9(2), 117–125.

The Muslim Council of Britain. (2015). British Muslims in numbers. A demographic, socio-economic and health profile of Muslims in Britain drawing on the 2011 census. https://www.mcb.org.uk/wp-content/uploads/2015/02/MCBCensusReport_2015.pdf

Vertovec, S. (2009). *Transnationalism*. Routledge.

Zimmerman, C. (2021, July 30). UPDATE: Catholics see challenging balance in Simone Biles' decisions at Olympics, Catholic News Service. https://www.catholicnews.com/update-catholics-see-challenging-balance-in-simone-biles-decisions-at-olympics/

Yousuf, S. (2022). Musings of a transnational intersectional UK practitioner psychologist. *Journal of Clinical Sport Psychology*, 1(aop), 1–9.

13
LIFE-LONG LEARNING

Life beyond the Training

Moira E. Lafferty and David Tod

Life-Long Learning: Life beyond the Training

In this chapter, we discuss how lifelong learning is central to practitioner development. We begin by discussing the relationship between Continued Professional Development (CPD) and Continuing Education (CE) and then provide our conceptualisation of lifelong learning drawing from the wider professional practice psychology literature and culminating with a sport psychology specific definition drawing on the work of Quartiroli et al. (2021). We then discuss the journey from novice practitioner to expert using Kneebone's (2020) three progressive stages and, through practitioner narratives, explore the reality of lifelong learning. We conclude with practical guidelines which we hope will help you plan and navigate your personal developmental journey toward expertise in applied practice.

Continued Professional Development, Education, and Lifelong Learning

Trainee Sport Psychologists about to embark on, currently undertaking, and those who have completed an accredited training pathway will be familiar with the concept of CPD. At a basal level, Golding and Gray (2006) describe it as those activities practitioners undertake to maintain currency and competency to practice. For those starting on the journey to registration, CPD activities will be recorded in a training diary, and for those newly registered, the training diary is replaced by CPD logs that are required in order to maintain registration. The list of activities recorded will undoubtedly differ from person to person but there will also be commonalities (e.g., conference attendance). Herein, we give our first word of caution. Attending a conference in and of itself does not contribute to development if no thought has been given to the learning or need that will be met through being present at

DOI: 10.4324/9781003196280-16

such events. Being physically present may present opportunities for networking and social support, both critically important (c.f. McEwan & Tod, 2015), but to truly develop practitioner skills we encourage you to reflect on the what, why and how. That is – What do I need to learn, develop, or improve? Why is that important? And ultimately, how will the conference aid this? The answer to the final question comes from a clear analysis of the conference offerings and the need to plan your own journey through the conference programme. Following this three-step process for all CPD activities will mean that more is gained from each opportunity and that time and financial investment are rewarded through professional growth.

However, focusing energy and attention on CPD in general terms negates two other areas of development that can contribute to growth and movement from novice to expert, that of CE and lifelong learning. Taylor and Neimeyer (2017) suggest that these processes are not divorced from each other but instead, both CPD and CE are subsets of the wider concept of lifelong learning as shown in Figure 13.1.

In Taylor and Neimeyer's (2017) conceptualisation, CE can be thought of as a process through which learning takes place and occurs on a continuum from formal through to non-formal. Formal learning for the trainee Sport Psychologist might involve, for example, undertaking a basic counselling course either online or at a College. Critically, the course will have educational aims, be a recognised qualification and have some form of assessment. In contrast, non-formal learning whilst still being structured is not credit or award baring. Engaging in all forms of continued learning will be of benefit to the developing practitioner and will ensure that they are well placed to meet Health Care Professions Council (HCPC) statutory CPD requirements. Failure to demonstrate CPD can result in removal from the HCPC register, meaning the title of practitioner Psychologist, Sport and Exercise Psychologist cannot be used, nor services utilising psychological skills offered. To aid planning and to illustrate the breadth of different learning options, in Table 13.1, we define each form of learning and offer examples recognised by the HCPC of each.

FIGURE 13.1 Relationship of CPD, CE with lifelong learning.

TABLE 13.1 Examples of the Differing Continuing Education Types

Continuing Education Area	Definition	Examples for the Sport and Exercise Psychologist Recognised by HCPC
Formal	Learning accompanied by predetermined objectives, the sport psychologist assumes the role of the student and is assessed	Courses accredited by a professional body (e.g., Safeguarding, Mental Health First Aid Training)
Informal	Self-directed learning that is neither supervised nor assessed	Reading journal articles/textbooks Knowledge development via the internet/documentaries/podcasts
Incidental	Express purpose is not learning (e.g., the learning occurs as a result of doing something else)	Teaching or giving presentations Mentoring Presenting at a conference Reviewing a journal article
Non-formal	Psychologist assumes the role of a student however there is no assessment or awarding body	Research seminar series Conference attendance

Note. The definitions are based on Taylor and Neimeyer (2016).

CE, engagement with learning opportunities and learning from other professions and professionals will contribute to practitioner growth and stem the tide of obsolescence that can occur when practitioners fail to keep abreast of field developments (Tod et al., 2020). The salutary lesson is that competence obtained can be lost if continued learning does not occur. However, we suggest that to develop as a practitioner there is a need to look beyond the myriad of knowledge-based opportunities and engage not only in activities that are professionally beneficial such as role plays but also in personal activities such as personal therapy that contribute to holistic development.

As previously discussed, Taylor and Neimeyer (2017) suggest that both CPD and CE are encased by the concept of lifelong learning. They describe and define lifelong learning as an active process; the participant has the purpose and drive to seek and search for knowledge and to cultivate their own growth and development. Furthermore, Taylor and Neimeyer argue that engagement in lifelong learning brings more to the table and practitioner development in that it also "enriches, enhances and extends the understanding of self" (p. 20). Quartiroli et al. (2021) through a Delphi survey study with sport psychology practitioners defines lifelong learning as "the individuals desire to explore and engage in on going information seeking and self-reflective activity to satisfy one's personal curiosity and self-development" (p. 178).

Engaging in lifelong learning, moving beyond CPD and CE activities ensures that not only will competence to practice be maintained but practice will be enhanced (Wise et al., 2010). When lifelong learning is entered into with an open mind the practitioner can begin a journey of discovery of who they are, what they do, with whom, when, and why (Tod et al., 2017). This self-exploration can lead to self-discovery and enlightenment; practitioners can pose questions in and of their practice, and explore their positionality both personally and professionally. This can allow applied Sport Psychologists to craft and subsequently strengthen the legs of what Skovholt and Starkey (2010) describe as the three-legged stool of expertise. They suggest that the legs represent practitioner experience, personal life and academic/research, and it is the combined strength of the three legs (in real terms the knowledge from these areas) that contributes to expertise. Whilst an interesting metaphor, we are left with questions such as: What are the three legs of the expert applied practitioners' stool? What experiences are carved into each leg as they move from training and newly qualified through to becoming an expert? And how can we align the journey from novice to expert with their lifelong learning experiences? Before we discuss lifelong learning through the voices of those on the journey, we discuss how one may conceptualise the movement from novice to expert through a review of Kneebone (2020), which we hope will allow you to understand where you are presently on your journey.

Describing Practitioner Growth

Over the last 25 years, researchers have explored how practitioners develop expertise (McEwan et al., 2019; Smith et al., 2019). Most work focuses on trainees, although a smattering examines experienced individuals (McEwan et al., 2019). Here, we synthesise the literature as a basis for understanding lifelong learning. The synthesis draws on Kneebone's (2020) three-stage model of how individuals become experts. The stages include *Apprentice*, *Journeyman*, and *Master*. Stage models get criticised for being overly linear and rigid. Kneebone, however, admits that expertise development is typically not as linear, nor the stages as clear-cut and independent, as his framework portrays. Nevertheless, the framework serves as useful scaffolding to integrate sport psychology literature.

Apprentice

Apprentices strive to become competent in their domain, generally by imitating how other people work, such as teachers, supervisors, and respected elders. Specifically, apprentices aim to acquire the necessary technical skills and to understand the domain in which they work. They achieve these aims by doing time, using their senses, learning to manage their workspace, and interacting with other people. Often, supervisors take responsibility for apprentices' work, both their output and their errors.

The theme of doing time echoes evidence that sport psychology trainees believe that supervised work experience is the key learning activity that allows them to develop competence (McEwan & Tod, 2015; Tod et al., 2007). Practical experience, however, is not a universal feature of sport psychology training (Hutter et al., 2018). The number of hours trainees need to complete to become qualified varies greatly across countries. For example, in Australia, trainees accumulate at least 1,000 hours of direct work with clients over two years (Psychology Board of Australia),[1] whereas in the USA, they need just 200 hours (AASP).[2]

The themes regarding using your senses and interacting with people highlight that trainees' understanding of how their own histories, characteristics, and foibles, along with the relationships they build with clients, influence the processes and outcomes of consultancy (Fogaca et al., 2018). Further, the theme of managing space reveals that trainees build their knowledge about the politics and demands involved in working in performance contexts, along with understanding sport psychology's position on the totem pole (Tod et al., 2011). The greater insights trainees have of themselves, their clients, and their work space allows practitioners to begin adapting their knowledge and skills to the needs of their clients (Tod et al., 2020), a theme that blossoms in the journeyman stage.

Journeyman

Journeymen are autonomous practitioners who have come out from under their supervisors' wings. Being independent means journeymen take responsibility for their work and must cope with the consequences, whether pleasant or not. Becoming a journeyman does not bring professional development to a close, and ideally, these individuals continue to extend and refine their skills and their understanding of the domain. Two pivotal shifts occur during the journeyman stage. First, individuals become less self-focused, and their attention moves from thinking about how they do the job to realising they need to concentrate on delivering a service or product that satisfies the client's needs and wishes. Second, journeymen rely less on working the way they were taught, or imitating others, and start to make choices about how they want to act. Along with taking responsibility for how they work, journeymen begin to develop their own style, and their work reflects their personalities. The individual's increase in self-expression is accompanied with an enhanced self-confidence that stems from having accumulated much experience in the domain.

Both these pivotal shifts appear in sport psychology research. First, as practitioners' self-confidence in their own abilities increases, they also report reduced narcissism and greater appreciation that they need to tailor their services to clients' unique needs and situations (Tod et al., 2017). Practitioner narcissism reduces because they realise that their interventions and expertise are not the main active ingredients in the helping relationships (Tod et al., 2019). Instead, practitioners acknowledge that the primary active ingredient, by far, is the client's active engagement, and practitioners are facilitators (McCarthy & Jones, 2013; Wadsworth et al., 2021).

Second, the integration of practitioners' personal and professional selves allows them to develop their own styles (McEwan et al., 2019). Just as esteemed Blues musicians, such as B. B. King, Buddy Guy, and Bonnie Raitt have unique styles, allowing aficionados to identify them within the first few bars of a song, sport psychology practitioners develop approaches that distinguish them from colleagues. Integration involves (a) increased coherence between practitioners' personalities and their theoretical beliefs and (b) their attempts to enhance the match between themselves and their clients or work environments (Rønnestad & Skovholt, 2013). Practitioners enhance the match between themselves and their work environments by either developing new ways of working (and shedding the old) or by deciding to work with specific population groups (McEwan et al., 2019).

Master

The absence of a clear definition and objective markers makes it difficult to identify who are master sport psychology practitioners, echoing a similar issue in counselling and clinical psychology (Tracey et al., 2014). Kneebone (2020) argues that masters develop a relationship of care and strive to pass on their wisdom to others through means such as providing supervision, writing books, and producing other educational materials. Although these behaviours have face validity, in sport psychology they are likely to be surrogate indicators of expertise at best. For example, in the UK, qualified practitioners with two years of professional experience can supervise trainees, but they are unlikely to be masters. The existing research has focused on respected and experienced individuals (McEwan et al., 2019; Simons & Andersen, 1995; Wadsworth et al., 2021), but again these criteria are fallible and may not help identify experts. Professionals in the field could direct future research to help understand the characteristics of master sport psychology practitioners, as opposed to journeymen.

Kneebone (2020) also suggests that masters have widespread influence over the domain community and change the direction of the field. Friesen's (2021) recent survey of AASP members about influential sport psychology literature may help identify individuals who have influenced the direction of the field. For example, based on the survey, Artur Pocwardowski could be considered a master sport psychology professional because he first authored the most influential journal article, was the only individual to first author more than one, and he first authored the fourth most influential textbook. Again, however, influential literature is at best a surrogate measure. For example, introductory textbooks are often highly cited and influential, but they typically do not change the direction of a field, but instead, reinforce the status quo.

A key change that underpins Kneebone's (2020) framework is an ontological shift. Part of becoming an expert is developing an identity. Individuals view themselves as becoming the type of performer they are striving to be, and not just someone who does the things those people can do. More specifically, consultants see themselves as sport psychology practitioners and not merely individuals who can help athletes with their sport psychology needs. Developing a professional or expert identity takes time and may be fraught with anxiety. The phrase *impostor syndrome* has entered the sport psychology practitioner lexicon (Hings et al., 2020). Imposter syndrome or imposter phenomena (Clance & Imes, 1978) occurs when someone believes erroneously, that they are intellectually and professionally inept despite evidence to the contrary. Characterised by self-doubt, anxiety, depression, and fraudulent feelings, it can lead to mental health problems (Tigranyan et al., 2021). Critically, feelings of imposter phenomena may be a sign that the individual has yet to develop a stable and resilient professional identity.

The examination of sport psychology practitioner identity is in its infancy. Most articles on identity are theoretical pieces or case studies (Tod et al., 2020; Williams & Andersen, 2012) and the field would benefit from an increase in research on the subject. An evidence-based understanding of practitioner identity could help professional organizations define a desired goal of training and allow them to design informed qualification pathways tailored to the needs of the community and neophyte consultants. Trainees and inexperienced practitioners may benefit from understanding how experts view themselves as situated individuals or beings-in-context. Knowing what they are striving to achieve may help trainees and inexperienced practitioners plan their professional development and engage in meaningful lifelong learning.

Illustrating Lifelong Learning across Kneebone's (2000) Three Stages

In this section, we present quotes from individuals in the apprentice, journeyman, and expert stages of Kneebone's (2020) model. These quotes illustrate features of lifelong learning that then form the basis of the applied implications we present in the final section.

Apprentice

The first two quotes are from a trainee on the cusp of completing the British Psychological Society (BPS) Stage 2 training and a newly registered HCPC consultant in the first two years of their career.

BOX 13.1   THE TRAINEE EXPERIENCE

As I write, I am waiting with quiet trepidation for my final QSEP feedback and hopeful invitation to VIVA. Upon deciding to retrain in my early thirties and after nearly eight years of hard work...actually no, it's a lot longer than that. Alongside a magnitude of theory studied and applied practice undertaken, although seemingly unrelated, I believe that every personal interaction, every professional role, every experience I have had in the last forty years has shaped me into the practitioner I am now, and to me this is only the beginning of a lifetime of learning. As a student and as a trainee sport psychologist, despite consistently gravitating towards a counselling approach, it was not until quite recently that I was able to identify a philosophy of practice which truly reflected my beliefs and values as both a person and a practitioner.

However, having embraced this approach, I feel there is still so much more to learn about the theoretical underpinning and also areas within its application that I wish to potentially adapt and refine to maximise its efficacy within the contexts of sport and performance. "Sponge" is a word that springs to mind when I think about lifelong learning! Over the years, I have observed that those who I admire and who are successful in any context, embody an openness to learning and absorbing information from seemingly limitless sources throughout their careers, and possess the flexibility of thinking to allow this to evolve and inform their practice. I certainly intend to emulate this in my own career.

BOX 13.2 THE NEWLY QUALIFIED CONSULTANT

Lifelong learning for me starts with passion. My roles as a lecturer and applied practitioner give my life a sense of purpose and meaning, which means I am constantly searching for new opportunities to learn and grow. Learning beyond formal education is difficult when it becomes something you "should" or "have to do" (attending conferences etc.). Lifelong learning is only truly possible when it becomes something you want to do. For me, 18 months post professional doctorate, most of my learning has come through personal growth. I have been to therapy as a client. I have become more self-aware through this process. I engage with critical friends, who both support and challenge me. This encourages me to reflect on myself and my practice. I surround myself with people from the field that share my passion and my frustrations. I am curious. I genuinely love learning because I love my job. I work in four separate, but connected areas; applied practice, teaching, research, and supervision and this provides me with variation and many challenges, which makes my job interesting. When I learn, I realise there is so much more I need to learn. I have been reading recently about "infinite purpose" ("be better than you were yesterday") and in my opinion, this sums lifelong learning up very well. It isn't a destination (learning to pass a MSc programme), it is a journey, which doesn't really have an end. Process over outcome. It can be about finding "answers" to questions external of yourself or about looking inward and asking yourself some very difficult questions.

Both individuals recognise that lifelong learning does not stop at graduation (the clue is in the name), despite not being easy. After graduation, individuals need to take responsibility for their learning and they can experience a range of emotions, from anxiety about one's acceptableness and competence as a consultant, to the passion and joy at personal development. Further, many aspects of lifelong learning take time (the name again gives it away), because they involve the synthesis of many ideas, such as finding a theoretical orientation. The trainee above mentions a theme that characterises apprentices: emulation or imitation. Neophyte consultants often intimidate professional elders, although as they gain experience working with athletes, they become confident in developing their own models of practice and approaches.

Journeyman

The next two quotes are from two consultants several years into their careers:

BOX 13.3 JOURNEY CONSULTANT 1

To me, lifelong learning means continued learning beyond education provision and across the lifespan. Our learning at university, through the lectures we attended and the reading we completed, becomes increasing "out of date" as each year passes. Lifelong learning involves being able to continue learning autonomously and independently well beyond our formal education, drawing upon self-motivation, confidence, and a broad skillset (e.g., finding good quality sources of information, critical thinking, time management).

I am grateful that I have developed into an independent and autonomous learner. When I have a question, wish to learn more about a topic, aim to stay abreast of current developments, or seek ideas and potential solutions, I draw upon a skillset that I developed steadily across my education, training, and career in sport and exercise psychology. I can ask helpful questions, find good quality sources of information, find key information within them efficiently, relate new material to what I already know, critically reflect on the research methods used to "create" the knowledge I am learning about, form my own perspective or viewpoint, and think critically about how I can apply what I have learned to a sport or exercise situation. I also benefit personally. I can follow my curiosities, gain insight into myself, reflect upon my experiences and my learning, and use critical thinking in my day-to-day live (e.g., to reach an informed opinion or decision).

Each part of my journey – An undergraduate degree in Psychology, a master's and PhD in Sport Psychology, my chartership training through BPS Stage 2, and teaching university students – contributed towards my development as a lifelong learner. They helped me to become increasing independent and autonomous, while drawing upon supervision and mentoring, and to identify a skillset that supports my continued learning and professional development.

> **BOX 13.4 JOURNEY CONSULTANT 2**
>
> Lifelong learning means moving through a continuum from informal learning to formal learning and back to informal learning. When we are young we learn about the world and ourselves through play and social interactions with others. When we go to school, then university we learn more formally – mostly about things (theories, principles) and sometimes, hopefully how they relate and apply to us. After formal education and training are over, I think we learn more about ourselves and our place in the world through the everyday informal interactions again. This informal learning can begin to explain and clarify some of the formal learning from earlier in our lives. So we might have studied the stages of grief at university, but only later in life, experience some of those stages and now know what they feel like. Along the same lines, we might have studied emotion on our degrees, then worked in applied sport psychology with a person who is struggling to manage their emotions (anger, frustration). When we draw on our own experiences, for example of my twins crayoning on the white walls in lipstick, I can begin to integrate the theory (of managing emotions in this case) to my own life and use it to help others. I hope that I can now understand and empathise with the client in a way that I couldn't before, because I have learned.

The quotes above illustrate one of the key themes in Kneebone's (2020) framework: individuation or the development of a personal consulting style. Freed from restrictions imposed by training programmes and professional elders, consultants now have the freedom to pursue avenues they believe will benefit them and their clients. Nevertheless, the freedom consultants have to explore areas they believe are useful comes with the need for them to take responsibility for their choices. Freedom and responsibility are two sides of the same coin (Sartre, 2007).

Also emerging from the consultants' words above are the ideas that professional development (a) leads to change in cognitions, emotions, and behaviour, and (b) information sources arise from inside and outside of the professional realm, again echoing individuation. As individuation intensifies and becomes increasingly apparent, we see Kneebone's (2020) suggestion around professional identity emerge. Consultants move from viewing themselves as individuals mastering the discipline's competencies, techniques, and procedures, to seeing themselves as a professional. In sport psychology, this professional identity involves individuals who see themselves as possessing skills and attributes that allow them to assist clients, as members of a community of like-minded people, and as individuals occupying specific social roles (Tod et al., 2020).

Expert

The final two quotes are from individuals, with many years of experience in the discipline:

BOX 13.5   REFLECTING ON THEIR JOURNEY CONSULTANT 1

In the early stages of my graduate studies, a professor asked us all "why do we do what we do?" In a mocking tone, he replied, "because that's the way we have always done it!" From there I was encouraged to consider impactful questions: "why do I do research?", "what makes my work meaningful?" and "what are the real-world questions that need asking?" Throughout my career, engaging in research related activities that inform my consultancy and knowledge development has been at the centre of my learning. I also remain excited by the ideas that can be generated from working in applied settings with colleagues, and through discussions with key stakeholders in performance organisations. Sport psychology is an ever-growing field and I'm motivated to stay contemporary (I don't want to become stale!), so I try to seek out new experiences and opportunities that help me to do this. A big part in my own learning and development is so I can also pass it on to the students I teach and supervise. I hope they feel excited and enthusiastic about pursuing a career in sport psychology. Sometimes it is easy to get pulled down by the busy-ness of work and objectives that are necessary to meet, but I remind myself to find time to engage in the activities that fuel my passion in sport psychology. A few years ago, a manager praised me for a temporary role that I had done, and added, "you didn't seem fazed at all by some difficult, unexpected issues that cropped up". It's feedback that has stayed with me and I have continued to learn from it. I would never have described myself in that way previously! It has reminded me that I am continuing to develop professionally and as a person – there is always room for that.

BOX 13.6   REFLECTING ON THEIR JOURNEY CONSULTANT 2

Lifelong learning means continually needing to explore new ideas and ways of working so that I remain able to help clients who live in a world that constantly changes. Using Schmidt's generalised motor programme theory as an analogy, the invariant features of applied work have not changed (such as the need for a solid consulting relationship), but the parameters constantly need evolving (e.g., how do you build and maintain a consulting relationship in a dynamic

> world). Working with clients is a huge part of my professional development because applied work helps me learn how to take research and theory (invariant features) and apply it to their specific situations (parameters). Research and theory is vital, but it tends to be generic and unless it can be tailored to clients' needs, it is not much use to them. Professional development over the years has flowed both ways, across both my personal and professional lives, as I have developed a better understanding of myself, my history, my values, my beliefs, my weaknesses (of which there are many), and my strengths. My world is an existential world and the longer I have worked with clients, the more I realise that. But I only see that because of the amount of reading, reflecting, and helping clients I have done over the years. This professional development is part of the reason why I find the job hugely rewarding. As much as I help clients, they teach so much about life and myself.

People want their lives to have meaning (Frankl, 1969) and in experts and other senior professionals, this urge is often expressed as leaving a legacy – a view apparent in the above quotes. Consultants achieve a legacy by passing on their wisdom to younger professionals and, in rare instances, by their impact and influence on the field more widely.

The quotes above also illustrate a key feature among experts: their passion for the domain. Even after decades of being involved in the discipline, these individuals continue to gain tremendous satisfaction and have a great desire to continue learning. From a related field, expert counsellors describe themselves as voracious learners with a high passion for self-improvement (Jennings & Skovholt, 1999), two ideas echoed in the above quotes. The above words also illustrate the difficulty experts can face in our field to ensure lifelong learning. Senior consultants and professionals in sport psychology often occupy roles that demand a great of their time and energy. Academics, for example, may be stretched across teaching, supervision, administration, research, and consulting. Some of these roles may pull them away from the tasks for which they originally trained and towards roles for which they may be ill-equipped (e.g., administration). They are also likely responsible for the growth and maturation of other people including students, supervisees, and colleagues. Experts who wish to continue maturing and developing need to extract time out of a full timetable if they are to engage in CPD or risk falling behind the arms race that is sport psychology.

We are grateful for the thoughts that the above consultants gave us to use in this chapter. The insights they offer serve at least two purposes: one theoretical and one applied. First, from a theoretical view, their words illustrate many of the themes contained in Kneebone's (2020) three stages of the journey towards becoming an expert and that researchers have uncovered as they have excavated the professional development landscape. Second, their words provide a basis for helping students, supervisees, and other consultants (both inexperienced and mature) identify ways to enhance their own professional development and lifelong learning. In the next section, we provide practical guidelines based on our conceptualisation of lifelong learning and the reflections of the above consultants.

Practical Guidelines for Professional Development through Lifelong Learning

In formulating the following practical guidelines, we have not produced a list of must-do's, or top ten activities as such a reductionist approach does not enhance practice or professional growth and is the antithesis of lifelong learning. A tick box of activities may form the requirements of some forms of continued registration but, we hold that merely doing does not represent travel from journeyman to expert. Instead, we present guidance to help you tailor specific activities to your situation and development needs

Identifying Who You Are to Define Where You Are Going

As we have seen through the reflections above, lifelong learning is described by our practitioners as having an openness to learn, a flexibility of thinking, a willingness to embrace new opportunities, and the confidence to follow curiosities. However, in doing and striving for all these there is a need to first engage in personal reflection to raise your awareness of self. Reflect on the skills you have, your professional philosophy and your core personal values, take time to think about areas of yourself you feel are both developed and underdeveloped and challenge your own biases, both conscious and unconscious, of who you believe you are. Time spent understanding who you are and reflecting on changes over time will undoubtedly uncover areas that you wish to explore. At this stage, write a list, think of it as your "bucket list" and identify what in the short term are the key areas to explore that will enhance your development as a practitioner at this point in your journey. Careful planning through reflection will give focus to any form of learning; critically however, also remember to remain open to changing direction in your journey as you acquire new knowledge or understanding.

Retaining Currency

As our practitioners identified, to remain effective and to continue to evolve as a Sport Psychologist, there is a need to remain contemporary in terms of knowledge and practice. The newly qualified practitioner has contemporary knowledge at the point of qualification; however, the field of applied sport psychology is continuing to evolve and there is a need to stay in the knowledge race to remain contemporary. Learning about the latest developments may come from a variety of sources such as textbooks, journals, conferences, podcasts, and webinars to name but a few. Most importantly, build time in your diary to do this be it a day, half-day, or evening every week or month. As an individual, you will know what works best for you.

Developing Formal and Informal Networks

Quite often, a trainee will have both formal and informal support networks. These provide not only social support but also a safe space for discussion and debate about research and professional practice. Even when qualified, it is important to retain such networks and or become part of new networks. We encourage each practitioner to engage with any formal networks organised by their professional body, for example, the Division of Sport and Exercise Psychology (BPS) Applied Hubs. These applied communities provide a space and place for trainees, supervisors and practitioners to meet and engage in training and CPD activities, ask questions, challenge practice and in doing so promote the profession to local communities. As well as these formalised opportunities, we encourage Sport Psychologists to reach out to other practitioners to develop personal informal support networks. As one of our practitioners noted, having critical friends is important as is surrounding yourself with like-minded people. For those newly qualified, creating these networks can seem daunting and challenging; one way to do this is by attending CPD events.

Getting the Most Out of CPD Events

As we previously discussed, planning which conferences you will attend and what you will listen to is critical if you are to learn from the event. Importantly though conferences and CPD activities such as workshops present the opportunity for peer interaction. Walking around posters at a conference gives you the chance to begin conversations, and awkward silences can be avoided as you are talking about the research. So, when at a conference think about using such sessions not only as a learning but also as a networking opportunity. Importantly, remember that your CPD planning should be informed by your "bucket list" discussed in tip 1.

Supervision and Mentoring

As an applied practitioner, it is important that even when qualified you engage in supervision and mentoring. Whilst not a requirement of sport psychologists in the UK at the present time, there is still much to be gained from supervision not least the space to discuss practice issues and reflect on challenges such as working in multi-agency organisations or systems, ethical issues, or even as you become a supervisor yourself your supervision practice.

Conclusion

In this chapter, we have introduced you to the concept of lifelong learning and shown how lifelong learning encapsulates both CPD and CE. Through introducing the concepts of Kneebone (2020), we have provided a framework for you to think about the journey from starting training through to expert, and through the voices of practitioners, we have given practical meaning to lifelong learning.

Our guidelines provide key practical pointers on how to continue the development journey and it is important that as you do this you remember that your journey and development are individual. There will be commonality with others; however, it is also just as rewarding to expand your thinking, drawing on other branches of science and psychology. Remember, your personal growth comes not only from your reflections on who you are but also your experiences, your beliefs, and philosophy of practice and self.

Notes

1 https://www.psychologyboard.gov.au/
2 https://appliedsportpsych.org/

References

Clance, P. R., & Imes, S. A. (1978). The imposter phenomenon in high achieving women: Dynamics and therapeutic intervention. *Psychotherapy: Theory, Research & Practice, 15*(3), 241–247.

Fogaca, J. L., Zizzi, S. J., & Andersen, M. B. (2018). Walking multiple paths of supervision in American sport psychology: A qualitative tale of novice supervisees' development. *The Sport Psychologist, 32*(2), 156–165. https://doi.org/10.1123/tsp.2017-0048.

Frankl, V. E. (1969). *The doctor and the soul: From psychotherapy to logotherapy*. Souvenir Press.

Friesen, A. P. (2021). A survey of applied impact of literature in sport psychology. *The Sport Psychologist, 35*(3), 250–258.

Golding, L., & Gray, I. (2006). What a difference a day makes. In L. Golding & I. Gray (Eds), *Continuing professional development for clinical psychologists: A practical handbook* (pp. 1–6). Wiley – Blackwell.

Hings, R. F., Wagstaff, C. R., Anderson, V., Gilmore, S., & Thelwell, R. C. (2020). Better preparing sports psychologists for the demands of applied practice: The emotional labor training gap. *Journal of Applied Sport Psychology, 32*(4), 335–356.

Hutter, R. I. V., van der Zande, J. J., Rosier, N., & Wylleman, P. (2018). Education and training in the field of applied sport psychology in Europe. *International Journal of Sport and Exercise Psychology, 16*(2), 133–149. https://doi.org/10.1080/1612197X.2016.1162189.

Jennings, L., & Skovholt, T. M. (1999). The cognitive, emotional, and relational characteristics of master therapists. *Journal of Counseling Psychology, 46*, 3–11. https://doi.org/10.1037/0022-0167.46.1.3.

Kneebone, R. (2020). *Expert: Understanding the path to mastery*. Penguin.

McCarthy, P., & Jones, M. (2013). *Becoming a sport psychologist*. Routledge.

McEwan, H. E., & Tod, D. (2015). Learning experiences contributing to service-delivery competence in applied psychologists: Lessons for sport psychologists. *Journal of Applied Sport Psychology, 27*(1), 79–93. https://doi.org/10.1080/10413200.2014.952460.

McEwan, H. E., Tod, D., & Eubank, M. (2019). The rocky road to individuation: Sport psychologists' perspectives on professional development. *Psychology of Sport and Exercise, 45*, Article 101542. https://doi.org/10.1016/j.psychsport.2019.101542.

Plutarch (n.d.). Retrieved from http://newstoryhub.com/2018/01/education-is-the-kindling-of-a-flame-how-to-reinvent-the-21st-century-university-otto-scharmer/

Rønnestad, M. H., & Skovholt, T. M. (2013). *The developing practitioner: Growth and stagnation of therapists and counselors*. Routledge.

Sartre, J. P. (2007). *Existentialism is a humanism* (C. Macomber, Trans.). Yale University Press. (Original work published 1945).

Simons, J. P., & Andersen, M. B. (1995). The development of consulting practice in applied sport psychology: Some personal perspectives. *The Sport Psychologist, 9*, 449–468.

Skovholt, T. M., & Starkey, M. T. (2010). The three legs of the practitioner's learning stool: Practice, research/theory, and personal life. *Journal of Contemporary Psychotherapy, 40*(3), 125–130.

Smith, M., McEwan, H. E., Tod, D., & Martindale, A. (2019). UK trainee sport and exercise psychologists' perspectives on developing professional judgment and decision-making expertise during training. *The Sport Psychologist, 33*(4), 334–343.

Taylor, J. M., & Neimeyer, G. J. (2016). Continuing education and lifelong learning. In J. C. Norcross, G. R. VandenBos, D. K. Freedheim, & L. F. Campbell (Eds.), *APA handbook of clinical psychology: Education and profession, Vol. 5* (pp. 136–152). American Psychological Association.

Taylor, J. M., & Neimeyer, G. J. (2017). The ongoing evolution of continuing education past, present, and future. In T. Rousmaniere, R. K. Goodyear, S. D. Miller, & B. E. Wampold (Eds.), *The cycle of excellence: Using deliberate practice to improve supervision and training* (pp. 219–248). John Wiley & Sons Ltd.

Tigranyan, S., Byington, D. R., Liupakorn, D., Hicks, A., Lombardi, S., Mathis, M., & Rodolfa, E. (2021). Factors related to the impostor phenomenon in psychology doctoral students. *Training and Education in Professional Psychology, 15*(4), 298–305. https://doi.org/10.1037/tep0000321.

Tod, D., Andersen, M. B., & Marchant, D. B. (2011). Six years up: Applied sport psychologists surviving (and thriving) after graduation. *Journal of Applied Sport Psychology, 23*(1), 93–109. https://doi.org/10.1080/10413200.2010.534543.

Tod, D., Hardy, J., Lavallee, D., Eubank, M., & Ronkainen, N. (2019). Practitioners' narratives regarding active ingredients in service delivery: Collaboration-based problem solving. *Psychology of Sport and Exercise, 43*, 350–358. https://doi.org/10.1016/j.psychsport.2019.04.009.

Tod, D., Hutter, R. I. V., & Eubank, M. (2017). Professional development for sport psychology practice. *Current Opinion in Psychology, 16*, 134–137. https://doi.org/10.1016/j.copsyc.2017.05.007.

Tod, D., Marchant, D., & Andersen, M. B. (2007). Learning experiences contributing to service-delivery competence. *The Sport Psychologist, 21*(3), 317–334. https://doi.org/10.1123/tsp.21.3.317.

Tod, D., McEwan, H., Chandler, C., Eubank, M., & Lafferty, M. (2020). The gravitational pull of identity: Professional growth in sport, exercise, and performance psychologists. *Journal of Sport Psychology in Action, 11*(4), 233–242.

Tracey, T. J. G., Wampold, B. E., Lichtenberg, J. W., & Goodyear, R. K. (2014). Expertise in psychotherapy: An elusive goal? *American Psychologist, 69*, 218–229. https://doi.org/10.1037/a0035099.

Wadsworth, N., McEwan, H., Lafferty, M. E., Eubank, M., & Tod, D. (2021). A systematic review exploring the reflective accounts of applied sport psychology practitioners. *International Review of Sport and Exercise Psychology*. Advance online publication. https://doi.org/10.1080/1750984X.2021.1975304.

Williams, D. E., & Andersen, M. B. (2012). Identity, wearing many hats, and boundary blurring: The mindful psychologist on the way to the Olympic and Paralympic Games. *Journal of Sport Psychology in Action, 3*, 139–152. https://doi.org/10.1080/21520704.2012.683090.

Wise, E. H., Sturm, C. A., Nutt, R. L., Rodolfa, E., Schaffer, J. B., & Webb, C. (2010). Life-long learning for psychologists: Current status and a vision for the future. *Professional Psychology: Research and Practice, 41*(4), 288.

Quartiroli, A., Wagstaff, C. R., Herms, M., & Kemmel, C. (2021). The future of continuing education and lifelong learning in sport psychology professionals: A Delphi study. *Professional Psychology: Research and Practice, 52*(2), 173.

INDEX

Pages in *italics* refer figures and **bold** refer tables.

accreditation: acquiring 64–67; realities of 58–64; requirements 56–58
Accreditation of Prior Experiential Competence (APEC) 30
Administrative/quality assurance processes, consultancy: note taking 129–130; reflection 130–135; setting up service agreements 128–129; standards of proficiency 126–128; supervision 135–139
American Psychological Association (APA) 127
Andersen, M. B. 147
Applied sport psychology 56–57, 63, 141–143, 179–183, 202
Apprentice: illustrating lifelong learning 199–201; practitioner growth 196–197
Arnold, R. 150
Asian South-Pacific Association of Sport Psychology (ASPASP) 57
Assessment, QESP: assessors 13–17; reflections 12–13
Assessor, QESP 13–17
Association for Applied Sport Psychology (AASP) 57, 128
Asylum 183

Biles, Simones 187
Black women 179–183
BPS Code of Practice 130
British Association of Sport and Exercise Sciences (BASES) 19–20, 127
British Association of Sport and Exercise Scientists Expert Statement on Burnout in Sport 151
British Psychological Society (BPS) 5, 39, 127
Broaden-and-Build theory 153–154
Burnout 151–154

Certified Mental Performance Consultant 58
Coakley, J. 187
Competencies, SEPAR **22–27**
Competency development, SEPAR 33
Competency profile completion, SEPAR 34
Consultancy practice, marketing 102–103; bringing audience to website 107–108; building trust/credibility 103; charging for services 106–107; directories 110–112; finding audience 107; memberships 108–109; paying for promotion 109–110; pricing 105–106; SEO 110; writing to the top 103–105
Consultancy, sport and exercise psychology: administrative/quality assurance processes 126–139; consultant mental health 145–157; enhancing 113–123; marketing 102–112; setting up/operating 89–101
Continued Professional Development (CPD) 39, 121, 143, 193

Continuing Education (CE) 193
Continuing Professional Development (CPD) 130
Core training, SEPAR 20
Cotterill, S. T. 115
Critical Race Theory (CRT) 179
Cropley, B. 10
Cultural competency 184–185

Day-Vines, N. L. 186
Devow, Serena 180
Diaspora 183
Digital technology, consultancy practice 113; consulting online 117–119; ethical/moral challenges 120–123; excelling online 119; marketing/promotion 120; social media account management 120; social media use 113–115; web design/management 119–120; website development 116–117

Engagement 147
Engagement continuum 151–154
Enrolment, qualification 9
Ethical imperative, consultants 146
Eubank, M. 6, 41
Eurocentrism 178–179
Experience, SEPAR 26–28
Expert *see* master
Expertise, sustaining, accreditation 63–64

Facebook 102–104, 108, 114
Feminism 179–183
Final recommendation, SEPAR 34–35
Fletcher, D. 154
Flourishing 147
Forshaw, M. 41
Friesen, A. P. 198
Full enrolment 9

General Data Protection Regulations (GDPR) 130
Glasgow Caledonian University (GCU) 39
Global competency model 86–87
Global trends, accreditation 59–61
Golding, L. 193
Governance, SEPAR 20
Government Disclosure and Barring Service 21
Graduate Basis for Chartered Membership (GBC) 7, 42
Gray, I. 193
Group consultancy 94–96

HCPC Standards of Education and Training and Standards of Proficiency 20
HCPC Standards of Proficiency and Education and Training for Practitioner Psychologists 40
Health and Care Professional Council (HCPC) 5, 39, 105, 127, 194
Higher Education Institution (HEI) 39
Hook, J. N. 185
How to Become a Sport and Exercise Psychologist (Eubank/Tod) 6
Humility 185–186

Instagram 100, 102–104, 108–109, 114, 117
international routes 54–56; accreditation realities 58–64; accreditation requirements 56–58; acquiring accreditation 64–67
International Society for Sport Psychology (ISSP) 114, 128
intersectionality: broaching conversations 186–187; broaching diversity in consultancy practice 176–177; contextualising work 178–183; doing work of 183–186; multiculturalism 177; practical/applied setting considerations 188
Islam 179–183
ISSP Position Stand on the Use of the Internet in Sport Psychology 115

Job demands 152–153
Job Demands–Resources Model 157
Job–Demands–Resource Theory 151–153
Job resources 153
Johnson, Dwayne 114
Journeyman: practitioner growth 197–198; illustrating lifelong learning 201–202

Keyes, C. L. M. 151, 156
Kneebone, R. 193, 198
Knowledge, SEPAR 21–23

languishing 147, 151
Lifelong learning: and continued professional development 193–196; continuing education types **195**; describing practitioner growth 196; guidelines for professional development through 205–207; illustrating 199–205
Life Story Interview 165, **166**
LinkedIn 114, 117
Liverpool John Moores University (LJMU) 39

Maslach, C. 151
Master: illustrating lifelong learning 203–205; practitioner growth 198–199
McCormack, H. M. 141, 147, 152
Mcintosh, Peggy 179
Mental health, consultants: applied implications 154–157; consequences 150–154; consulting at Olympic Games 150; ethical imperative 146; multi-dimensional model of mental health 146–147; practitioner recommendations 154–157; professional challenges 147–150; shared mandate 145–146
Messi, Lionel 114
Miller, G. E. 21
Moran, A. 145
Multiculturalism 177

Nassar, Larry 187
Neil, R. 10
Neimeyer, G. J. 194–195
Neo-racism theory 182
Note taking 129–130

Olympic Games, consulting at 150

Pay-per-click (PPC) 104
Performance Interview Guide 186
Pocwardowski, Artur 198
Portenga, S. T. 61
Practice-informed research 45–46
Practitioner growth, describing 196–199
Pricing, consultancy 105–106
Professional challenges, consultants 147–150
Professional Doctorates (PDs) 39–40; current enrolments/completions 40; developing into competent psychologist 50–52; getting most out of supervised practice 48–49; navigating writing-up/assessment process 49–50; programme director perspective 42–46; research-informed practice 45–46; supervision 'plus,' 44; taught continued professional development content 43–44; trainee perspective 46; training 40–42; training route strengths 46–48; unique selling points of 42–46
Professionalism, accreditation 61–63
Professional, Statutory, Regulatory Bodies (PSRB) 40–41
Provisional enrolment 9
Psychological flexibility 167–168

Qualification in Sport and Exercise Psychology (QSEP) 5–6; assessment 12–17; enrolment 9–11; supervision 9–11; training 6–9
Qualification in Sport and Exercise Psychology (QSEP Stage 2) 57
Quality assurance, SEPAR 20
Quartiroli, A. 193, 195

Race 178–179
Racism 178–179
Recordkeeping 129–130
Reflection, consultancy 130–135
Reflection, trainees 8–9
Reflective account, SEPAR 33–34
Reflexivity 185
Register of Applied Psychology Practice Supervisors (RAPPS) 10, 71
Relation-Inferred Self-Efficacy (RISE) 134–135
Research-informed practice 45–46

Saliency of Race in Sport Questionnaire (SORIS-Q) 188
Sarkar, M. 150
Schinke, R. 58
Search Engine Optimisation (SEO) 117
Self-assessment, SEPAR 31–32
Self-awareness 165
Self-care 160; barriers to implementing 168–169; definition of 167; engaging in 164; foundational mechanisms of 164–168; interconnection of one's practices 168; outset considerations 163–164; payoff of 169–170; plan 170–172; reflective questioning on 167; responsibility 161–162; understanding 162–163
Self-care plan 170–172
Self-development/management, SEPAR 25–26
Self-reflection 165–167, 185
Sensitivity 185
SEPAR Advisory Group (SEPAR AG) 20
Service agreements, setting up 128–129
Service charging, consultancy 106–107
Skills, SEPAR 23–25
Skovholt, T. M. 196
Slade, L. 151, 156
Social media, using 113–115
Socio-economic status (SES) 177
Sport and Exercise Psychologist in Training (SEPiT) 20

Sport and exercise psychology: BSP qualification in 5–18; international routes to 54–67; intersectionality in 176–189; marketing consultancy practice 102–112; professional development 19–38; Professional Doctorates 39–52; self-care 160–172; sport and exercise psychology consultancy 85–101; supervisor–trainee relationship 70–83

Sport and Exercise Psychology Accreditation Route (SEPAR) 19–20, 57; competencies **22–27**; completing process of 28–30; core training 20; entry requirements/enrolment 20–28; experience 26–28; governance 20; knowledge 21–23; knowledge-based competencies **22**; quality assurance 20; reflection/supervisor tips on 30–35; self-development/management 25–26; skills 23–25; skills-based competencies **23, 24**; supervisor role 35–38

Sport and exercise psychology consultancy, developing 85, 89–90; client checklist *91*; first workshop 93–94; global competency model 86–87; group consultancy 94–96; items to consider *92*; launching private practice 97–98; managing time/resources 99–101; operation 97; personal timeline *91*; physician know yourself 85–86; private practice 90; securing first clients 90–93

Sport and Exercise Psychology Qualification Board 10

Sport and Exercise Psychology Review (SEPR) 6

Sport, exercise, and performance psychology (SEPP) 176

Sport Interviewing Protocol (SIP) 186

Sport psychology, defining 145–146

Sport psychology practitioners (SPPs) 160; barriers to implementing self-care plan 168–169; engaging in self-care 164; foundational mechanisms of self-care 164–168; outset considerations 163–164; understanding self-care 162–163; unique challenges of 161

Sport Psychology Self-Care (SPSC) 162

Standards of Proficiency (SOPs) 126–128
Starkey, M. T. 196
Supervised practice 13–17
Supervision, consultancy 135–139
Supervision, qualification 10–11
Supervisor–trainee relationship 70–71; managing 79–83; potential trainees 77–79; selecting supervisor 71–74; supervisor operation 74–77; supervisor requirements **72**

Taught continued professional development content 43–44
Taylor, J. M. 194–195
TikTok 114
Tod, D. 6
Tokyo 2020 Olympic Games 115
Toner, J. 145
Trainees, reflections of 8–9
Training, QESP 6–9
transnational perspectives 179–183
Triplett, Norman 145
Twitter 100, 102–103, 108–109, 114, 117, 120

Unique selling points (USPs) 39
United Kingdom (UK) 56, 105
United States of America (USA) 56
United States Olympic and Paralympic Committee (USOPC) 187
University of Portsmouth (UoP) 39

Virtual Learning Environment (VLE) 8

Wagstaff, C. R. D. 154
Website, developing 116–117
WhatsApp 76, 114
Williams, Serena 180
Women 179–183
World Health Organisation (WHO) 147
writing-up process 14–17

Your Pathway, Your Choice, SEPAR 28; final submission 30; initial 3-month submission 29; mid-point submission 29–30

Zizzi, S. J. 58

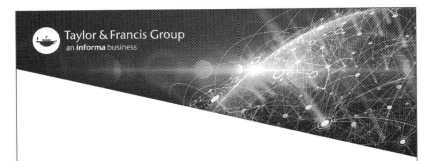

Printed in the United States
by Baker & Taylor Publisher Services